Understanding Global Media

Understanding Global Media

Second edition

Terry Flew

 palgrave

First edition published 2007
This edition published 2018 by
PALGRAVE

Palgrave in the UK is an imprint of Macmillan Publishers Limited,
registered in England, company number 785998, of 4 Crinan Street,
London, N1 9XW.

Palgrave® and Macmillan® are registered trademarks in the United States,
the United Kingdom, Europe and other countries.

ISBN 978–1–137–44654–1 hardback
ISBN 978–1–137–44653–4 paperback

This book is printed on paper suitable for recycling and made from fully
managed and sustained forest sources. Logging, pulping and manufacturing
processes are expected to conform to the environmental regulations of the
country of origin.

A catalogue record for this book is available from the British Library.

A catalog record for this book is available from the Library of Congress.

Printed and bound by CPI Group (UK) Ltd, Croydon, CR0 4YY

Contents

List of figures and tables

Figures

Tables

Preface

Any current book on global media has to face up to three challenges. First, there is a need to reconcile an interest in the global dimensions of media with a preparedness to critically scrutinize claims that we now live in an unprecedented era of 'the global' that supersedes earlier stages of human history, particularly those where the nation-state had primacy. Such perspectives have been associated with globalization theories and, as we will see in this book, there are considerable grounds for questioning the claim that nation-states and territorially based forms of culture and identity are in inexorable decline. Understanding the global dimensions of media without succumbing to an ideology of globalism is an important test of scholarship in this field.

The second challenge is to clarify what is now meant by 'the media' in an age of digital networks, convergent platforms and user-generated content. Key perspectives considered in this book, such as modernization theory and critical political economy, were initially framed around film and broadcast media, and have had to be significantly retooled for understanding the global internet and social media. As with globalization, the divide between 'old' and 'new' media can be overstated – television is now clearly a digital media platform, and many of the world's most accessed websites are the online versions of traditional media brands – but there are clearly challenges in setting the parameters of the media in an age where digital platforms carry virtually everything. It reminds us of the need to conceive of media in terms of technologies that enable people to communicate, rather than tying it to particular industry structures, types of content or forms of carriage.

Finally, there is the question of 'media-centric' approaches and those that stress the social, political, economic and cultural contexts in which media operate. All media theories have had to balance this question, from mass communication debates about media effects to questions of whether the internet presages a new version of what Marshall McLuhan termed the 'Global Village' (McLuhan & Fiore, 1967). This book does place a stress on the relationship of media to social relations, and particularly power relations, as they play out on local, national and global scales. But in doing so, the intention is not to subsume what is interesting and important about the media itself in the thickets of social theory.

In developing the ideas that underpin this book, I have benefited from engagement with the International Communication Association (ICA), and particularly the Global Communication and Social Change division, of which I was Vice-Chair from 2013 to 2015 and Chair from 2015 to 2017. Thanks to Rashmi Luthra, Silvio Waisbord, Robert Huesca, Joe Khalil, Antonio la Pastina, Joe Straubhaar, Karin Wilkins, Daya Thussu, Jack Linchuan Qiu, Colin Sparks, Anthony Fung, Ju Oak Kim, Will Youmans, Shiv Ganesh, Radhika Gajjala and others with whom I have shared ideas in the Division. And of course thanks to the wider ICA community, particularly Cynthia Stohl, Amy Jordan, Francois Heinderyckx, Peter Vorderer, Patricia Moy, Peng Hwa Ang, Paula Gardner, Larry Gross, Michael Haley and Laura Sawyer.

The book benefited from the opportunity to present key ideas at conferences and university symposia in the United States, China, South Korea, Russia, Indonesia, Austria, New Zealand and Australia. Thanks to Wenshan Jia, David Craig, Clayton Dube, Jiannu Bao, Wen Wen, Elena Vartanova, Donald Matheson, Shin Dong Kim, Josef Trappel, Li Benqian, Li Jiashan, Zhu Lian, Zhang Xiaoyang, Xiao Han, Endah Triastuti, Billy Sarwono, Wang Xiaohua, Li Xiaomu and Haiyan Wang for inviting me to speak to their colleagues and to graduate students. Parts of this book have been presented at:

ICA-SJTU International Forum on New Media, Shanghai Jiao Tong University, Shanghai, China.

National Institute for Cultural Development, Beijing International Studies University, Beijing, China.

Center for Information and Communication Technologies & Society, Department of Communication Studies, University of Salzburg, Austria.

Institute for Cultural Industries, Shenzhen University, Shenzhen, China.

U.S.-China Institute, USC Annenberg School of Communication and Journalism, University of Southern California, Los Angeles, USA.

Asia Media Forum, Communication University of China, Beijing, China.

Thanks to my colleagues in the Creative Industries Faculty at the Queensland University of Technology for their insights and support. Among those who have helped to shape the arguments in this book are Stuart Cunningham, Jean Burgess, Axel Bruns, Nic Suzor, Adam Swift, Brian McNair, Stephen Harrington, Greg Hearn, Emma Baulch, Patrik Wikström, Liangen Yin, Bonnie Liu and Donna Hancox. Thanks to my graduate students, notably

Jiajie Lu, Fiona Suwana, Rido Panjaitan, Callum McWaters, Falk Hartig, Angela Lin Huang and Seiko Yasumoto. Others who have helped me shape ideas in various ways include Julian Thomas, Michael Keane, Brian Yecies, Nina Li, Bill Dutton, Steve Wildman, Sandra Braman, Paulo Faustino, Leah Lievrouw, Hilde van den Bulck, Eli Noam, Tim Dwyer, Jonathan Hutchinson, John Hartley and Mark Gibson.

Finally, all the very best to my daughter, Charlotte Flew.

Acknowledgements

The author wishes to thank the following copyright holders for permission to reproduce the following:

Table 1.1 from John B. Thompson (1995) *The Media and Modernity* (p. 17). Cambridge: Polity. Reproduced with permission of Polity and Stanford University Press.

Figure 1.2 from Robert Picard (1989) *Media Economics: Concepts and Issues* (p. 21). London: SAGE. Reproduced with permission of SAGE Publications.

Figure 2.1 from Everett M. Rogers (1974) 'Communication and Development', *Annals of The American Academy of Political and Social Science* 412(1) (p. 49). Reproduced with permission of SAGE Publications.

Figure 4.1 from Roland Robertson (1992) *Globalization: Social Theory and Cultural Change* (p. 27). London: SAGE. Reproduced with permission of SAGE Publications.

Figure 4.2 from Anthony Giddens (1990) *The Consequences of Modernity* (p. 59). Cambridge: Polity. Reproduced with permission of Polity and Stanford University Press.

Table 5.1, Figure 5.1 and Table 5.2 from UNCTAD *World Investment Report 2016*, published by the United Nations Conference on Trade and Development. http://unctad.org/en/Pages/DIAE/World%20Investment%20Report/Annex-Tables.aspx.

Figure 5.2 from AusFilm (2000) *A Bigger Slice of the Pie: Policy Options for a More Competitive International Film and Television Production Industry in Australia*. Report prepared by Malcolm Long Associates, November. Reproduced with permission of AUSFILM.

Table 6.1 from Jan Nederveen Pieterse (2015) *Globalization and Culture: Cultural Mélange* (p. 55). Boulder, CO: Rowman & Littlefield. Reproduced with permission of Rowman & Littlefield Publishers.

CHAPTER 1

Introduction to global media: key concepts

Media as technologies, institutions and culture

Communications media have long been central to the major developments of modern societies. The creation of nation-states and national identities; ideas of citizenship and freedom; the development of political culture and the public sphere; the growth of capitalist commercial enterprises; and modern consumer culture – all of these developments owe a great deal to the development of communications media. Historically, communications media have been integral to the rise and fall of empires, to diplomacy, war, the spread of languages and cultural norms, and to the processes we refer to today under the general terms of globalization and modernity. In the twenty-first century, we find that social media, carried through digital networks and the global internet, are enabling a highly diverse array of individuals, groups, organizations and movements to produce and globally distribute media content. This presents new challenges to how we understand the media, as it blurs mass communication era distinctions between media producers and audience-consumers, and between professional and amateur creators and distributors of media content.

When we refer to *media*, we are using the term in a threefold sense. First, it refers to the *technological means of communication*. The term 'media' is an extension of 'medium', or the technical means through which a message is sent and received, and associated questions of how messages are stored and distributed over time and space. Technical media that have been prominent through human history have included print (paper and movable type), broadcasting (radio and television), telecommunications and the internet.

When thinking about a media technology, we need to acknowledge that the particular technological device we are referring to constitutes only one of an ensemble of elements requiring our attention. We also need to consider the practices that were associated with that technology, as well as the institutions that have shaped, and are shaping, its ongoing development. Lievrouw and Livingstone (2006) argued that communications and media studies needs to get beyond the level of artefacts and devices, or technologies in the narrow sense. To understand why a new media device, or indeed a new content form, is new, we always need to ask not only why this is a new device or form, but also what is new *for society* about it. They argued that this requires a threefold concern with:

1. The *artefacts or devices* that enable and extend our capacities to communicate;
2. The *activities and practices* that people engage in to use these devices for communication;
3. The *social institutions and organizational forms* that develop around those devices and practices.

They make the point that the relationship between these three elements is circular rather than linear. This ensemble of relationships between technological devices, communication practices and social institutions is shown in Figure 1.1:

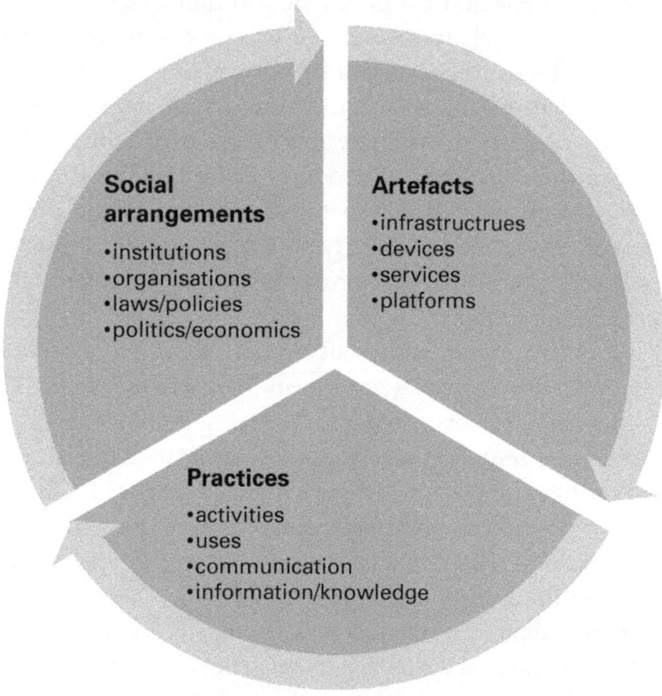

Social arrangements
•institutions
•organisations
•laws/policies
•politics/economics

Artefacts
•infrastructrues
•devices
•services
•platforms

Practices
•activities
•uses
•communication
•information/knowledge

Figure 1.1 Constituent elements of media

Source: Author's own diagram based on Lievrouw & Livingstone (2006).

Adapting this framework, we therefore think of the media in three dimensions. First, it consists of the technologies of production, distribution and reception, and the associated infrastructures that enable media messages to be shared, which is the first precondition of technologically mediated communication, i.e. all forms other than direct, face-to-face communication. Second, the media consists of the industries and institutions through which decisions are made about what media content is produced and distributed for audiences or other groups of users larger than those that can be gathered together for direct interpersonal communication. Third, the media consists of its content, or the cultural and symbolic forms that are shared, and which generate meaning for individuals, communities, nations and – potentially – the global population. It is noted later in this chapter that these three dimensions of media interact with four overarching frameworks: the economic framework; the policy framework; the cultural framework; and the digital framework.

Media technologies and infrastructures

In order to better understand the relationship between media forms and social change, there is a need to reflect upon the relationship of mass communications media to the emergence of modern societies. The rise of mass media is generally associated with the print revolution of the fifteenth and sixteenth centuries, which enabled the dissemination of written works in the forms of books, newspapers, magazines, pamphlets etc., as well as the rise of a 'reading public' that had both the capacity to read and write – print literacy – and a preparedness to engage collectively with ideas and insights derived from such printed works. In *The Media and Modernity*, John Thompson (1995) observed that 'the important point about mass communication is not that a given number of individuals … receives the product, but rather that the products are available in principle to a plurality of recipients' (Thompson, 1995, p. 24). Thompson argued that mass communication forms have five characteristics:

1. They make use of a *technical medium* that allows information and symbolic content to be 'fixed and transmitted from producer to receiver' (p. 18);
2. They are the products of *media industries*, as 'organizations which … have been concerned with the commercial exploitation of technical innovations' (p. 27);
3. They are associated with a '*structured break between the production of symbolic forms and their reception*' (p. 29), which may be over space, over time, or both;

4. They become *increasingly mass media forms*, i.e. they 'are made available to more individuals across larger expanses of space and at greater speeds' (p. 30);

5. Mass communication involves 'the public circulation of symbolic forms', playing a key role in *ordering (and transforming) public space and public culture* through being 'made visible and observable to a multiplicity of individuals who may be, and typically are, scattered across diverse and dispersed contexts' (p. 31).

The technological means of communication constitute the *infrastructure* that makes media communication possible. While the component elements of this infrastructure may be technical mediums – printing presses, TV and radio antennas, copper wires, broadband cables, satellites orbiting the globe, and so on – their broader impacts are social and cultural. Questions of 'how to infrastructure' (Star & Bowker, 2006), have frequently been approached from a technical or engineering perspective, but there is also a need to consider their impacts upon social relations and human interactions, alongside an awareness of the technical properties of different media. The history of media infrastructures also reveals a complex and ongoing relationship between the national and global scales. The internet emerged as a global information infrastructure developed by and for the US scientific community and the military, but it possessed an 'architecture of openness' and freedom from government controls that have been a vital part of its evolution as a global communications network ever since (Castells, 2001).

At the same time, as the internet became more of a global network from the mid-1990s onwards, the role played by nation-states, most notably the United States, in shaping its evolution became increasingly apparent. In particular, the development of a National Information Infrastructure (NII) strategy by the Clinton Administration in 1993, and Vice-President Al Gore's guidelines for a Global Information Infrastructure (GII) at the International Telecommunications Union Summit in Buenos Aires in 1994, were critical moments in shaping the global internet in the preferred interests of dominant players. The associated policies were by no means value-neutral and purely technical: the guiding principles of the GII as articulated by Clinton and Gore favoured private investment over public in infrastructure provision, free markets and competition over national monopolies, and the removal of all barriers to foreign investment in telecommunications systems (Mattelart, 2003, pp. 117–123; Flew & McElhinney, 2006).

Media industries and institutions

The second sense in which we refer to media is in terms of *the media industries*. Media industries provide the *institutional and organizational forms through which media content is produced and distributed*. The study of media industries draws attention to *media economics*, and the distinctive features of media economics and markets will be discussed below. It is important to note that there are different traditions in media economics, most notably between those who approach the field from the perspective of mainstream economic theories, also known as neoclassical economics (Picard, 1989; Finn *et al.*, 2004; Albarran, 2010; Doyle, 2013), and those who analyse media industries from the perspective of critical political economy (discussed at length in Chapter 3). While these have been antagonistic traditions, there is significant recent work which suggests the possibility of reconciling them. Drawing upon analytical tools provided by media economics to develop critical accounts of media industries, Napoli (2009), Picard, (2011a), Winseck (2011), Ballon (2014) and others have drawn attention to the implications of concentration of media ownership and the relationship between the economic power of media companies and the 'public interest' expectations that exist around media as technologies of public communication.

The media industries perspective draws attention to the critical position of *media production*. Media producers include those who generate original creative content, and include actors, animators, producers, directors, designers, journalists, photographers and camera people. There are also other professionals whose work contributes to the sustainability and growth of media industries, such as advertisers, marketers, public relations professionals, lawyers, accountants, etc. (Deuze, 2007). In the influential theory of the *creative class* proposed by Richard Florida (2002), those directly engaged with the generation of new ideas, concepts, designs and creative works were the 'creative core', and their work was supported by creative professionals working across a range of knowledge-intensive industries. For Florida, this creative class was the fastest-growing segment of the US economy, and its values of individuality, creative self-expression, meritocracy and commitment to diversity and openness were transforming society and culture, particularly in those urban centres where they were most concentrated (Florida, 2002, pp. 72–80).

From a more critical perspective, Hesmondhalgh (2013) and McRobbie (2016) have identified that distinctive features of cultural labour, such as the desire for creative autonomy, are often pursued in the context of irregular employment and uncertain career prospects, making such work often highly stressful and prone to exploitation and self-exploitation. Creative workers have distinctive relations to creative managers, with the latter often preferring 'soft control' and management by contract over direct oversight of the creative process, and to cultural intermediaries in industries such as advertising, fashion, public relations, publishing, arts management and other sectors, who undertake 'the symbolic work of shaping the perception and reception of goods, services, and ideas', and are 'key market makers in contemporary consumer economies' (Matthews & Maguire, 2014, pp. 3–4).

Understanding media as institutions has a dual element to it. At one level, they are firms that produce, package and distribute media content in particular ways in order to achieve particular objectives, be they profit maximization for commercial media enterprises, or a range of 'public interest' goals for publicly funded media (Doyle, 2013, p. 5). But an institution is much more than a 'black box' through which inputs are turned into outputs. From an institutional economics perspective, Douglass North has defined institutions as 'the humanly devised constraints that shape human interaction', arguing that they 'reduce uncertainty by providing a structure to everyday life ... [and] a guide to human interaction' (North, 1990, p. 3). Formal and informal institutions shape the *rules of the game* by which media systems operate, which can be changed through conscious human action, but which also appear as historically derived constraints at any point in time.

Following Williamson (2000), we can think about media institutions as operating across four levels, with each having its own historical timeframe:

1. Institutional arrangements within the media organization itself (e.g. how production and distribution of content are organized internally) and its dealings with other key market participants (interactions between media buyers, advertising agencies and corporate clients, dealings with rights holders, etc.);
2. Interactions between media institutions and policy and regulatory institutions that shape regimes of media policy and governance;
3. Interactions with formal institutions that shape the institutional environment and enforce its rules, which include media companies, but also government agencies, trade unions and producer guilds, industry associations, lobby groups etc.;
4. Relationships to informal institutions, which include the norms of behaviour, conventions, customs, traditions, norms and values, codes of conduct, ideologies and belief systems through which institutional arrangements are shaped, which differ from one nation to the next and are subject to historical path dependency.

As institutions are culturally embedded in society, there is more to understanding media institutions than simply approaching them as either profit-maximizing agents indifferent to the society in which they operate, or as the neutral arbiters of the public good as it pertains to media and culture. Moreover, there are both national and international institutions associated with media governance, and the interactions between these two levels as they shape media industries is a matter that will be considered in detail in this book.

Media content and cultures

The third sense in which we understand the media is in terms of culture. The media can be formally described as *the informational and symbolic content received and consumed by readers, audiences and users*. This is the 'common sense' understanding of what the media are, as it refers to the content that comes to us through our newspapers, magazines, radios, televisions, personal computers, mobile phones and other devices. It is received through the technical infrastructures and institutions that enable its production, distribution and reception.

When we consider the nature and significance of media content as it is received in the public domain, the question that arises is the extent to which media now define the culture of modern societies. Thompson has referred to 'the *mediatization of modern culture* ... [where] the transmission of symbolic forms becomes increasingly mediated by the technical and institutional apparatuses of the media industries' (1990, pp. 3–4). Douglas Kellner has argued that 'we are immersed from cradle to grave in a media and consumer society, and thus it is important to learn how to understand, interpret and criticize its meanings and values' (Kellner, 1995, p. 5).

As we will note in later chapters, culture is a notoriously slippery term to define. Thompson (1990) identified two principal conceptions of culture. One is the *descriptive* conception of culture as what people do in a particular place or at a particular time, or 'the varied array of values, beliefs, customs, conventions, habits and practices characteristic of a particular society or historical period' (p. 123). The other is the *symbolic* conception of culture, or the underlying system of social, cultural, linguistic and psychological relationships through which people, in different places or at particular times, are engaged in making sense of their wider social environment and acting within it. Media are particularly important to symbolic and signifying systems, and it in this capacity that they are taken to shape the everyday lives of people and communities, and notions of 'common sense', truth and falsehood, and right and wrong. Theories that give a central role to dominant ideologies in shaping social order tend to give the media a central role in this, as in the case of critical political economy theories of global media.

These three interconnected elements of the media – technical infrastructures, institutional forms, and cultures of reception – provide the context for a critical evaluation of global media. They focus attention on questions of *media power*, and the extent to which communications media 'structure culture, politics and economics ... [and] determine how a life may be lived' (Jordan, 1999, p. 1). In order to properly address this question, we need to consider the relative significance of *media-centric* and non-media-centric or *society-centric* explanations of society and culture, to work out the extent to which methods for analysing global media should be focused on the media as such, as distinct from other social, economic, political and cultural forces.

Media-centric and non-media-centric approaches to global media

In his account of the historical origins of international communications research, Mowlana (2012) made the point that the first US-sponsored programmes established in developing countries had relatively little interest in the mass media as such. They were primarily concerned with developing leadership communication skills for elites, and with the process of public opinion formation, insofar as political leadership in these countries played a critical role in global geopolitical alliances. At the same time, because these were rarely stand-alone programmes; they tended to be highly interdisciplinary, 'relating to and drawing from fields as diverse as economics, international studies, politics, sociology, psychology, literature and history' (Mowlana, 2012, p. 272).

Early mass communication research was strongly influenced by the *media effects* paradigm, which sought to use social science methods to identify whether exposure to particular forms of media content had direct effects on individual behaviour, e.g. does political advertising change voting behaviour? Does violent content in the media lead to anti-social behaviour? The question that was invariably raised in such research was the role played by *intervening variables*, e.g. is anti-social behaviour more associated with economic disadvantage or dysfunctional family environments than with the media? (Newbold, 1995). The critique of *media effects theories*, and functionalist theories of the media more generally, pointed to the limits of media-centrism insofar as it was associated with approaching the impact of communication on society independently of an understanding of underlying social relations. Critical theorists identified the importance of the political-economic context of the media in capitalist societies, and how different social classes and other groups related to it, arguing that these social forces were neglected in what Gitlin (1995) termed the 'dominant paradigm' of mass communication (cf. Hall, 1982).

The impact of critical theories on media studies was ambiguous. It undermined the media effects model, by demanding that media studies take account of the complex social totality within which the media operated, pointing in the direction of more society-centric accounts of media and communications. At the same time, as media studies came to be increasingly influenced by political economy and critical cultural studies, 'the reconceptualization of the media as powerful came about ... [through] neo-Marxist macro-analysis of media as "ideological apparatuses" of social reproduction' (Newbold, 1995, p. 120). The question thus came to be one of: if the media are powerful, to what ends does that power operate? And can that power be resisted, or are there instances where it fails to operate? As James Halloran posed the question in relation to these debates, 'A theory of society is needed ... but what theory?' (Halloran, 1995, p. 41).

In global media studies, the most significant integration of media theory and social theory has come from critical political economy. The first generation of critical global media theorists, such as Herbert Schiller, combined an analysis of the global political economy (dependency theory) with an analysis of the cultural impacts of uneven global media flows (cultural imperialism). While more recent work in this field tends to shy away from the stronger variants of cultural imperialism theories (see, for example, Miller & Kraidy, 2016, pp. 26–32), there is nonetheless a continuing connection made between macro-analyses of where media sit in contemporary global capitalism as a political-economic system, with perspectives on the dominant ideologies associated with this system variously labelled neoliberalism, globalism and consumerism. Criticisms of these approaches tend to either question the media theory, particularly assumptions about ideological dominance, or the political economy, but typically do so in a way that does not propose a new synthesis. Globalization theories, for instance, are less clearly constituted as a distinct paradigm than critical political economy.

An example of a 'media-centric' analysis is provided by Grabe and Myrick's (2016) account of the role of media in enabling citizen participation in political life and developing informed citizenship. They argue that conventional political theory routinely underestimates the significance of media in democratic theory, because it works with a 'rational actor' model of politics that does not adequately consider 'the deliberate entanglement of emotion with knowledge acquisition and political participation' (Grabe & Myrick, 2016, p. 216). When the role of media is considered, the focus is on information media and so-called 'hard news', and not on entertainment and 'soft news' genres; this is also reflected in a preference for words over images as the primary mode of political communication. Grabe and Myrick make the argument that not only do images, entertainment media, infotainment, etc. matter in shaping citizen participation in political life, but that this is consistent with a growing body of work in the neurosciences as well as the social sciences indicating that 'affect – in concurrence with rational thought – is instrumental to living a collaborative life' (2016, p. 221). In other words, a more media-centric approach to understanding informed citizenship enables a better understanding of trends in contemporary politics, such as the role of social media in forming 'affective publics' that engage in political action (cf. Papacharissi, 2015), political engagement outside of traditional channels such as elections and political parties, and the role of fictional media depictions of politics (e.g. *The West Wing, House of Cards*), political satire, and hybrid 'infotainment' formats in shaping contemporary politics worldwide (see McNair *et al.*, 2017 for analysis in the Australian context).

By way of contrast, the cultural theorist David Morley has recently called for a *non-media-centric* approach to media studies. By this, Morley means that:

> We need a new paradigm for the discipline, which attends more closely to its material as well as its symbolic dimensions. If improvements in the speed of communications are central to the time-space compressions of our era, emphasis has recently fallen almost exclusively on the virtual dimension (the movement of information) to the neglect of the analysis of the corresponding movements of objects, commodities, and persons ... We should aim to develop a model for the integrated analysis of communications, which places current technological changes in historical perspective and returns the discipline to the full range of its classical concerns. (2009, p. 114)

This means, for example, thinking about communications and transport as together constituting the global infrastructure that moves people, images, information, and commodities, and observing how such networked flows can be blocked as well as facilitated (e.g. nation-state restrictions on the movement of certain groups of people, or inequalities of access to information infrastructure). It rejects the idea of a sharp distinction between 'old' and 'new' media, arguing that 'material' and 'virtual' geographies are intertwined, and that it is possible to 'map' global communication and media flows just as one would map the movement of goods and people through shipping, aircraft travel, etc. It would also guard against presumptions about growing global mobility and developments associated with it (e.g. declining attachment to particular places, or the waning of a sense of national identity), to instead ask:

> *Who* is mobile in relation to *which* material and virtual geographies ... who has access to what, how that access is patterned and what consequences that access has for everyday experiences of movement. What we need to avoid is ... the idea that we're all mobile now, and in much the same way. (Morley *et al.*, 2014, p. 688)

The two perspectives here are not presented as polar oppositions, and the point is not that one needs to prefer one over the other. Both provide vitally important insights into contemporary media. But it is to note that an important methodological question in global media studies is the significance that one wishes to give to media technologies, industries and content, as distinct from other social, cultural, political and economic factors, in shaping global media developments.

Media and power

The question of the relationship of media to power is a vitally important one in global media studies. Thompson has defined power as 'the ability to act in pursuit of one's aims and interests ... to intervene in the course of events and to affect their outcome' (Thompson, 1995, p. 13). In a similar vein, Manuel Castells (2009, p. 10) defines power as 'the relational capacity that enables a social actor to influence asymmetrically the decisions of other social actors in ways that favour the empowered actor's will, interests and values'. Castells makes the point that power can be 'exercised by means of coercion (or the possibility of it) and/or by the construction of meaning on the basis of the discourses through which social actors guide their actions' (2009, p. 10). Media power is particularly important with regards to power exercised through consent and compliance rather than through coercion. Freedman (2015, p. 274) defines media power as referring to 'the relationships – between actors, institutional structures, and contexts – that organize the allocation of the symbolic resources necessary to structure our knowledge about, and by extension our capacity to intervene in, the world around us'.

Power can be both relational and structural. The concept of *relational power*, or power as possession, owes a particular debt to the work of sociologist Max Weber, who defined power as 'the chance of a man or of a number of men [*sic*] to realize their own will in a communal action even against the resistance of others who are participating in the action' (Weber, 1946, p. 180). In this perspective, power constitutes a form of action based on identifiable decisions, issues and social actors, or what Steven Lukes describes as 'the power of *A* to get *B* to do something they would not otherwise do' (Lukes, 2005, p. 16). Freedman associates relational power with consensus-based understandings of the social order, where 'power is widely distributed, pluralistically organized, and contributes to a relatively stable social arrangement' (Freedman, 2015, p. 275). From this perspective, the media perform both an integrative function, binding individual citizens to the nation-state and the broader society, and provide the 'mixed economy' of outlets that can cater to the diverse needs and interests of the wider society, subject to a limited degree of state regulation of the 'marketplace of ideas'.

Structural power refers to the power, not only of one party over another in actual decisions, but power over the agenda as to what is or is not deemed important and hence requiring decisions to be made. Steven Lukes' 'three-dimensional' view of power, which involves 'power [by A over B] ... by influencing, shaping or determining his [*sic*] very wants' is an example of a structural power framework (Lukes, 2005, p. 27). Theories of *hegemony* inspired by the Marxist political theorist Antonio Gramsci provide another example of structural power, with its notion that '"common sense" becomes one of the stakes over which ideological struggle is conducted' (Hall, 1996a, p. 43). It is also consistent with what Freedman terms the *contradiction* model of media power, where:

> The media as a set of institutions and practices ... are implicated in the regular advocacy of 'common sense' ... But ... when pushed to do so by popular mobilizations and mass struggles, the media may be able to ... enhance prospects for change. (2015, pp. 204–285)

The concept of structural power, or power as being enmeshed in complex networks that entail not only domination but also consent, can be also found in the work of French philosopher Michel Foucault. Foucault argues that there was a need to focus not on power in the abstract, but on *power relations*, or 'the strategies, networks, the mechanisms, all those techniques by which a decision is accepted and by which that decision could not but be taken in the way it was' (1988, pp. 103–104). In his later work, Foucault became particularly interested in the relationship of strategies of power to the conduct of government, and what he termed *governmentality*, or the 'new governmental techniques' that balanced 'political power wielded over legal subjects with pastoral power wielded over live individuals' (1988, p. 67; cf. Dean, 2014). The legal dimension of power is particularly important since, for Foucault, the distinctiveness of power in modern societies is that it is exercised over free individuals: 'power is exercised over free subjects, and only insofar as they are free' (Foucault, 1982, p. 221). For Foucault:

> The exercise of power consists in guiding the possibility of conduct and putting in order the possible outcome. Basically power is less a confrontation between two adversaries or the linking of one to another than a question of government. This word must be allowed the very broad meaning which it had in the sixteenth century. 'Government' did not refer only to

political structures or to the management of states ... but also modes of action, more or less considered and calculated, which were destined to act upon the possibilities of action of other people. *To govern, in this sense, is to structure the possible field of action of others.* (1982, p. 221, emphasis in the original)

Thompson (1995, pp. 16–17) identified four forms of power that operate in modern societies: political, economic, coercive, and cultural or symbolic (see Table 1.1):

1. *Political* – institutions and practices primarily concerned with coordination and regulation; this form of power is primarily held through government and the state;
2. *Economic* – the ability to control processes of production, distribution, prices in markets, and accumulation; such power is most notably held by corporations, but may also be held by other institutional agents, such as trade unions or producers' associations;
3. *Coercive* – the capacity to use actual or potential force against others, particularly in combination with political power, notably associated with the armed forces, the police, security agencies, etc.;
4. *Cultural/symbolic* – power associated with the ability to control the production, transmission and reception of symbolic forms, or the means of information and communication.

Table 1.1 Forms of power

Forms of power	Resources	Paradigmatic institutions
Economic power	Material and financial resources	Economic institutions (e.g. commercial enterprises, trade unions, producers' groups)
Political power	Authority	Political institutions (e.g. nation-states, regulatory agencies)
Coercive power	Physical and armed force	Coercive institutions (e.g. military, police, prisons)
Symbolic power	Means of information and communication	Cultural institutions (e.g. religious institutions, schools and universities, media industries)

Source: Thompson (1995, p. 17). Reprinted with permission of Polity and Stanford University Press.

Thompson argued that media are primarily associated with forms of *cultural power*, or *symbolic power*, that arise from the capacity to control, use and distribute resources associated with the means of information and communication. Symbolic power matters because it is the principal means by which the actions of others can be shaped through the transformation of values, beliefs and ideas, or the practices and institutions of *culture*. Media are particularly important in terms of Thompson's schema, since they are not only institutional sites through which cultural or symbolic power may be exercised, but are also major corporations that invest in resources, employ people, and produce goods and services, and therefore exercise significant economic power. The shift from mass communications traditions of media research to critical media theories entailed a shift in the focus of studies of power from relational power to structural power. Whereas earlier approaches to media focused upon power in terms of influence and the impact of particular media messages, the critical media studies tradition understood the question of media power in terms of *ideology* and structural power, and the complex relationship of dominant ideologies to questions of representation, consent, and the social construction of reality, or what Hall (1982, p. 64) referred to as 'the power to define the rules of the game'.

The second major issue in theories of media power is the extent to which media power is largely reflective of other systems of social power (economic, political and coercive), or whether it has its own internal dynamics and relative autonomy from other spheres. It has been the process of drawing the interconnections between these two dimensions of media power – the cultural-symbolic and the political-economic – that has historically defined the critical political economy approach. While the mass communications tradition, and associated approaches such as modernization theories, have tended to approach economic, political, coercive and cultural power as relatively discrete in their nature and operations, the critical paradigm saw these as being interconnected.

The relationship between different forms of power, and how these play themselves out in terms of global media, also constitutes an important point of difference between political economy and globalization theories. Whereas political economists identify strong overlaps between economic, political and cultural/symbolic power, globalization theorists have often pointed to disjunctures between these forms of power. Globalization theorists tend to see power relations globally as being more diffuse and decentred, whereas political economists tend to view such power relations as highly concentrated, and becoming increasingly concentrated in fewer hands over time.

The remainder of this chapter will provide an overview of the key concepts that will inform the discussion of different approaches to global media, such as modernization theories, critical political economy, and globalization theories. It proposes four frameworks to global media that provide analytical lenses through which key concepts can be understood. They are:

- The economic framework
- The policy framework
- The cultural framework
- The digital framework.

The economic framework

As media power is related to economic power, it is therefore important that we understand the economic environment in which media businesses operate. The field of media economics provides important insights in this regard, although it is in some key respects fragmented due to the limited history of engagement, and the often intense intellectual rivalry, between the mainstream tradition and critical political economy.[1] Nonetheless, the economics of media is important, not least because, as Gillian Doyle (2013, p. 1) has observed:

> as a discipline [economics] is highly relevant to understanding how media firms and industries operate ... [because] most of the decisions taken by those who run media organizations are, to a greater or lesser extent, influenced by resource and financial issues.

As with other branches of economics, media economics focuses upon how firms and consumers interact through two types of structures: markets and industries. Media companies operate in three types of markets. First, there is the *market for creative content*, or the ability to produce and/or distribute material that is sufficiently compelling to audiences, readers or users for them to exchange money and/or time for access to such content. This creates a market for creative talent, professionals and specialist labour. Second, there is the *market for financial resources*, or the ability to generate capital to finance their ongoing operations as well as new investments in technology, distribution platforms or territorial expansion of their operations. Finally, there is the *market for audiences* (also referred to as readers, users or consumers), and the competition both for people's spending behaviour and the time and attention they devote to accessing the content of a particular media company, as against other uses of their time. Garnham (1990) proposed that media companies are simultaneously competing for consumer expenditure, for advertising expenditure, and for the free time of people, in what has been termed the 'experience economy' (Gilmore & Pine, 2011).

The range of media products is heterogeneous and highly complex, and Doyle (2013, p. 12) has observed that it is 'difficult to define what constitutes a unit of media content'. For example, if one purchases a newspaper or magazine, the content is the whole product, whereas with radio and television, one consumes particular programmes, rather than the whole content of a network or service. One distinctive feature of media markets that media economists have observed is that they are typically *two-sided markets*, or even *multi-sided markets*. Media businesses provide platforms that bring together two or more agents operating on different sides of a market, but whose relationships are interdependent. For example, broadcasters compete for the time of audiences with their products and services, selling access to audiences to advertisers, and hence to the producers of other goods and services who advertise on their channels (Ballon, 2014, p. 78). Similarly, digital platform providers such as Facebook reduce transaction costs for multiple agents – including both commercial agents and individual users – by easing interaction between them, and profiting from the network effects of making it a requirement to be on these platforms in order to derive such benefits (Bauer, 2014). Media organizations compete for both audiences and advertisers in particular *geographical markets*, which may be local, national or international (see Figure 1.2). In some instances, particularly in relation to the allocation of broadcasting spectrum, government regulatory authorities determine the geographical reach of the market area in terms of audiences. In other instances, most notably in relation to the internet, the global reach of the medium enables media organizations to compete in a market space that is at least potentially borderless and global.

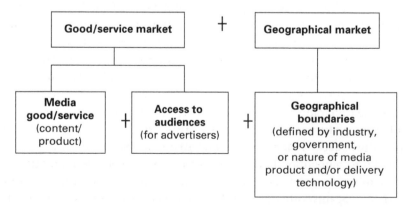

Figure 1.2 The nature of media markets

Source: Picard (1989, p. 21). Reprinted with permission of SAGE publications.

A characteristic of media industries has been a tendency towards *concentration of media ownership*. Various studies (Finn *et al.*, 2004; Noam, 2009, 2016; Albarran, 2010) have found no media industries to be perfectly competitive, and a characteristic market structure to be that of *oligopoly*, with few sellers and very limited price competition. Gomery (1989, p. 50) observed that 'economic theory has a hard time with oligopolists', because they have a wide range of options in terms of market behaviour, and a degree of control over market pressures. Competition between oligopolists is also often marked by periodic collusion, including lobbying of politicians to maintain favourable policy conditions, and maintaining barriers to entry for potential new competitors. Expansion in the media sector involves not only competitive strategies to expand market share within particular markets, but also what is known as *vertical expansion*, or takeovers, mergers and acquisitions of related production and distribution interests within the industry supply chain, and *conglomeration*, which involves expansion into complementary activities, either through mergers and acquisitions or the development of new enterprises (Doyle, 2013, pp. 9–21). A key aim of media conglomerates is to enable productive synergies to be developed across multiple product lines 'by retooling content for additional uses, by trying to create successful cross-media concept products in films, books and games, and using staff from one media operation to provide services to another' (Picard, 2011b, p. 212). Where such strategies are successful, as they have been for many years with Disney, and as seen today with the *Harry Potter* franchise, or the cinematic adaptation of Marvel comics characters such as *Spiderman*, *Iron Man* and *X-Men* since the merger with Disney in 2009, conglomeration can develop very powerful and recognizable global media products.

The policy framework

Policy institutions have a central role in regulating the ownership, production and distribution of media in all forms. Although the precise institutional forms and underlying principles vary across nations, the regulation of communication itself is, as James Michael (1990, p. 40) has observed, 'as old as blood feuds over insults, and … as classic an issue as deciding whose turn it is to use the talking drum or the ram's horn'. Different branches of social theory identify distinctive rationales for media policy, and there are different forms that regulation can take, that can involve a mix of state and non-state actors. It is also important to note that media policy and regulation sit within the wider framework of media governance, which can include 'the totality of institutions and instruments that shape and organize a policy system – formal and informal, national and supranational, public and private, large-scale and smaller scale' (Freedman, 2008, p. 15).

In economic theory, three key arguments that underpin state intervention in media markets is commonly justified in terms of *market failure* (Picard, 2011b). Three issues in particular feature in such discussions. First, there is the *concentration of media ownership*, and undesirable consequences that stem from it, including restricting entry to potential new competitors, restricting the 'marketplace of ideas', and giving too much power and influence over the political process to 'media moguls'. Second, there are *externalities*, or costs and benefits borne by parties other than those directly engaged in producing or consuming the good or service in question. Externalities may be negative or positive: excessive violence in the media may be seen to generate negative externalities by promoting anti-social behaviour, whereas locally produced media content may promote positive externalities such as enabling citizens to develop a better understanding of their national culture, or encouraging overseas travellers to visit the country. Policies such as content standards regulations or local content rules may provide ways of minimizing negative externalities or promoting positive ones in such instances. Finally, media can constitute *public goods* that are: (1) non-rivalrous, in that one person's consumption does not prevent another person from consuming them; and (2) non-excludable, where price-based discrimination between consumers would not be appropriate. Both broadcast media and internet-based content have public good elements, and it may be that private provision leads to undersupply of some forms of content. Government support for non-profit public service broadcasters (PSBs) is often justified on this basis, as PSBs can be required by law to provide programme types that are undersupplied by commercial media and which are considered to have cultural value or positive externalities, such as children's programming, documentaries, arts and science programmes, and programmes for cultural and linguistic minorities.

The issues around the role of the media in public communication has a breadth and significance that cannot be captured by purely economic arguments. In democratic societies, plurality of ownership and dispersed distribution structures allow for a breadth of voices and representations that will most closely approximate the breadth of viewpoints in society itself (Curran, 2005). Moreover, as Baker (2007, p. 16) argued, 'the widest possible dispersion of media power reduces the risk of the abuse of communicative power'. Our concerns about media moguls such as Rupert Murdoch, Silvio Berlusconi and others have never been purely about their economic impact. It has also been a concern that their control over media can be used to shape the political system itself, from using media to prevent the enactment of laws and regulations that may restrict media concentration to active intervention in the structure of the main political parties themselves (or, in Berlusconi's case, forming his own governing party, Italy's *Forza Italia*). In the twenty-first century, there may be a 'battle of the moguls' taking place, between the traditional media barons such as Murdoch, and the digital media giants such as Facebook's Mark Zuckerberg, Amazon's Jeff Bezos and Silicon Valley entrepreneurs such as Peter Thiel and Elon Musk.

The precise forms that media policy and regulation take are shaped by the overall national media system. One influential account of national media systems has been that of Hallin and Mancini (2004), which distinguishes between market liberal, democratic corporatist and political partisan models. The democratic corporatist models – characteristic of Germany, Austria and the Scandinavian countries – have tended to be associated with the strongest forms of public interest media regulation, although strong PSBs can exist in some market liberal environments, as seen with the BBC in Great Britain (cf. Syvertsen *et al.*, 2014 on the Nordic nations). Curran and Park (2000) proposed differentiating media systems on a fourfold axis between authoritarian and democratic societies on one axis and neoliberal and regulated media systems on the other. Such taxonomies are informed by the perception that 'ways of understanding the world's media system are unduly influenced by the experience of a few, untypical countries' and that this 'distorts understanding not only of non-Western countries but also of a large part of the West as well' (Curran & Park, 2000, p. 15).

The combination of media convergence and media globalization poses fundamental questions about the sustainability of media policy models developed in the twentieth century for contemporary media environments. As Konrad von Finckenstein, then-Chair of the Canadian Radio-Television and Telecommunications Commission (CRTC), observed:

> The [media] industry is going through fundamental change in technology, in business models and in corporate structures. It has become a single industry, thoroughly converged and integrated. Yet it continues to be regulated under … Acts which date from 20 years ago. Authority continues to be divided among different departments and agencies. (Finckenstein, 2011, p. 1)

Media convergence refers to the combination of computing, communications, and media content around networked digital media platforms. It involves the rise of new, digitally based companies such as Google, Apple, Microsoft, Amazon and others as significant media content and access providers, the metamorphosis of established media institutions as digital content producers and distributors, the rapid growth of social network media platforms, the proliferation of user-created content, and multi-screen accessing of media content (e.g. accessing TV programmes from tablet computers). The policy challenge posed is whether these broader patterns of media convergence also point towards global policy convergence, with pressures to respond to the challenge of digital content platforms that lack a clear territorial basis.

The cultural framework

As the media are central to the provision of cultural or symbolic resources globally, integral to the exercise of cultural or symbolic power, and at the forefront of contemporary forms of cultural identity, debates about the cultural impact of global media are vitally important to any discussions of globalization. The ways in which the media are linked to culture more generally are complex. One approach, which has elements of conventional aesthetic theory as well as being influenced by the neo-Marxist 'Frankfurt School', questions whether we should consider mass media to be 'culture' at all. From this perspective, the mass media – developed in advanced capitalist economies as the culture industry – have been engaged in a debasement of culture, by industrializing its production, commodifying its consumption and reducing its content to either pro-capitalist propaganda or 'mere' entertainment that provides a distraction and temporary salve to the masses (Steinert, 2003). From this perspective, mass media are seen largely as ideological supports to the dominant corporate and political interests, and 'meaningful' culture is that which is engaged in political struggle against such interests. This is not an approach that will be considered at length in this book, although elements of such an approach feature in the critical political economy tradition of studying global media, particularly where global media are seen as promoting a dominant ideology that has variously been termed neoliberalism, globalism or consumerism.

A quite different approach comes from the anthropological understanding of culture, which has been less concerned with the 'great works' works of art and literature than with culture as the lived experience of people and communities, or what Edward Tylor described in 1903 as 'that complex whole which includes knowledge, belief, art, morals, law, custom, and any other capabilities acquired by man [sic] as a member of society' (quoted in Thompson, 1990, p. 128). This is a definition of *culture as lived experience*, or what people do in a given social situation, with the resources available to them, to both produce and consume culture. Culture is understood here less as a showcase for human excellence and more as a diverse repository of symbolic forms. Raymond Williams, one of the founding figures of cultural studies, proposed that culture was not simply an 'ideal' concept concerned principally with art and aesthetics, but that it existed in the anthropological sense of being 'a particular way of life, whether of a people, a period [or] a group' (Williams, 1976, p. 18). For Williams, this 'social' definition of culture referred to 'meanings and values not only in art and learning but also in institutions and ordinary behavior' (Williams, 1965, p. 57).

The study of culture has been a key element of the discipline of cultural studies, which has grown in significance since the 1960s. In a key essay in the field, Stuart Hall (1986) described the *two paradigms* of cultural studies as being culturalism and structuralism. Drawing attention to the formative texts of British cultural historians such as Richard Hoggart, Raymond Williams and E. P. Thompson, Hall observed that these authors developed an understanding of culture as lived experience that moved beyond dichotomies between 'high' and 'low' culture, to instead 'conceptualize culture as interwoven with all social practices, and those practices, in turn, as a common form of human activity ... through which men and women make history' (Hall, 1986, p. 39). This understanding of culture has been central to what Hall terms the *culturalist* tradition, with its focus upon the lived experience of ordinary people.

The alternative paradigm of *structuralism* was concerned less with what people did than with the overarching social conditions under which they did it. It drew attention to the ways in which individuals were the 'products' of a system of social, cultural, linguistic and psychological relationships that existed independently of the actions of particular individuals, which possessed an underlying structural 'code' that was not in itself immediately accessible to those individuals who were expected to adopt it. Structuralism was strongly influenced by developments in the field of semiotics, and its understanding of language as a system or code where, as Umberto Eco argued, 'every act of communication ... presupposes a signification system as its necessary condition' (Eco, 1976, p. 9).

The relationship between culture as lived experience (culturalism) and culture as a complex signifying system (structuralism) generates some interesting tensions when applied to popular mass media forms, and in particular to the question of the relationship of critical media and cultural theories to popular media and culture. This question has been approached at the empirical level, aiming to map the relationship of media to their audiences and how people use the media, such as the *uses and gratifications* approach to audience studies in mass communications research (Curran, 1990), and at the structural level of the *dominant ideology* thesis, where it is argued that the dominant meanings of popular media reflect the class interests of those who own and control these institutions. Mark Gibson has observed that cultural studies has faced a recurring tension around how it approaches power, between viewing culture as 'a general pattern of social organization', with its own logics and determinants, and as ideology, 'requiring everything to be referenced to "real relations" at the social level' (Gibson, 2007, p. 107). It will be argued in this book that critical theories of global media have typically worked with the second interpretation, of culture as an ideological system that serves dominant interests, and that a number of the weaknesses of the critical approach stem from this.

The other key issue raised by the relationship of global media to culture is whether there is a tendency towards a common global culture, whose shape is at least partly attributable to common exposure to the cultural products of global media. Theories of global media as otherwise diverse as Marshall McLuhan's concept of the 'Global Village', modernization theories, and dependency or 'cultural imperialism' theories all posit some version of the argument that global media are vectors for some or other form of global culture. But it is useful to think about how the terms 'culture' and 'media' are being defined in such debates. If culture is understood in the more structural sense of a shared symbolic order, with the media increasingly at the heart of such systems of communication, then global media may indeed be generating forms of global culture. It would mark the globalization of what John Thompson (1995, p. 46) termed the 'mediatization of culture' as a core feature of a globalizing capitalist modernity. If, however, the concept of culture is understood in the anthropological sense of being a *lived and shared experience*, or 'way of life of a people', then it is hard to maintain that we live in a global culture, or that we are heading towards one. Insofar as claims about a global culture entail a convergence of the customs, beliefs and ways of living between the different people of the world, then there is considerable evidence to suggest that such a convergence is not happening, even as globalization entails more interaction among different peoples and cultures.

The digital framework

The information and communications technology (ICT) revolution that has gained momentum from the 1980s onwards has fundamentally transformed the global media environment. The global popularization of the internet in the 1990s and 2000s saw all media content take a digital form, and digital media has itself been transformed with the rise of social media from the mid-2000s onwards (Meikle, 2016) and the migration of digital content from networked personal computers to a diverse array of mobile devices (smartphones, tablet devices, e-readers etc.), and to traditional media platforms such as television through digital streaming services (Netflix, Amazon Prime etc.). Transformations in digital media and ICT capabilities need to be understood in the context of what has been termed the 'Fourth Industrial Revolution', defined as:

The staggering confluence of emerging technology breakthroughs, covering wide-ranging fields such as artificial intelligence (AI), robotics, the

Internet of things (IoT), autonomous vehicles, 3D printing, nanotechnology, biotechnology, materials science, energy storage and quantum computing ... [and] the fusion of technologies across the physical, digital and biological worlds. (Schwab, 2017, p. 1)

The impact of digital media is particularly profound as it is associated with *media convergence*, or the integration of ICTs, communication networks and media content, combined with a decoupling of relationships between platforms and types of media content, as content now moves seamlessly across digital platforms and media devices. It is also a force for *media globalization*, as the internet enables the global distribution of information and media content across common digital platforms, with far less formal gatekeeping at a national level than has characterized cinema or broadcasting. Media convergence occurs in parallel with a series of other changes in the global media and communications environment that include: (1) increased access to high-speed broadband internet; (2) the globalization of media platforms, content and services; (3) accelerated platform and service innovation, that makes it increasingly difficult to define the 'industry' that major digital companies are operating in; (4) the proliferation of user-created content, and the associated shift of media users from audiences to participants; and (5) a blurring of public–private and age-based distinctions, as all media content is increasingly distributed and consumed online (Flew, 2016a).

These radical changes in the media landscape require a rethink of core media policy principles, as well as how we understand the digital media economy. Identification of the key *media industry actors* has changed, with 'new' media giants such as Google, Apple, Amazon, Facebook, Netflix, Alibaba, Baidu, Tencent etc. possessing a different relationship to media laws, policies and regulations from more traditional media giants such as Time Warner, News Corporation, Disney and other big media conglomerates. For example, media ownership rules have traditionally been premised upon a relatively stable definition of a media industry, whereas a feature of the new digital players is that they aim to move across conventional industry boundaries, having a promiscuous relationship to the traditional content providers and distribution channels. This opens up questions of regulatory parity between 'old media' and 'new media' platforms and services. Similarly, there are difficulties in applying media content rules, as there are questions of the equivalent treatment of media content across platforms as digital content now moves easily between print, broadcast and online, as well as a growing fuzziness around the distinction between 'media content' and personal communication, and between mass media that is subject to government regulations and user-created content which is for the most part free of government controls (Flew, 2014a).

As the internet is a global network, and major developments in digital platforms have happened largely independently of national governments, there has been the question of whether the turn to digital media is a factor in the weakening of nation-states. Digital media platforms have proven to be hard to regulate at the national level, partly because of jurisdictional issues – the major platforms are not territorially based in most nation-states in the world – and partly because of the bottom-up, user-driven nature of content on the platforms, which makes content monitoring by external agencies extremely difficult and time-consuming. In some instances, the rise of digital and social media has been seen as a factor behind why nationally based regulations are giving way to greater management of media content by the social media platform providers themselves, as with user flagging of inappropriate content on sites such as Google and Facebook (Crawford & Lumby, 2013). There is also the issue of whether new supranational forms of regulation are coming into play, and whether non-governmental organizations (NGOs) can work more productively with supranational agencies and perhaps with the platform providers themselves around shared policy objectives, as national forms of law, regulation and governance become increasingly ineffectual in the face of these globalizing forces (Mansell & Raboy, 2011).

An argument that is made in this book is that claims about the 'demise of the nation-state', and the inability to manage digital media flows at a national level, are overstated (Flew & Waisbord, 2015; Flew, 2016b). There are clearly parts of the world where there is, and always has been, a significant degree of monitoring and filtering of internet content: China, Russia, Iran and Saudi Arabia are countries that come to mind in this regard. In other cases, crackdowns on political dissent have been accompanied by the periodic banning of particular social media platforms, as in countries such as Pakistan, Egypt and Turkey at various times. Outside of the context of authoritarian states, there are disagreements about the appropriate jurisdictional reach of government with regards to global media platforms, as seen with regulations adopted by the European Union towards platform providers such as Google with the 'Right to be Forgotten' laws and associated privacy provisions (Holt & Malčić, 2015; Rustad & Kulevska, 2015). More generally, as Iosifidis (2016, p. 29) has argued, 'states retain a central role in the growth and institutionalization of global governance', not least because 'the most significant shifts in economic globalization and the rise of multinational enterprises are heavily dependent on state support in order to provide an environment of smooth functioning'. The apparently deterritorialized nature of digital media platforms as compared to traditional, territorially based print and broadcast media, should not be conflated with the assumption that such entities can operate completely independently of the legal, policy and institutional infrastructures that have historically been associated with governments and nation-states.

Conclusion

This chapter has identified key concepts that will inform the approach taken to understanding global media throughout the book. It has observed that when we speak of 'media' of any form, we are referring to technological means of communication, with the term 'technology' understood in its widest sense to refer to practices and institutions associated with technologies, as well as the devices and platforms themselves. The media are therefore a combination of technologies and enabling infrastructures, industries and institutions, and content that forms part of wider cultures.

A recurring challenge in communication and media studies is that of balancing media-centric and society-centric accounts of communications. Media theorists often point to the 'blind spots' that exist in other branches of social theory, such as the explanations of political behaviour and citizenship that exclude the increasingly central role of the institutions and practices of the media, in both its traditional forms and increasingly online. At the same time, the need to situate the media in a wider socio-cultural and political-economic context places limits on the need to avoid simple cause-and-effect arguments around the media and societal developments. The complexities of these relationships become apparent when we consider the relationship of media to power. Media are associated with cultural or symbolic power, as distinct from political, economic and coercive forms of power, but these are clearly categories that intersect with and overlap with one another.

Finally, the chapter sought to situate the media in four broader fields of study. First, it considered the economic framework of media, and some of the distinctive insights that economic approaches can provide to understanding media markets and ownership structures. Second, it considered the policy framework and the degree to which the activities of media organizations are tied up within nationally based structures of laws, policies and regulations, and whether and how these are being transformed by media globalization. Third, it considered the cultural framework, with particular reference to debates about whether culture is best understood in terms of distinctive ways of life or as signifying systems with their own structural logics. The relationship between the 'culturalist' and 'structuralist' approaches to media is important in the global context, as media can only operate as socially meaningful cultural forms insofar as their codes and meanings are accepted across societies and cultures: the wider cultural influences of media cannot be derived solely from the technologies themselves, or even from their industry and ownership structures. Finally, the chapter considered the digital framework, and the challenge presented to traditional approaches to media by the internet and convergent digital technologies and platforms. The argument made, which will be returned to at different points in this book, is that we need to both recognize profound changes taking place in media around the globe and avoid falling into a determinist trap of assuming that media globalization means the end of nation-states, national cultures and identities, and territorially defined systems of production, distribution and governance. In that respect, understanding global media also requires us to set limits to 'the global' as a structural force that overrides all other ways of thinking about media and society.

Note

1 These divisions in media economics speak to much wider methodological and philosophical divides within the discipline of economics. Earl and Peng (2012) identified 12 distinct 'brands' of economic thought, meaning that the mainstream neoclassical approach is confronted not only by radical political economy, as in media economics debates, but by areas as diverse as 'old' and 'new' institutional economics, behavioural economics, evolutionary economics, Austrian economics, Post-Keynesian economics, feminist economics and others. These multiple 'heterodox' forms of economics differ not only in their underlying assumptions and their methodologies, but also in their perspectives on the capitalist economic system itself, with some being very positive (e.g. Austrian economics) and others highly critical.

CHAPTER 2

Modernization theories and development communication

The rise of nation-states

The origins of the modern nation-state can be found in Europe during and after the period of absolutist monarchies. In 1500, there were about 150 independent political entities in Europe; by 1900, there were 25. Gianfranco Poggi (1990, p. 19) has defined the modern nation-state as:

> an organization or set of organizations ... [where] political power must be vested and exercised through a set of purposefully contrived arrangements – a body of rules, a series of roles, a body of resources – seen as concerned with and committed to a distinctive, unified and unifying set of interests and principles.

Other features of the modern nation-state are that:

1. In its sovereign possession of political power, it is clearly differentiated from other organizations (churches, corporations, political parties, trade unions, etc.) within that territory, who constitute the various branches of civil society;
2. It possesses a monopoly of legitimate violence within that territory, but has also engaged in the 'pacification of life within the state's boundaries' (Calhoun, 1997, p. 67) that enable it to provide populations with peace and security from non-state, or illegitimate, forms of violence;
3. It is sovereign within its own defined territory, possessing the unique capacity to police its own borders, collect taxes and duties within that territory, and administer populations through the provision of economic, social and other resources;
4. It possesses territorial jurisdiction, or 'exclusive control over a portion of the earth – its territory, over which it routinely exercises jurisdiction

and law enforcement, and whose integrity it is committed to protecting against encroachment from any other political power' (Poggi, 1990, p. 21).

A number of other factors were coexistent with the rise of the modern nation-state. The capacity to exercise sovereign power entailed improvements in the administrative capacity of states and the rise of bureaucratic forms of organization, as well as broader measures to develop national economies and enhance overall prosperity which would give states the resources to exercise their powers of government. Long-distance trade, the regional differentiation of production and the migration of people from the countryside to cities were also features of economic modernization. The development of advanced transport and communications systems acquired a growing importance in modern nation-states as 'more and more of social life took place through forms of mediation – markets, communications technologies, bureaucracies – which removed relationships from the realm of direct, face-to-face interaction' (Calhoun, 1997, p. 68).

The acquisition of new powers held by the state in its sovereign capacity raised the question of its legitimacy to exercise such powers over subject populations. As the historian Eric Hobsbawm has observed, 'the equation nation = state = people, and especially sovereign people, undoubtedly linked nation to territory, since the structure and definition of states was now essentially territorial' (Hobsbawm, 1990, p. 19). But it also entailed a new form of political community, whereby the people became citizens of a state, and where 'membership of a political community i.e. citizenship, bestows upon the individual both responsibilities and rights, duties and powers, constraints and liberties' (Held, 2006, p. 64). In the modern liberal-constitutional state, this also meant that:

> government exists to safeguard the rights and liberties of citizens who are ultimately the best judges of their own interests ... government must be restricted in scope and constrained in practice in order to ensure the maximum possible freedom of every citizen. (Held, 2006, pp. 64–65)

But it also entailed what Calhoun (1997, p. 69) described as:

> An ascending account of political legitimacy ... [where] political power could only be legitimate when it reflected the will, or at least served the interests, of the people subject to it ... [and] 'the people' constituted a unified force, capable not only of rising *en masse* against an illegitimate state, but capable of bestowing legitimacy on a state that properly fitted with, and served the interest of, the people.

Nations and nationalism

The rise of the nation as a political formation forged new relationships between the institutions and agencies of the state and the people as a national citizenry. But any account of the modern nation-state also needs to recognize the cultural dimensions of nationhood and national identity. Calhoun pointed out that 'recognition as a nation clearly requires ... some level of integration ... and collective identity – the recognition of the whole by its members, and a sense of individual self that includes membership in the whole' (1997, p. 4). But many forms of groupings can provide a sense of social solidarity and collective identity, from families and corporations to religions, political parties, armies, trade unions and much more. Membership of a nation also entails belonging to what Benedict Anderson (1991, pp. 6–7) termed an *imagined community*, where people feel 'connected to people that they have never seen'; not to humanity as a whole, but rather to those people with whom they perceive themselves to share a 'deep, horizontal comradeship' based on history, culture, and other markers of identity. This brings forth the question of *nationalism*, as a distinctive form of imagining collective identity and social solidarity associated with the modern nation. Calhoun (1997, pp. 4–5) identified ten features of nationalism, of which the majority will apply to all nations to greater or lesser degrees:

1. Boundaries of territory, or population, or both;
2. Indivisibility – the notion that the nation is an integral unit;
3. Sovereignty, or at least the aspiration to sovereignty, and thus formal equality with other nations as an autonomous, self-governing state;
4. An 'ascending' notion of legitimacy, where government is just only when it serves the interests of the nation and its people;
5. Popular participation in collective affairs, and a population that can be mobilized on the basis of national membership;
6. Categorical equivalence of individuals within a nation as a part of the nation as a whole;
7. Culture, including some combination of language, shared beliefs and values, habitual practices, and common rituals and ceremonies;
8. A sense of the nation as having existed through historical time;
9. Shared kinship relations or ethnic/racial characteristics;
10. Special historical or even sacred relations to a certain territory.

The German social theorist Karl Deutsch placed culture and communication at the centre of his account of nationalism. Deutsch observed that people are bound to a national community on the basis of 'complementary habits and facilities of communication', and that 'membership in a people consists in wide complementarity of social communication ... [and] the ability to communicate more effectively, and over a wider range of subjects, with members of one large group than with outsiders' (Deutsch, 1994, pp. 26, 27). Such a capacity for social communication is not simply a matter of a common language or a shared history; it is supported and reinforced by institutions and technologies of mass communication, public libraries, public monuments and collective rituals (cf. Mihelj, 2011, p. 22).

Defining nationalism as 'the fusing of culture and polity' (p. 13), Ernest Gellner stressed the role played by 'high' culture – the arts, literature, performance, historical artefacts held in galleries and museums – in the formation of national identities, as well as the role played by mass education in disseminating this national 'high' culture to a nation's people (Gellner, 1983, pp. 35–38). Anderson identified the fusion of capitalism and print technologies as promoting national languages and a reading public, as well as creating languages of power and public administration (Anderson, 1991, pp. 39–45). Hobsbawm (1990, pp. 141–142) saw mass media as an important driver of nationalism in two key respects. First, mass media enabled popular ideologies to be 'standardized, homogenized, and transformed, as well as ... exploited for the purposes of deliberate propaganda by private interests and states'. Second, mass media were able to 'make what were in effect national symbols part of the life of every individual, and thus to break down the divisions between the public and local spheres in which most citizens normally lived'. He described the humanization of the British Royal Family as both a domestic family and public icons of national identification as an example of this. Also important has been the fusion of the mass media with other critical symbols of national identity, most notably those in the burgeoning popular pursuit of sporting competitions.

Any discussion of nationalism needs to note the strong critiques that exist of such nationalistic sentiments and claims to a historically distinct national identity. Marxism has long presented itself as an alternative to nationalism, proposing working-class internationalism under the communist movement as an alternative to identifying with the ruling classes of particular nations. The experience of World War I, where the Second International fragmented in the face of conflict among the European powers, the question of 'socialism in one country' posed by the Russian Revolution of 1917, and the subsequent isolation of the Soviet Union have demonstrated the historical vicissitudes of the national question for Marxists (Hobsbawm, 1990, pp. 124–125). More generally, nationalism has been associated with wars, racism, colonialism, feelings of superiority of one nation over another, and the driving out, segregation or extermination of other races and ethnicities in the name of a racially and ethnically homogeneous nation. The desire for a form of post-national or cosmopolitan citizen identity that can transcend nationalism has long been a significant force, particularly among intellectuals. Stuart Hall has observed that the view of nationalism as an archaic discourse that can be trumped by modernist notions of rationality and reason has been associated with the belief that it will disappear over time:

> The great discourses of modernity – in this respect Marxism no less than liberalism, both in their different ways Enlightenment 'grand narratives' – led us to expect, not the revival but the gradual disappearance of the nationalist passion. Attachments to nation, like those of tribe, region, place, religion, were thought to be archaic particularisms which capitalist modernity would, gradually or violently, dissolve or supercede. (Hall, 1993a, p. 353)

Attitudes to nationalism in general, and cultural nationalism in particular, will be a recurring theme of this book. Different approaches to global media understand the relationship of nations to global media in different ways, from the preference for cultural hybridity associated with globalization theories to the questions of unequal power and cultural domination that political economists have focused upon. A complicating factor is the ambivalent place of nationalist discourses in anti-colonial struggles and the formation of identities in the 'Third World' or 'Global South'. Nationalist ideologies were deployed by the European powers to justify colonial expansion and the formation of empires; the military strength and self-proclaimed moral superiority of the colonial power could be counterposed to the alleged inferiority of those races and peoples that had permitted themselves to be colonized.

But struggles against colonial rule themselves very often took a national form, as they allowed for mass movements to form around the claim that a unique national identity was being suppressed by the colonialist powers. As Calhoun has observed, nationalism itself became a 'cosmopolitan discourse', that could be 'transplanted from one setting to another', and leaders of anti-colonial movements 'drew upon the discourse of nationalism to frame their opposition to colonial rule [as] they combined indigenous traditions and international rhetoric in ways that could be strikingly innovative and which could transform both indigenous and international ideas' (1997, pp. 106, 107). To take one example, the Chinese Revolution of 1949, led by Mao Zedong, fused anti-colonial nationalism and Marxism in ways that would have global implications, including endorsement by the Chinese Communist Party (CCP) of the notion of a 'Third World' of nations not aligned to the United States or the Soviet Union.

New nations, the mass media and national cultural identities

In 1945, at the end of World War II, there were 72 sovereign nations, of which 45 were admitted as members to the newly established United Nations. In 2016, there were 195 sovereign nations, of which 193 were UN members. In the period prior to the break-up of the Soviet Union and Eastern European communism in 1989, the vast majority of these new nations were from Asia, Africa, the Middle East and the Americas. There were 85 new nations created between 1945 and 1975, of which more than half (44) were in Africa, with another 17 in Asia, eight in the Americas and the Caribbean, eight in the Middle East, six in Oceania and two in Europe. In the vast majority of cases, these new nations had previously been colonies of major European powers such as Great Britain, France, the Netherlands, Belgium, Spain and Portugal. The period from 1975 to 2016 saw 39 new nations emerge, with a particular surge in Europe and West Asia after the dissolution of the Republic of Yugoslavia in 1990 and the Soviet Union in 1991 (see Table 2.1).

Culture is one of the means by which nation-states seek to integrate otherwise diverse groups of people into common national communities. Michael Schudson (1994, p. 64) has made the point that 'language, symbols, rituals, and stories – culture, in a word – bring individuals and families of varying circumstances and backgrounds together in a collectivity with which people may strongly identify, take primary meanings from, and find emotionally satisfying'. The modern nation-state 'self-consciously uses language policy, formal education, collective rituals, and mass media to integrate citizens and ensure their loyalty' (p. 65). The question of what contributions media, communications and cultural policies could make to the development of these newly independent nations was a vitally important one, with the United Nations Educational, Scientific and Cultural Organization (UNESCO) playing a key role in brokering international conferences and disseminating information about the role that could be played by culture and mass media in national development (Mattelart, 1994, pp. 148–156).

Table 2.1 The creation and disappearance of states 1813–2016

Time period	States created	States disappearing
1816–1876	24	15
1876–1916	12	1
1916–1945	16	7
1945–1975	85	1
1975–2016	39	4

Sources: Author's own table based on Thompson and Krasner (1989), Holton (1998), Wikipedia (2017).

Schudson (1994, pp. 68–74) identifies the mass media, in both print and broadcast forms, as being among a number of cultural policy instruments that the nation-state consciously uses for the integration of national populations. Others include mass education, particularly in language and the promotion of reading 'national' texts, collective rituals that commemorate particular national events and identities, and galleries, libraries and museums that document and illustrate aspects of national history and culture. There are also 'nationalizing' forces in commercial popular culture, including large-scale sporting events, food and fashion. But broadcasting has been identified as having a particular role in consolidating national languages, promoting collective rituals, developing a shared sense of political as well as cultural identity, and projecting the nation globally and among other nations. With the major exception of the United States, broadcasting was typically 'under the strict control or regulation of the state', and 'legislation establishing broadcast systems has clearly identified national, integrative, and participatory goals for them' (Schudson, 1994, p. 74). In doing so, it was reflective of the role played by nation-states as 'the leading advocate[s] of the theory that a common culture is necessary for societal integration' (Schudson, 1994, p. 78).

The dynamics of national development in post-colonial states after World War II was driven not only by domestic factors but by the global geopolitical context of the 'Cold War' between the United States and its allies in the one camp ('the West'), and the Soviet Union and its allies on the other ('the Eastern Bloc'). McPhail (2009) attributes the origins of development communication to the 1949 Presidential Address of US President Harry S. Truman. In that speech, Truman committed to 'embark on a bold new program for making the benefits of our scientific advances and industrial progress available for the improvement and growth of underdeveloped areas' (quoted in McPhail, 2009, p. 4). Truman drew attention to the problem of underdevelopment, observing that:

> More than half the people of the world are living in conditions approaching misery … Their economic life is primitive and stagnant. Their poverty is a handicap and a threat to them and to more prosperous areas. For the first time in history, humanity possesses the knowledge and the skill to relieve the suffering of these people. (Quoted in McPhail, 2009, pp. 4–5)

Such humanitarian statements would become central to modernization theories, and to development communication as a component of these, during the 1950s and 1960s. But the onset of the Cold War was impossible to ignore as a driver of such apparent beneficence. In 1948, occupied Germany split into two states: the Soviet-aligned East Germany and the Western-aligned West Germany. Europe was dividing between an Eastern Bloc of the states of Poland, Czechoslovakia, Hungary, East Germany, Romania and Bulgaria, who would form the Warsaw Pact as a military alliance, while nations of Western

Europe would join with the US in the formation of the North American Treaty Organization (NATO). The year 1949 saw the Communist Party of China led by Mao Zedong gain power and proclaim a People's Republic of China, while two governments had formed in Korea – the communist North Korea and the pro-American South Korea – leading to the onset of the Korean War in 1950.

Communications media would be central to the Cold War in two respects. In the first instance, there was the direct transmission of communication services around the world for propaganda purposes, such as the Voice of America, Radio Free Europe and the Soviet TASS news agency. Second, advice on the development of communications infrastructure, media industries and professions, and media content was seen as enabling newly independent nations to determine their primary alignment in terms of economic and foreign policies. Political alignment to the West would enable the major global corporations to 'continue to control raw materials and develop potential markets for Western products' (Thussu, 2006, p. 24).

Modernization theories and development communication

Development communication was born in the context of theories of *modernization*, in the countries of Latin America, Asia and Africa. Modernization theories identified the cause of the 'misery' and 'stagnation' that President Truman referred to as having cultural roots, arising from the absence of dynamism in less developed societies, whether due to low levels of economic growth, the dead hand of cultural traditions, or the absence of nation-building institutions. They pointed to 'a necessary fitness between a "modern" culture and economic and political development' (Waisbord, 2001, p. 3). The problem of underdevelopment was seen as having essentially local or national causes (i.e. they were internal to the regions in question), and the route to national development was associated with the transition from 'tradition' to 'modernity', as marked by indicators such as urbanization, higher agricultural productivity, higher rates of economic growth, the development of manufacturing industries, and political institutions that enabled broader participation in public life. Coleman and Almond defined a modern society as:

> characterized ... by a comparatively high per capita income, extensive geographical and social mobility, a relatively high degree of commercialization and industrialization of the economy, an extensive and penetrative network of mass communication media, and, in general, by widespread participation and involvement by members of the society in modern social and economic processes. (1960, p. 532)

Everett Rogers, one of the leading early theorists of development communication, defined modernization as 'the process by which individuals change from a traditional way of life to a more complex, technologically advanced and rapidly changing style of life' (Rogers, 1974, p. 45).

Development communication was an important element in instilling cultural change, where 'the role of the media would be one of preparing traditional societies for modernization by helping to change traditional values, attitudes and behaviors' (Fair, 1989, p. 131). Modernization was explicitly defined around the need to emulate contemporary Western industrial societies. Eisenstadt (1966, p. 1) observed that 'historically, modernization is the process of change towards those types of social, economic, and political systems that have developed in Western Europe and North America', while Barrington Moore (1967, pp. 89–90) saw modernization as requiring 'a total transformation of a traditional or pre-modern society into the types of technology and associated social organizations that characterize the ... nations of the Western World'. Such analyses drew upon the sociology of Max Weber, particularly his notion of a modern 'mental type', and the idea that 'the most important opponent with which the spirit of capitalism has had to struggle was that type of attitude and reaction to new situations which we may designate as traditionalism' (Weber, 1978, p. 59). In the context of the Cold War, it was apparent that modernity could be socialist as well as capitalist. The industrialization of the Soviet Union under Stalin had a significant impact on economic thinking in the developing world, and Daniel Lerner, in his famous study of media and development in the Middle East, proposed that people in developing nations 'more than ever want the modern package, but reject the label "made in the USA" [or, for that matter, "made in the USSR"]. We speak, nowadays, of modernization' (Lerner, 1958, p. 45).

The dominant paradigm of development communication was emerging through the works of authors such as Daniel Lerner (1958, 1963, 1968), Lucien Pye (1963), Ithiel de Sola Pool (1963), Wilbur Schramm (1964) and Everett Rogers (1969). It was disseminated worldwide during the 1950s and 1960s through development programmes supported by US foreign aid, as well as through bodies such as UNESCO with its 'Decade of Development' programmes in the 1960s. It was influenced by concepts from development economics such as the 'vicious circle of poverty', which proposed that low incomes prevented savings and investment, which in turn inhibited improvements in productivity and economic growth, and Walt Rostow's 'Stages of Economic Growth' thesis, which proposed that all societies could experience a 'take-off' from traditional society to a modern consumer society by concentrating resources in industrial development and advancing science and technology (Nafziger, 2006, pp. 128–131). The belief that the Western path of development was a universal model that pointed the way to overcoming poverty and backwardness, and was available to all societies and cultures, was unequivocal. It was described by Lerner in these terms:

> The Western model of modernization exhibits certain components and sequences whose relevance is global. Everywhere, for example, increasing urbanization has tended to raise literacy; rising literacy has tended to increase media exposure; increasing media exposure has 'gone with' wider economic participation (per capita income) and political participation. (1958, p. 46)

The role attributed to mass media in such modernization processes – or what was referred to as the 'virtuous circle' of modernization (Lerner, 1968, p. 386) – related to transforming the mental states of individuals, to make them more open to innovation and receptive to change, and through such processes to transform the overall national culture. Ithiel de Sola Pool (1963, pp. 281–282) described the values and modes of behaviour of a 'modern' individual as being 'characterized by aspirations to achieve and improve their material condition, the ability to empathize and think at the level of the wider society, and the ability to think freely and independently of customs and superstitions'. A modernized society, for de Sola Pool, would be one that was increasingly secular and meritocratic, would reward personal effort rather than ascribed status, and would make greater use of technologies to create, acquire, retrieve and distribute information.

The contribution of mass communications media to such a modernization process would be targeted at two levels. First, for those already engaged with current issues, the mass media would provide them with richer and more detailed sources of information. Drawing upon the *two-step flow of communication model* first proposed by Katz and Lazarsfeld (1995), this group would be the potential opinion leaders in the new social order. Second, for the broad mass of the population, mass media would provide new forms of entertainment where the audience could 'find in it characters with whom they can identify and topics that bear on their own lives' (de Sola Pool, 1963, p. 287). De Sola Pool was clear that commercial entertainment media had a modernizing function, proposing that they contained 'propaganda for modernity', where 'the request for a particular purchase preference is only a small part of a plea for a whole modernized way of life' (de Sola Pool, 1963, p. 289).

The influence of Max Weber on modernization theories can be seen in their understanding of social change: change happened in the first instance at the level of the mental states of individuals, and then radiated outwards to the wider social order (Hernandez-Ramos & Schramm, 1989; Sparks, 2007). Nonetheless, as development communication strategies were typically tied to government-to-government forms of foreign aid and assistance, national strategies were developed for communication and social development. Wilbur Schramm (1964) saw the roles of communication as being: (1) to build a sense of national identity; (2) to be the voice of national development planning; (3) to teach necessary skills; (4) to expand the market for new products and services; (5) to help people to adjust to the social changes brought about by development and modernization; and (6) to enable the nation's people to understand their place in the wider global system. Everett Rogers (1974) proposed that mass media played a complementary role to interpersonal channels of communication, by promoting the diffusion of innovations, promoting higher levels of literacy, and generating more positive attitudes towards the process of social change. The relationship between mass media, the climate for modernization, adoption of innovations and behavioural change as outlined by Rogers is shown in Figure 2.1.

MODERNIZING INFLUENCES	→	CLIMATE FOR MODERNIZATION	→	ADOPTION OF INNOVATIONS	→	CONSEQUENCES IN MORE MODERN BEHAVIOUR AND DEVELOPMENT
		1. Active information-seeking		1. Awareness and correct information about innovations		1. Higher agricultural productivity
1.Mass media exposure (combined with subsequent interpersonal communication		2. Favourable attitude toward change		2. Favourable attitude toward innovations		2. Fewer children per completed family
		3. Higher aspirations		3. Adoption of innovations		3. Better health and nutrition
		4. Perceived self-control (rather than fatalism and perceived other control)		4. Continued adoption (rather than discontinuance) of innovations		4. Wider Political participation

Figure 2.1 Mass media, modernization and behavioural change
Source: Rogers (1974, p. 49). Reprinted with permission of SAGE publications.

Crisis of the modernization paradigm

From the late 1960s, the modernization paradigm faced a growing crisis. As with many of the US-led development programmes of the period, there was a significant and growing gap between the rhetoric of modernization and 'take-offs' to development and the modest outcomes of such foreign aid and investment on improving the everyday lives of people in the developing world. Development communication theorists themselves worried that the promised 'revolution of rising expectations' was turning into a 'revolution of rising frustrations' (Lerner, 1963, p. 349). The 1960s and 1970s saw rising political tensions throughout the developing world, with many nations rejecting Western development models entirely and seeking inspiration from the Soviet Union, China, or locally developed alternative models: African socialism, pan-Arabism, etc. Other nations became military dictatorships: Mattelart (1994, p. 154) estimated that the number of military dictatorships in the world doubled between 1967 and 1972.

The latter phenomenon exposed an ambiguity at the heart of the development communications project, as the spread of democracy was clearly projected as an explicit outcome of modernization, yet nation building was increasingly being pursued by authoritarian governments, often with support from the United States and other Western governments. While some came to embrace the military themselves as the modernizing agents and opinion leaders (Mattelart, 1994, pp. 152–156), others became more critical of the whole development communication paradigm. It was increasingly being observed that the paradigm had neglected 'questions of power ... [and] who had access to messages and who benefited from receiving those messages' (Fair, 1989, p. 134). The failure of modernization projects applied through the mass media to generate the anticipated forms of social and behavioural change led to the possibility that:

> the entire theory and practice of development through the dissemination of western modernity was alien to the developing world, and that its promoters, whether they were foreign experts or local officials, were distant from the realities and values of the mass of the population. (Sparks, 2007, p. 40)

Critiques of development communication as not only factoring in inequalities of power at the local, national and international levels, but in fact being complicit in the preproduction of unequal power relations, became increasingly common. The Latin American scholar Luis Ramiro Beltrán (1976) argued that the inattention to power relations in society was indicative of methodologies that combined a focus on the individual and how they should 'adjust' to social change with an underlying functionalism that was based around adjustment within the framework of existing power relations. By contrast, Beltrán argued, it was widely understood among the mass of the people in Latin America that development along the lines sought by modernization theorists would require transformation of these power relations to achieve social change. A range of researchers were also arguing that the media in developing countries were promoting Western values of commercialism and consumerism to the detriment of their local cultures and the needs of their people, and that 'these values, along with elite and/ or government ownership of the media, created a lack of media credibility' (Fair, 1989, p. 133).

In 1976, Everett Rogers, one of the pioneers of the field, referred to the 'passing of the dominant paradigm' of modernization theory in development communication, acknowledging problems with the underlying development paradigm and its assumptions about the relationship of communication to development. Rogers (1976) conceded that the dominant approach was viewed as intellectually ethnocentric, devaluing non-Western forms of knowledge and applying an individualistic approach to poverty and economic backwardness rather than one focused on social inequalities. The failure to recognize external constraints on development aspirations, combined with the focus on large-scale capital-intensive technologies, had also promoted inappropriate development models that accentuated the distance between Western 'experts' and the communities whose lives they sought to improve. The application of a top-down, communication-as-transmission approach also meant that there had been insufficient attention given to audiences as members of communities and a wider society, and the complex and socially differentiated ways in which they received and valued mass media messages.

The modernization paradigm had also overstated the potential for mass media to generate social change, relying upon a strong media effects model that was increasingly at odds with trends in mainstream media and communications scholarship, which was increasingly engaged with questions of social structure, cultural complexity, and sources of inequality and conflict in society (Hall, 1982; Jensen & Rosengren, 1990; Servaes, 1999). The critiques came in the context of a wider questioning of dominant development discourses. While the traditional approach had stressed economic growth and cultural modernization above all else, global institutions such as the World Bank were observing by the 1970s that more redistributive economic policies could simultaneously improve aggregate economic indicators and the lives of the majority of the population (Wilber & Jameson, 1988).

Participatory communication and rethinking development communication

In the wake of the crisis of the modernization paradigm, there was a significant rethinking of development communication goals, strategies and modes of engagement with local communities. Most significantly, there was a turn towards *participatory communication* that aimed to be more inclusive of and better targeted to local communities and more bottom-up in its orientation, that would address structural inequalities as a cause of poverty in developing nations rather than simply focusing upon individual behavioural change. Karin Wilkins defines participatory approaches to development communication as ones which 'centre their attention on the people engaged in and affected by social change interventions. Development is accorded to communities over nations, while communication is envisioned as dialogic rather than linear' (Wilkins, 2008, p. 1230).

The participatory communication paradigm became the dominant theoretical approach in development communication from the 1980s onwards. For participatory communication advocates such as Servaes (1989, 1999), Waisbord (2001), Huesca (2003), Wilkins (2008), Melkote (2010), Manyozo (2012) and many others, participatory communications offered the opportunity to 'build upon communication processes and technologies towards social change', and to 'broaden the vision of development communication to encompass concerns with development ... in terms of what visions of social change and communities are articulated' (Wilkins, 2008, p. 1232). In this context:

> participatory communication ... recognizes diversity in approaches to development, as opposed to assuming social change occurs along one universal path [and] the role of the development communicator then becomes one of facilitator rather than outside expert, such that local knowledge is privileged over external advice. (Wilkins, 2008, p. 1230)

The turn to participatory communication came in the context of a wider cognitive shift in development thinking towards approaches that rested less upon quantitative indicators of national economic performance and more upon human-centred approaches that identified evidence of people improving not only their material standard of living but also the quality of their lives. The Nobel Prize-winning economist Amartya Sen has argued that measures such as real income are at best only proxy indicators for what he termed the 'capability to function' (Sen, 2003). The ability to make choices about how to direct one's life is clearly an element of personal well-being, and it is in turn shaped by many aspects of one's life, ranging from personal health to personal mobility and self-esteem, and the ability to participate in the life of a community (Todaro & Smith, 2015, pp. 18–20). In general terms, development has come to be associated with: (1) increasing the availability and widening the distribution of basic life-sustaining goods such as food, shelter, health and protection; (2) raising incomes and making more jobs available, but also providing better education and access to cultural resources that enhance not only material well-being but also self-esteem; and (3) expanding the range of economic and social choices available to individuals by freeing them from relations of servitude and dependence (Todaro & Smith, 2015, p. 24). One can see parallels in such thinking with the participatory communication model, with its notion of there being a plurality of pathways to development, and the associated need for development experts to work with local communities to identify what they see as the most important goals and the best means of achieving them.

Among the features of the participatory communication approach are:

1. A focus upon people and communities as the key agents for change and participants for development;
2. An orientation towards meeting basic needs and building community resilience and sustainability;
3. An emphasis upon the local community rather than the nation-state as the primary constituency to be engaged with by external communication specialists;
4. A focus on dialogue and participation, and learning from the local customs, traditions and knowledge of these communities;
5. Understanding development in terms of the empowerment of people and more democratic decision-making practices, including greater opportunities to participate in the media and access to the means of communication.

An important influence on participatory communication has been the radical Latin American education theorist Paolo Friere. Waisbord (2001, p. 19) identified Friere as 'offer[ing] the concept of liberating education that conceived communication as dialogue and participation ... that prioritized cultural identity, trust and commitment ... communication should provide a sense of ownership to participants through sharing and reconstructing experiences'. Drawing upon the contributions of Friere and others, Servaes (1999) described the participatory model of communication as one that 'stresses the importance of the cultural identity of local communities and of democratization and participation at all levels – international, national, local, and individual' (p. 88). The focus of the participatory model is on dialogue and reciprocal communication, where 'the focus moves from a "communicator-centric" to a more "receiver-centric" orientation, with the resultant emphasis on meaning sought and ascribed rather than information transmitted' (Servaes, 1999, p. 89). Melkote (2010) defined such an approach as an *empowerment model* of development communication, and drew upon post-structuralist and postmodern theories to argue the need for 'epistemological plurality', against universalist knowledge claims in development communication theories.

A common feature of participatory communication approaches has been their application of *participatory action research* (PAR) as a research methodology. With its origins in the humanistic turn in organizational sociology undertaken by Kurt Lewin and colleagues in the 1940s, action research has been widely adopted in the social sciences in recent years. With a strong orientation towards applied problem-solving research, learning through practice, and engaging the human subjects of research in the process of research, action research has sought to 'dissolve the apparent dichotomy of science and democracy – of methodical knowing and authentic dialogue, instrumental rationality and life-world communication' (Chevalier & Buckles, 2012, p. 4). Characteristic features of action research when applied to projects are that: (1) it is associated with practice and problem solving, rather than theory development for its own sake; (2) it involves action, evaluation and critical reflection and – based on the evidence gathered – changes in practice are then implemented; (3) it is participative and collaborative, as well as situation-based and context specific; (4) knowledge is created through action and reflection at the point of application, and is developed jointly with the participants; and (5) action research findings will emerge as action develops, but findings are always provisional, and do not acquire the status of conclusive fact (Koshy *et al.*, 2011).

Beyond their distinctions with modernization theories, participatory communication approaches have often prided themselves on their theoretical eclecticism and absence of an overarching developmental narrative. For example, Servaes (1999, pp. 276–277) concludes his account of participatory communication by arguing that 'there is no universal development model and ... development is an integral, multidimensional and dialectic process that can differ from one society to another'. There are clear influences on the participatory approaches, including feminist theories (Wilkins, 2008), post-structuralist theories (Melkote, 2010), social movement theories (Huesca, 2003) and postcolonialism (Manyozo, 2012). But in line with the general bottom-up, inductive approaches to knowledge that characterize action research approaches, there is a reluctance to posit any overarching theory that either positions people as solely the objects of research enquiry, or which posits a singular path to development or social change.

Critics such as Sparks (2007) have identified this theoretical agnosticism as being a weakness of the participatory communication model. It is certainly conceivable that movement towards a genuinely participatory and demo-cratic society would challenge dominant power interests within a society or community, and that the question becomes one of political engagement rather than one of simply working with communities. Moreover, since access to such communities may well be contingent upon the support – whether active or tacit – of local and national governments, the question of the rela-tionship of communications practitioners to these communities has a further political dimension. Development communication thus has both a 'negoti-ated' and a 'radical' variant (Sparks, 2007, pp. 72–78). In the 'negotiated' version, development communication experts engage in relatively small-scale interventions with local communities, with the support of govern-ments and other elite interests, around the resolution of particular problems. While the models employed are different to those that characterized earlier modernization theories, the relationship of the expert to the community in question is broadly similar, since 'it is the official representatives of the local community, whose activities are sanctioned by the state, who will define the problems and their possible solutions' (Sparks, 2007, p. 74). In the more 'radical' variant, community empowerment is seen as being integrally linked to a wider democratization of communication and a redistribution of politi-cal power through popular mobilization. At some point, as critical political economists argue, and as we will see in the next chapter, this is likely to move such issues beyond questions of participatory communication towards broader challenges to political and economic power, and local, national and international levels.

Modernization 2.0? ICTs for development (ICT4D)

At one level, the participatory turn in development communication marked a move away from the top-down approaches to communication and the narrowly defined terms of development associated with moderni-zation theories. While the modernization paradigm as presented by the first generation of development communication theorists certainly went out of fashion in the 1980s and 1990s – which allowed Rogers (1976), Fair (1989), Wilkins (2008) and others to speak of the 'passing of the dominant paradigm' – it would be a mistake to ignore certain continuities between the modernization and participatory paradigms. Morris (2003) observed that although the diffusion and participation approaches are presented as polar opposites, in actual development projects they were often comple-mentary to one another rather than being opposed. Community engage-ment in developing, implementing and evaluating projects had become the developmental norm, even if they remained reliant upon Western experts to work with these communities, and upon the use of advanced communication technologies to achieve developmental goals (Mefalopulos, 2008). The focus on more localized and decentralized projects was associated with another major shift in this period, away from a focus on mass media and development tools and towards information and communication technologies (ICTs) as the critical variable in communication for development and social change.

A central feature of development communications in the 2000s was the rise of the Information and Communication Technologies for Development (ICT4D) agenda. From the late 1990s onwards, a range of international agencies, non-governmental organizations (NGOs), corporate interests and academic researchers began to focus on the potential of ICTs for development, both through their contribution to economic growth and their ability to empower poor people and communities. The United Nations Millennium Summit in September 2000 proclaimed eight Millennium Development Goals, of which Goal 8 was to develop a Global Partnership for Development, with Target 8F being 'in cooperation with the private sector, [to] make available benefits of new technologies, especially information and communications' (United Nations, 2003). In 2000, the World Economic Forum launched its Global Digital Divide Initiatives, while the Group of Eight nations created a Digital Opportunities Taskforce (DOT) (Unwin, 2009, pp. 126–127, 132–134). The United Nations Development Programme (UNDP) Human Development Report for 2001 was titled *Making Technologies Work for Human Development* (UNDP, 2001), and in the same year a UN ICT Task Force was created. The World Summit on the Information Society (WSIS) events organized by the International Telecommunications Union (ITU) and held in Geneva in 2003 and Tunis in 2005 also focused on the ICT4D agenda of making better use of ICTs for development and the eradication of poverty.

Ogan *et al.* (2009) have noted that references to ICTs and the ICT4D agenda surged in the academic literature on development communication from about 2002 onwards. They also observe that over half of these studies were framed within modernization paradigms, or ones that combined modernization and participatory paradigms (p. 661). Critics of ICT4D have termed the approach 'Modernization 2.0' (Shade, 2003) and 'Developmentalism Redux' (Sundaram, 2005), as it reinstitutes key elements of the earlier modernization approaches to development communication, infused with more recent sociological theories such as Daniel Bell's 'information society' thesis (Bell, 1980; cf. Mattelart, 2003, pp. 75–79). As with earlier modernization concepts such as the 'Stages of Growth', the 'information society' thesis was posited around a series of evolutionary stages, in this case from agrarian society to industrial society, and then to the information (or post-industrial) society. It offered policy makers in developing nations the opportunity to achieve the attributes of the most technologically advanced societies through strategies that could 'leapfrog institutional obstacles ... on the ground' (Wade, 2002, p. 445).

An important contextual factor in driving ICT4D initiatives was the question of the *digital divide*. The term was first used in the United States during the Clinton Administration to identify gaps between 'information-haves' and 'information-have-nots' in relation to access to computers and the internet, and associated concerns about 'unequal advantage being derived from [the] benefits' of new media access (Rice & Haythornthwaite, 2006, p. 93). On a global scale, it was believed that unequal access to ICTs mattered:

> because of the widely held belief that inclusion and involvement in the global information and knowledge economy is an important measure of the 'quality of life' in the 21st century ... [and] being excluded by this emerging economy is deemed a significant deprivation. (Thomas, 2010, p. 332)

Wade (2002) observed that organizations such as the World Bank and the Organisation for Economic Co-operation and Development (OECD) came to be very focused on the role that ICT4D could play in addressing the digital divide. These agencies called for development communication theorists to engage more actively with information systems theorists and the IT community, to develop impact assessment strategies for ICT4D and reduce the degree to which design and implementation of ICT4D strategies were being driven by actors external to the development field.

The ICT4D agenda has sought to learn from earlier modernization programmes by avoiding top-down solutions imposed from outside, engaging local populations, focusing upon grassroots community participation and meeting the basic needs of the poorest sections of the community. Associated with this was the focus upon a *multi-stakeholder approach to development* that involved NGOs, civil society organizations and community leaders, as well as corporations in the ICT and related sectors. The focus on multi-stakeholder approaches was consistent with the growing influence of NGOs and civil society organizations on development projects as part of the 'participatory turn' in development communication (Sparks, 2007, pp. 75–80). It also paralleled a turn towards developing world markets among the world's leading ICT corporations, and what C. K. Prahalad (2005) described as capturing 'the fortune at the bottom of the pyramid', or the 3 billion people receiving less than $US2 a day. Programmes such as One Laptop Per Child, established by MIT Media Lab founder Nicholas Negroponte, were able to get support from companies such as Google, eBay and

Nortel, as well as from the UNDP, to provide very basic laptop computers valued at $US100 to children in the least developed countries. In *The End of Poverty*, the economist Jeffrey Sachs emphasized the need to empower villages to take up ICTs, arguing that 'rapid economic development requires that technical capacity suffuses the entire society from the bottom up' (Sachs, 2005, p. 257).

There is a commonly stated view that ICT4D needs to avoid the top-down presumptions of older modernization discourses, and avoid substituting what Wade (2002, p. 450) describes as an earlier technological faith in 'tractors for all' with a new belief in the transcendent power of 'laptops for all'. At the same time, critics of the ICT4D agenda, such as Wade (2002), Shade (2003), Sundaram (2005) and Leye (2007), have all identified important traces of the earlier modernization discourses in it. In particular, the analysis of underdevelopment as equating with lack of access to the latest technologies is pervasive in the ICT4D discourse. The perception remains that 'technology, which was regarded as neutral and entirely beneficial, would bring the underdeveloped areas material progress, innovation and results' (Leye, 2007, p. 979). Wade makes the point that the importance of 'bridging the digital divide' as the principal development issue had become so pervasive in the leading international agencies that, according to an anonymous World Bank official, the only major speaker at a forum they had heard question the importance of internet access to human development was Bill Gates, such had become the degree of what he termed 'group think' within the organization (Wade, 2002, p. 444).

The critique of ICT4D is not only that it misdiagnoses the problems of developing nations, and hence misdirects development assistance towards investments in ICT hardware and infrastructure, it is also argued that ICT4D agenda promotes greater economic dependency by integrating the nations of the Global South into a global information economy on highly unequal terms, where 'the developing world is adequately and sufficiently connected [and] will become fully integrated into the global economy and hence become an equal partner of the rich countries' (Leye, 2007, p. 978). The emphasis upon acquiring computer hardware and software, which require regular systems upgrades in order to be compatible with leading users, locks developing country users, and particularly their governments, into highly unequal contractual arrangements, with scarce foreign exchange needing to be used on ICT investments rather than meeting basic needs.

It is also a feature of the ICT4D literature, and modernization theories of development more generally, that broadening access to new technologies, and particularly of spreading the adoption of digital technologies in the developing world, is taken to be a positive to the point of barely being worth discussing. But Pierskala and Hollenbach (2013) raise the point that the greatly enhanced availability of mobile phones in Africa not only enabled new forms of collective action, but also particularly violent forms of collective action. This is not to say that mobile technologies lead to violence, or that acts of organized rebellion against government cannot be justified. It is, however, to note that we need to understand digital media technologies in a complex ecology of social, political, economic and other arrangements, and not simply view them as one-dimensional forces for transparency and accountability, or the bearers of democratic transformation.

Debates on the current and future shape of global ICTs, and the policies and institutions surrounding this development, remain dominated by the rich countries. Global internet governance sites such as ICANN (Internet Corporation for Assigned Names and Numbers) are not transparent in their operations, and the World Intellectual Property Organization (WIPO) has only shown limited engagement with developing country concerns about global software monopolies. As Wade (2002, p. 443) puts it, 'the technologies and "regimes" (international standards governing ICTs) are designed by developed country entities for developed country conditions'. It is thus argued that net effect of the ICT4D agenda to bridge the 'digital divide' may 'have the effect of locking developing countries into a new form of dependency on the West' (Wade, 2002, p. 443). In this respect, the unequal terms on which global technological and economic integration are proposed in developmental models such as ICT4D come to ultimately reproduce patterns of uneven development and unequal exchange that have been the subject of sustained analysis by dependency theorists and critical political economists.

Modernization and globalization

While modernization theories are being presented here as a standalone paradigm, it is important to note several points of overlap with globalization theories. It has been argued that there was a turn 'from modernization to globalization' since, as Currie and Thobani argued, 'globalization makes visible the inseparability of technology and power in ways not apparent in modernization discourse' (2003, p. 150). At the same time, there are clear affinities between modernization and globalization, particularly around the notion that access to communications media increases the extent to which people are exposed to different ideas and cultures from other parts of the globe, and hence more likely to question ideas that are based upon tradition, custom and convention. Moreover, insofar as contemporary development theories incorporate notions of popular participation and an emphasis upon attentiveness to local context, it could be that more participatory approaches to communication have continuities with earlier modernization theories, albeit without the Eurocentric and ethnocentric underpinnings that were frequently overt in the earlier development communication discourses. Influential analyses of the shift from modernization to globalization discourses among Chinese academics have identified the continuities as well as the differences, noting that:

> Despite their differences in emphasis, the two are actually complementary to each other and mutually explanatory. Modernization theory stresses the development of a country or region while globalization theory places more emphasis on the interrelationship among countries of the world and the process in which these countries, to a certain degree, become 'one'. (Jiafeng, 2009, p. 74)

Mefalopulos (2008) has made the observation that participatory communication has come to be adopted by the United Nations and other international agencies such as the World Bank. One reason for this is that participatory approaches are perceived to be more cost-effective forms of service delivery that require local stakeholders to take ownership of the project implementation process (Mefalopulos, 2008, p. 51). The participatory turn in development communication may therefore have had the ironic effect, noted by Huesca (2003), of rescuing the modernization paradigm by couching it in more notionally pluralistic terms. The ICT4D agenda was clearly envisaged as one where corporate interests and civil society organizations would work in partnership with local and national governments, in contrast to earlier strategies where development exports would be flown in from the West to implement a pre-determined development communications strategy.

Political economy of non-governmental development organizations

It has been the case that greater engagement of NGOs in development strategies, and the turn from top-down directives to multi-stakeholder engagement, are consistent with broader turns in global governance. Participatory communications theories can broadly align with globalization theories in terms of the three models of global media being developed in this book. While they often share with political economists a critique of unequal communication structures under global capitalism, the natural constituency for such ideas has been international NGOs as they have both the will and the capacity to engage with 'global' challenges at the level of local communities. Moreover, many of the core concepts of participatory communication – participation, community, democratization, social justice, empowerment – draw at some level upon shared human values with some claim to universality, even despite the apparent disavowal of the sort of universalist claims originally made around the benefits of modernity for all peoples and cultures.

This raises the question of where NGOs sit within the political economy of global media. Questions of whether NGOs should have a greater role in promoting development feed not only into debates about national sovereignty, cultural identity and the impact of global modernity, but also into questions of political and economic power on a global scale. As Enghel (2015) has noted, such questions are often glossed over in development communication, which tends to see such questions as 'theoretical', in opposition to the more 'practical' tasks of working with communities to improve people's lives. But Enghel identifies two reasons why it may not be sufficient to isolate the 'applied' world of development communication from broader theories of global media.

First, the largest players in the global media and communication industries are themselves increasingly involved in development communication programmes, as funders, partners and relationship brokers. The example of the Bill & Melinda Gates Foundation, established from the wealth accrued by Bill Gates as CEO of Microsoft and now one of the world's leading funders of development programmes, 'suggests a correlation between the economic power derived by privileged individuals from the media industries and the ensuing possibility to influence international policy agendas through their philanthropic arms' (Enghel, 2015, p. 18), that clearly warrants critical scrutiny.

Second, there is the continuing centrality of nation-states, and national government agencies, to the deployment of development communication interventions. Contrary to the 'declining state' paradigm of global media and communications, where supranational governmental institutions and NGOs increasingly engage directly with local communities, it can be argued that nation-states remain central to development communication, both in setting the conditions under which NGOs and others operate within their territory, and also in the inter-state dialogues that inform projects funded at a government level.

As will be discussed in later chapters, questions of whether NGOs should have a greater role in promoting development, and whether development communications specialists have a particular role in this regard, intersect with wider debates about the possibility of a global civil society. Whereas 'first generation' modernization theories may have suffered from being too closely identified with the dominant Western political powers, it is proposed that NGOs constitute a third sector that is independent of nation-states and corporations, whose actions can prefigure emergent forms of global governance. The experience of programmes such as ICT4D suggests grounds for doubting such an optimistic scenario, but it will be returned to in later chapters of this book.

CHAPTER 3

Critical political economy

Defining critical political economy

From the 1960s to the present, critical political economy has provided one of the most influential frameworks through which developments in global media are understood and interpreted. Political economists have insisted upon the importance of questions of power and ideology, and upon economic, political and symbolic power interact in the sphere of culture, particularly in the mass media, which Stuart Hall (1977, p. 340) described as 'having established a decisive and fundamental leadership in the cultural sphere' in contemporary societies. Political economists have critiqued approaches such as mass communications theory and modernization theories of development communication, arguing that these approaches failed to give suitable weight to the significance of economic processes in the media and communications industries that set limits to the diversity of ideas and opinions in circulation through the media, in contrast to liberal ideals of a 'free press' (e.g. Siebert *et al.*, 1956).

Central to critical political economy is the proposition that the media have to be understood as *a central part of capitalist economies*. Political economists place a particular primacy upon the structure of economic relations under capitalism, because structures of domination based upon class relations are at the core of what defines a capitalist economy and generates its dynamics, including its sources of conflict and contradiction. Nicholas Garnham (1995, p. 70) argued that 'political economy sees class – namely, the structure of access to the means of production and the structure of the distribution of the economic surplus – as the key to the structure of domination'.

Vincent Mosco (2009, p. 24) has defined political economy as involving 'the study of the social relations, particularly the power relations, that mutually constitute the production, distribution, and consumption of resources'. Oliver Boyd-Barrett (1995, p. 186) observed that, with regard to the media and communication, political economy has 'a broadly "critical" signification, often associated with macro-questions of media ownership and control ... and other factors that bring together media industries ... with political, economic and social elites'. Among the economic processes it is concerned with are those of 'commercialization, internationalization, the working of the profit motive in the hunt for audiences and/or for advertising, and its consequences for media practices and media content' (p. 186). Jonathan Hardy defines critical political economy of media as examining 'how the political and economic organization ... of media industries affects the production and circulation of meaning, and connects to the distribution of material and symbolic resources that enable people to understand, communicate and act in the world' (2014, p. 9).

There is a strong focus on media industries and markets, but Murdock and Golding (2005, p. 61) propose that critical political economy differs from mainstream economics in that it 'goes beyond technical issues of efficiency to engage with basic moral questions of justice, equity and the common good'. At the same time, the cultural dimensions of communication preclude a simple economic determinism and render media industries different to other industries, insofar as the transmission of information and the social construction of meaning have cultural, cognitive and subjective dimensions. There is an insistence upon analysis of the *social totality*, or 'the relationship among commodities, institutions, social relations, and hegemony, and ... the determination among these elements' (Wasko, 2004, p. 110). Mosco has observed that political economy is 'characterized by an interest in examining ... the *totality of social relations* that make up the economic, political, social, and cultural areas of life' (Mosco, 2009, pp. 3–4). This entails a commitment to interdisciplinary scholarship, based on the recognition that political economy needs to be concerned with 'the mutual determination and multiple constitution of social life ... and to the relationships among many aspects of social life' (Mosco, 2009, p. 28).

In this chapter, I want to focus upon three elements of the critical political economy of media approach: critical political economy as economics; critical political economy as critical theory; and the global political economy of communication. With regards to the latter, it will be noted that there are different generations of scholarship, from the pioneering early work of scholars such as Herbert Schiller, Kaarle Nordenstreng and Oliver Boyd-Barrett to contemporary applications by such authors as Robert McChesney, Toby Miller and Dan Schiller. The latter part of the chapter will consider some critical issues associated with the critical political economy approach, including the role of the nation-state in global communication, the question of whether US media and cultural dominance remains in the twenty-first century, and issues relating to the internet and digital media.

Critical political economy as media economics

A defining feature of critical political economy is its stress upon the importance, and in some instances the analytical primacy, of the economic dimensions of media. In an early contribution to the field, Murdock and Golding argued that a defining feature of the political economy of communication was 'the recognition that the mass media are first and foremost industrial and commercial organizations which produce and distribute commodities' (Murdock & Golding, 1973, pp. 205–206). In a more recent statement on the field, these authors argued for the primacy of analysing media industries and cultural production, observing that 'different ways of financing and organizing cultural production have traceable consequences for the range of discourses, representations and communicative resources in the public domain and for the organization of audience access and use' (Murdock & Golding, 2005, p. 60).

Critical political economists have placed considerable importance on the history of economic thought, and particularly the schism that occurred in economic thought in the nineteenth century between the marginalist or neoclassical school on the one hand, and Marxist political economy on the other. The classical political economists, such as Adam Smith, David Ricardo and John Stuart Mill, were broadly supportive of the capitalist market economy, but were also insistent that economists had to deal with the big questions of how economic wealth was produced and distributed at a society-wide level (Wasko, 2004, pp. 309–310; Mosco, 2009, pp. 32–33). From the 1850s onwards, economics turned towards what came to be known as the neoclassical model, with its particular focus on how relative prices emerge in markets through the interaction between individual consumers and producers. This also came to be known as marginal economics, as the focus was on how individuals would rationally respond to changing market signals at the 'margins' of decision making. For example, by how many units would demand for a particular product or service fall if its price rose? At the same time, Karl Marx was developing a radical critique of capitalism that drew upon key themes of classical political economy but used them to demonstrate tendencies towards crisis, inequality and exploitation at the core of the capitalist economic system. This divergence between neoclassical economics and Marxism was also marked by a series of other dichotomies that demarcated the economic mainstream from its radical critics: focusing on rational individuals or collective agents; economics as a stand-alone discipline or as interconnected with other areas of the social sciences; differing views on the importance of history and culture; and so on (Ingham, 1996; Jackson, 2009). A summary of the differences between the two approaches is provided in Table 3.1:

Table 3.1 Differences between mainstream neoclassical economics and critical political economy

Mainstream economics	Critical political economy
Focus on the individual	Focus on collective entities (e.g. social classes)
Individual rational choice	Socially determined belief systems
Analysis of market exchange	Analysis of circuits of production, distribution and consumption
Study of market equilibrium situations (micro)	Study of socio-historical processes (macro)
Focus on individual choices and mutual benefits of interaction through markets	Focus on power, social conflict and forms of collective agency
Economics as a stand-alone discipline	Political economy as inherently interdisciplinary
Preference for formal models and quantitative methods	Preference for descriptive analysis and qualitative methods
Scholarship as a value-neutral activity (separation of facts and values)	Scholarship as a form of political and ethical engagement (facts and values interconnected)
Markets lead to social harmony	Capitalism based on social conflict

Source: Cunningham *et al.* (2015, p. 3).

Critical political economists are thus particularly focused upon the economic dynamics of media corporations and industries. However, they differ from more conventional approaches to media economics (see, e.g., Albarran, 2010; Cunningham *et al.*, 2015, Chapter 1) in their focus upon 'the organization of property and production ... within the cultural industries and more generally' (Murdock & Golding, 2005, p. 62). This approach also insists upon situating economic analysis within 'wider sets of social relations and the play of power', as well as aiming to show how 'particular micro contexts are shaped by general economic dynamics ... [such as] the ways that communicative action is structured by the unequal distribution of material and symbolic resources' (Murdock & Golding, 2005, p. 62).

There is also a particular concern with questions of ethics, and the politics of engagement with media policy and other issues. For example, Freedman (2014) argues that engaging with media ownership debates cannot rely solely upon the use of quantitative indicators to determine whether particular media markets are functioning effectively. He argues that this must also be informed by the values that one wishes to see driving a diverse and pluralistic media system, such as the existence of alternative voices and limits on the exercise of media power. The neo-Marxist concept of *praxis* is sometimes used to describe such an approach (e.g. Mosco, 2009, pp. 34–36), where intellectual engagement is explicitly linked to normative positions and questions of moral philosophy to provide guidance to action. Examples of such praxis would be a commitment to working with trade unions in the media industries, or campaigns to reform media ownership laws along more democratic and pluralistic lines.

Critical political economy as critical theory

The understanding that critical political economists are engaged in a battle of ideas about the media and its societal role stems from the view that media are central to the shaping of how people understand society and culture, and the political economy of the societies in which they live. The media are seen as being not simply the neutral conveyors of information but as being critical to defining 'reality'. Moreover, this capacity to define social reality is itself political, with dominant media interests tending to generate images and understandings of events that align with the interests of the dominant economic classes and those of the state. The result is what Stuart Hall, following from the Marxist tradition associated with Antonio Gramsci, referred to as the production and reproduction of *hegemony*, or 'the operation of one class upon another in shaping and producing consent (through the selective forms of social knowledge made available) ... [that is] one of the principal kinds of work that the dominant ideologies perform' (Hall, 1977, p. 339). If the media are engaged in the production and dissemination of dominant ideologies, through the 'selective forms of social knowledge' they make available to the public, then the work of political economists is seen to require a critical orientation and a preparedness to intervene on behalf of subordinate groups in society in the shaping and defining of social reality.

The 'critical' element in critical political economy, then, refers to its relationship to *critical theory*, and with that to Marxist theories of ideology. David Held (1983, p. 183) identified critical theory with the 'Frankfurt School' of neo-Marxist social philosophers, originally centred around the Institute for Social Research established in Frankfurt in 1923. This group of philosophers, which included Theodor Adorno, Max Horkheimer and, later, Herbert Marcuse and Jürgen Habermas:

> tried to develop a critical perspective in the discussion of all social practices, that is, a perspective which is preoccupied with the critique of ideology – of systematically distorted accounts of reality which attempt to conceal and legitimate asymmetrical power relations ... Through an examination of these systems they hoped to enhance awareness of the roots of domination, undermine ideologies and help to compel changes in consciousness and action. (Held, 1983, p. 183)

In general terms, the proposition is that the realm of culture and ideas cannot be understood independently of the political and economic forces that shape it and ultimately constrain it, which makes the concept of *ideology* central to a Marxist theory of culture, and necessitates critical theory.

Within critical theories of ideology, there are three important variants. The first is what may be termed the simple class/ideology relationship, derived from Marx and Engels' proposition in *The German Ideology* that 'the ideas of the ruling class are in every epoch the ruling ideas i.e. the class which is the ruling material force of society, is at the same time its ruling intellectual force' (quoted in Barrett, 1991, p. 9). One example of this 'simple' proposition would be the *propaganda model* of media developed by Edward Herman and Noam Chomsky (Herman & Chomsky, 1988). Herman and Chomsky proposed that the United States media largely functioned through a class-based monopoly of ideas, whereby 'money and power are able to filter out the news fit to print, marginalize dissent, and allow the government and dominant interests to get their messages across to the public' (Herman & Chomsky, 1988, p. 2). This was the result of five 'filters' that impact upon the flow of ideas through the mass media: concentration of ownership; reliance upon advertising revenues; the reliance of journalists upon 'official' sources; the role played by right-wing media in generating 'flak' towards social critics; and the influence of dominant ideas such as anti-communism and the threat of terrorism (Herman & Chomsky, 1988, p. 2).

A second, more complex approach that is also derived from Marx proposes that culture and ideology exist as a level in a social formation where economic relations have a dominant, but not necessarily determinant, role. It is through the relationship of the political and ideological 'levels' to the political and economic that social relations are largely understood and contested. As Marx put it in *A Contribution to the Critique of Political Economy*:

> In the social production of their lives, men enter into definite relations that are indispensable and independent of their will, relations of production which correspond to a definite stage of development of their material productive forces. The sum total of these relations of production constitutes the economic structure of society, the real foundation, on which rises a legal and political superstructure and to which correspond to definite forms of social consciousness. *The mode of production of material life conditions the social, political and intellectual life process in general.* (Quoted in Larrain, 1983, p. 42; emphasis added by Larrain)

This approach to the relationship between media and power sees economic power relations under capitalism as dominant but not determinant. In their overview of the political economy of media, communication and culture, Murdock and Golding (2005) propose that there are factors that set structural limits to the diversity of media forms and representations, which include the corporate interests of private media owners, assessments of the most profitable audience segments in the market, and inequalities of access to communication resources. In doing so, however, Murdock and Golding stress that the media are sites of contradiction and contestation, in a world where 'owners, advertisers and key political personnel cannot always do as they wish ... [but] operate within structures that constrain as well as facilitate' (Murdock & Golding, 2005, p. 74).

A third approach that some critical political economists have developed argues that the current phase of capitalist development is one where the economic and media/cultural spheres increasingly overlap. Raymond Williams made the observation:

> The major modern communications systems are now so evidently key institutions in advanced capitalist societies that they require the same kind of attention ... that is given to the institutions of industrial production and distribution ... these analyses force theoretical revision of the formula of base and superstructure and of the definition of productive forces, in a social area in which large scale capitalist activity and cultural production are now inseparable. (Williams, 1977, p. 136)

Drawing upon this insight, Nicholas Garnham (1990) argued that the base/superstructure model and its variants misunderstood Marxism in conflating the 'material' with industrial production and the 'ideological' with cultural production. Garnham instead proposed that the key question for a materialist theory of culture was to understand the processes through which cultural forms became 'industrialized', or subject to the general forms and practices of capitalist commodity production.

Global critical political economy: dependency theory and the 'first generation' of theorists

A global perspective has long been a central, if sometimes implicit, element of the critical political economy tradition. As Hamid Mowlana (2012) has observed, the field of international communication was initially dominated by the modernization paradigm, but the crisis of that field from the late 1960s onwards, combined with a growing assertiveness on the part of critics of United States foreign policy more generally, saw a radical perspective emerge in the field. A central figure in this regard was the US communications scholar Herbert Schiller. In *Mass Communications and American Empire*

(Schiller, 1969), Schiller argued that that the international movement towards the commercialization of broadcasting was driven by the rise of the US entertainment, communications and information (ECI) industries. The media and communications industries had been moving towards the centre of the political economy of the United States, and this had cultural as well as economic implications for the world generally, given the power and influence of the US in global affairs. In particular, the influence of the ECIs is never simply political or economic; these sectors differ from other branches of commercial enterprise through their 'direct, though immeasurable impact on human consciousness', as well as their capacity 'to define and present their own role to the public' (Schiller, 1996, pp. 115, 125).

Authors such as Schiller were strongly influenced by *dependency theory*. With its roots in Latin American political economy, scholars associated with dependency theory argued that global capitalism is associated with what Andre Gunder Frank (1973) termed the 'development of underdevelopment', whereby the nations of the 'Third World' are subject to systematic exploitation by the metropolitan 'core'. It was argued that economic exploitation of the 'periphery' occurred through unequal terms of trade, the imposition of a primary-products-based economic structure, and the development of highly exploitative systems of labour control (Amin, 1980). This was accompanied by the manipulation of local politics through the cultivation of political, intellectual, business and military elites who identify their interests as synonymous with those of the dominant metropolitan powers (Amin, 1980). In the economic sense, dependence referred to the resulting shaping of national systems by more powerful international forces, defined by Theodor dos Santos in the following way:

> By dependence we mean a situation in which the economy of certain countries is conditioned by the development and expansion of another economy to which the former is subjected. The relation of interdependence ... assumes the form of dependence when some countries (the dominant ones) can expand and be self-sustaining, while other countries (the dependent ones) can only do this as a reflection of that expansion (dos Santos, 1973, p. 10).

The economic historian Immanuel Wallerstein (1974) argued that the resulting division of the world into a capitalist core, a semi-periphery, and an exploited periphery had been a defining characteristic of what he termed the *capitalist world-system* since European colonial expansion and the creation of empires commenced in the fifteenth century. A critical way in which an unequal capitalist world-system was reproduced was political. Dependency theorists argued that the ruling elites in dependent nations were more closely aligned to global elites than to their own people, and that their access to power and resources were contingent upon their positioning within the global capitalist system. In Frank's terms, they are comparadors, who direct state policies to serve the interests of the global powers on whom they are dependent (Frank, 1973).

Dependency theories proved to be one of the most enduring elements of early work in global critical political economy (Brewer, 1980; Hout, 1993). A focus upon colonialism and imperialism has always been a feature of Marxist political economy, although Marx himself was ambiguous about its impact on the colonized societies: on the one hand, it involved exploitation and appropriation of the wealth of the colonies, but on the other it introduced capitalist social relations, and hence was a force for modernization. In the most influential study of imperialism in the early twentieth century, that of V. I. Lenin (1965), this position had hardened to the proposition that under monopoly capitalism, the imperialist powers systematically exploited their colonies in order to stave off crises in their own national economies, and working-class movements in these nations had been 'bought off' to support imperialism, aligning with their own nations rather than with socialist internationalism. It was this argument, shaped in the post-World War II period by neo-Marxists such as Paul Baran and Paul Sweezy (Baran, 1973; Baran & Sweezy, 1968), that would form the political-economic basis for the highly influential dependency theories developed by writers such as Immanuel Wallerstein (1974), Andre Gunder Frank (1973) and Samir Amin (1980).

Schiller argued that the economic power of the ECI sector, combined with the global reach of Western cultural commodities and media messages, led to *cultural imperialism*. In *Communication and Cultural Domination*, Schiller defined cultural imperialism in the following terms:

> The concept of cultural imperialism ... describes the sum of processes by which a society is brought into the modern world system and how its dominating stratum is attracted, pressured, forced, and sometimes bribed into shaping social institutions to correspond to, or even promote, the values and structures of the dominant centre of the system. (Schiller, 1976, p. 9)

Oliver Boyd-Barrett (1977) used the term *media imperialism* to refer to the ways in which Anglo-French-American domination of international news agencies, combined with the dominance of Hollywood studios in global film and television markets, led to global inequalities in media power that could prevent the development of national media forms in less powerful countries that could effectively question the global political-economic order. Kaarle Nordenstreng and Tapio Varis (1974) developed a major study for UNESCO, finding that television content flows were largely a 'one-way street' from a small number of Western nations to the developing world. Jeremy Tunstall argued in *The Media Are American* (Tunstall, 1978) that advertiser dominance of commercial media funding worldwide led to a convergence of media forms towards a template derived from US broadcasting. Dallas Smythe (1977) argued the global media were a 'consciousness industry' that reproduced relations of domination and dependency whose roots were psychological as much as they were economic.

For these global critical political economists, a formative moment in international relations was the struggle within UNESCO for a New World Information and Communication Order (NWICO). The NWICO was 'a concept ... born in an aggressive wave of decolonization ... in the first part of the 1970s' (Nordenstreng, 2012, p. 478). In the context of wider struggles to transform power relations in the global economic order, the Non-Aligned Nations of the Third World had concluded that in relation to global media and communication 'technical assistance did not alter their dependency status, that information inequality persisted, and that in fact their cultural sovereignty was increasingly threatened' (Hamelink, 2015, p. 140). The demands for an NWICO focused in particular upon the largely one-sided flow of media content from the 'Global North' to the Third World, the resulting distortions in images of the world – particularly with regard to news and information – and the ways in which flows of media technology failed to fully promote development and ultimately increased relations of dependence.

In 1980, the International Commission for the Study of Communications Problems, established by UNESCO and chaired by Sean MacBride, the Irish-born founder of Amnesty International, released its final report on global communications, *Many Voices, One World*, also known as the MacBride Report (1980). The MacBride Report was highly critical of what it saw as the 'one-way flow' of information from the developed Western nations to the Third World that arose from the control of multinational corporations over information technologies and resources. It saw arguments promoting the global 'free flow' of information as needing to be weighed up against the rights of national governments, particularly in the developing world, to manage such flows in order to maintain national sovereignty, build cultural identity and harness communication resources more effectively to developmental goals. The recommendations of the MacBride Report were adopted by UNESCO at its 21st General Conference, held in Belgrade (then in Yugoslavia) in 1980.

'First generation' global political economy: an assessment

'First generation' critical political economy theories of global media had considerable institutional as well as intellectual influence around the world.[1] Coinciding with a wider uptake of political economy perspectives in media and communication studies (Mosco, 2009), the work of authors such as Herbert Schiller, Kaarle Nordenstreng, Cees Hamelink, Dallas Smythe, Oliver Boyd-Barrett and others was central to fundamentally rethinking the underlying assumptions surrounding global media. Whereas modernization theories identified the communication gaps in the developing world as arising from inadequate local institutional structures and attitudinal mindsets, and saw Western development aid, foreign investment and international communication experts as providing the solutions (reversing the so-called 'vicious circle of poverty'), critical political economists identified the absence of development in these nations as having its roots in Western colonialism and the unequal economic and political relations that had formed the basis of the modern capitalist world-system.

Drawing upon a wider critique of global capitalism associated with neo-Marxist dependency theories, critical political economists saw the further integration of post-colonial nations into the capitalist world-system, and an unequal global communications order, as perpetuating inequality and elite domination both within and between nations. They instead demanded transformation of the global communication system, associated with the demands for a NWICO, and radical political-economic change in the developing world along the lines of the socialist revolutions in countries such as Cuba under Fidel Castro and the People's Republic of China under Mao Zedong.

Over the course of the 1980s and 1990s, four significant lines of critique emerged of the cultural imperialism thesis as it had developed in critical political economy:

1. The underlying assumption of a 'one-way flow' of media content from the major Western nations to the rest of the world was becoming less applicable over time, as significant new players emerged in global media and entertainment markets;
2. Assumptions that the consumption of media content meant greater global cultural homogenization were not supported by research into active audiences and cross-cultural interpretations of media texts;
3. Theories of cultural imperialism underestimated both the resilience of local cultures and cultural diversity within nation-states, as they took the nation as the primary unit of analysis;

4. National media and cultural producers in the developing world were adaptive in their responses to media globalization and continued to possess significant advantages in their relevant markets, as measured by various media consumption indicators.

When the cultural imperialism thesis was originally developed in the late 1960s and early 1970s, the United States overwhelmingly dominated world media and entertainment markets. The UNESCO study by Nordenstreng and Varis (1974; cf. Varis, 1974) found that over half of the world's television content was imported from a small number of Western countries, with the United States accounting for about 90 per cent of imported entertainment content. A subsequent study by Varis (1984) found that about one-third of TV content was imported, with the highest levels of importation by the poorest countries, but also found that there were significant regional sub-markets for television content which complicated the picture of global media flows being a 'one-way street'. In particular, the period since the 1970s had seen the rise of significant media production centres outside of the United States and Western Europe that catered for particular regional and language-based sub-markets. Sinclair *et al.* (1996) termed these *geo-linguistic regions*, finding that there were major content producers among the so-called developing nations such as Hong Kong in the Chinese-speaking world, Brazil and Mexico for Portuguese and Spanish speakers, and Egypt in the Arab world, as well as countries such as Canada and Australia having some significance in the English-speaking world.

Defenders of the cultural imperialism thesis such as Schiller (1991) and Boyd-Barrett (1998) argued that this did not affect the overall pattern of dominance by Western transnational media corporations. They did acknowledge that, as Curran and Park (2000, p. 6) observed, there was 'a certain fuzziness in the way in which three different categories – American, Western, and capitalist – can be used almost interchangeably' in the cultural imperialism argument. It also suggested that national governments could develop local media production centres and 'national champions' that could compete effectively with Hollywood, particularly in those parts of the world where English was not the first language.

The second set of criticisms concerned the assumptions being made about media audiences and how they used imported media content. The cultural imperialism thesis had worked with the operating assumption that exposure to certain types of media content influenced attitudes and behaviour in relatively predictable ways. By contrast, new approaches to audience studies, such as reception studies and the encoding/decoding model derived from British cultural studies, were opening up new questions about the relationship between media content, or what were referred to as media texts, and their multiple and diverse audiences (Morley, 1989; Ang, 1991; Fiske, 1998). In particular, they opened up the possibility that the 'readings' made of imported media content by local audiences were highly variable and grounded in aspects of local culture and identity: influential studies included Ien Ang's analysis of viewers of the US serial drama *Dallas* in The Netherlands, Elihu Katz and Tamar Liebes' (1990) study of *Dallas* viewers among different ethnic communities in Israel, and Rogers and Antola's (1985) study of how and why *telenovelas* were replacing US dramas in the television schedules of Latin American countries. Drawing upon this diverse array of cross-cultural ethnographic research and reception studies, Ien Ang argued that there was a need for closer analysis of how global media content is 'actively and differentially responded to and negotiated in concrete local contexts and conditions' (Ang, 1996, p. 153), and that there is never a simple process of cultural homogenization, but rather 'it is in the particular appropriation and adaptation of such standardized rules and conventions within local contexts and according to local traditions, resources and preferences that the non-linear, fractured nature of cultural globalization displays itself' (Ang, 1996, p. 154).

The third critique of cultural imperialism theories concerns the understanding of local cultures. Authors such as John Thompson (1990, 1995) and John Tomlinson (1991, 1999, 2007) were critical of the critical political economy approach which, they argued, 'tries to infer, from an analysis of the social organization of the media industries, what the consequences of media messages are likely to be for the individuals who receive them' (Thompson, 1995, p. 171). They argued that such an approach fails to adequately understand the moment of consumption in the circulation of media forms. In arguments that have become central to globalization theories – to be considered in the next chapter – it was argued that as societies and cultures have become increasingly diverse and differentially integrated into global flows of media and culture it is increasingly difficult to speak of a relatively homogeneous national culture that would exist independently of the influence of global media flows. Tomlinson (1991) also argued that theories of media imperialism and cultural imperialism had a tendency to conflate media with culture – thereby blurring the relationship between culture as forms of symbolic representation and culture as lived experience. Insofar as globalization involves the movement of people and cultures as well as images and commodities, such questions of cultural complexity can intensify, as Joseph Straubhaar observed:

> Very few nations are ethnically homogeneous ... Most have fairly large minorities. If language is a primary characteristic of culture, then most nations are multilingual and not homogeneous nation-states. This opens up a large area of interest in media ... which addresses media audiences of smaller than national scope. (Straubhaar, 1997, p. 286)

It was also argued that the cultural imperialism thesis consistently under-estimated the continuing significance of national media industries, as well as local audience preferences for locally produced content. While it can be argued that local media industries have responded to the presence of global media by adapting to or even imitating US generic models as the exemplars of what Sinclair *et al.* (1996, p. 13) term 'international best practice', it is nonetheless the case that activist media and cultural policy can be success-ful in promoting viable 'national champions' which dominate local markets and achieve a level of export success. The success of the Latin American *telenovela* with audiences in the Spanish- and Portuguese-speaking worlds, Hong Kong-produced 'Canto-pop' and action/martial arts films in Chinese-speaking media markets, the 'Korean Wave' of films, television programmes, games and popular music, and Australian serial dramas or 'soaps' in English-speaking markets were among the examples of such 'indigenization' or 'hybridization' of global cultural forms. Joseph Straubhaar (1991, 2007) developed the argument, based upon Latin American (and particularly Brazilian) case studies, that domination of television programming sched-ules by media content imported from the US was a feature of less developed national media systems, but as these systems evolved over time this content tended to be displaced by locally produced material. Straubhaar argued that this tendency towards the 'localization' of media content was reflective of a process he termed *asymmetrical interdependence*, whereby the requirement to compete with US media content forced producers in countries such as Brazil to develop more innovative programme genres to capture local audi-ences, and in doing so they were able to expand their presence in regional markets. In contrast to the cultural imperialism thesis, which stressed disen-gagement from the capitalist world-system as the condition for developing strong national media cultures, Straubhaar's argument suggested that it is the context of global competition that stimulates innovation among media producers in developing countries.

More generally, the empirical work of Straubhaar, Sinclair *et al.* and others suggested a tendency in the critical political economy literature to systemati-cally underestimate the continuing significance of local advantage. Straub-haar (1991) drew attention to the competitive advantages enjoyed by local producers in having a greater degree of *cultural proximity* to their audiences than the producers of 'global' media content have in such local and regional markets. Moreover, they are able to periodically deploy the threat of 'Ameri-canization' or cultural imperialism to strategic advantage in policy forums to buy time and/or resources in order to strengthen their own competitive position in the context of emerging international threats. In Western Europe, for instance, the spectre of 'Americanization' has been invoked as providing a case for developing pan-European audiovisual markets, so that European media multinationals can compete on a more level global playing field (Schlesinger, 1997).

Finally, the changing geopolitics of the 1980s and 1990s were also a factor. The UNESCO campaign for a NWICO suffered a slow and painful death over the course of the 1980s, with the unequivocal hostility of the United States to this agenda strengthened when the Reagan administration came to power in 1980, to the point where the US government, along with the governments of Great Britain and Singapore, withdrew all financial support from UNESCO in 1984. It was not until 2004 that the US rejoined UNESCO, by which time the NWICO and related arguments about cultural imperialism had long been abandoned. There was also the criticism that the NWICO and related agendas arose out of relations between nation-states, which could be criticized for being overly nationalistic and state-centred, downplaying the suppression of media freedoms that was occurring within many of the participating nation-states (Roach, 1990, 1997; Sparks, 2007, pp. 112–115). As we will see in the next chapter, globalization theories have sought to downplay the role played by nation-states and national media systems, focusing instead on the possibilities of civil society and the global internet.

The end of the Cold War was also a significant change factor. With Soviet leader Mikhail Gorbachev developing a new policy of *glasnost* (openness) with the West from the mid-1980s, the sense that the two superpowers were engaged in an information war rapidly receded. German reunification in 1989 and the dissolution of the Soviet Union in 1991 only added to the sense of the NWICO struggles being part of the past, rather than the future, of global communications. The 1980s also saw a dissipation of energies associated with Third World radical nationalism. In the Asian region in particular, economic growth in countries such as South Korea, Taiwan and Singapore threw into question the proposition that global capital and multinational corporations necessarily block economic development in the non-Western world (Warren, 1980; Amsden, 1989; Wade, 1990). The post-Mao era in China from 1978 saw the process of reform and opening up (*găigé kāifàng*) commence under Deng Xiaoping's leadership, meaning that China – long the champion of anti-colonial thought and 'Three Worlds' theory – was increasingly turning towards better relations with the Western powers and economic programmes that actively sought investment from multinational corporations.

Global critical political economy in the twenty-first century

Many of the criticisms of the critical political economy perspective on global media discussed above would become associated with globalization theories, which will be considered in the next chapter. Critical political economists such as Schiller (1991) and Boyd-Barrett (1998) accepted some of the criticisms, but rejected most. It was acknowledged that the United States may not have the unquestioned hegemony in global media and communications that was sometimes assumed in theories of cultural imperialism, that the relationship of audiences to media content can be complex and multifaceted, and that the NWICO and dependency theory often placed relations of inequality and exploitation at the level of nation-states rather than social classes. But these authors continued to defend concepts such as media imperialism and cultural imperialism, and argued that globalization theories downplayed the extent to which it was global *capitalism* that needed to be critically evaluated, and not just globalization.

The radical critique of global media associated with critical political economy experienced a resurgence of interest in the late 1990s and 2000s. In the United States in particular, there was growing concern about media ownership concentration and its effects on public discourse, as argued by authors such as Robert McChesney, Noam Chomsky, Edward Herman, Dan Schiller and others. The proposition that media ownership worldwide was also subject to growing concentration, leading to reduced competition and increasingly commercialized and globally homogeneous media content, was a core theme of Robert McChesney and Edward Herman's 1997 book, *The Global Media: The New Missionaries of Global Capitalism*. Picking up on the themes of earlier authors such as Herb Schiller, McChesney and Herman argued that 'the ... global media system is dominated by three or four dozen large transnational corporations (TNCs) with fewer than ten mostly U.S.-based media conglomerates towering over the global market' (McChesney & Herman, 1997, p. 1). They argued that such a system was marked not only by concentration of media ownership and power but also by 'an associated marked decline in the relative importance of public broadcasting and the applicability of public service standards' (p. 1), a weakening of the public sphere, and the promotion of 'a "culture of entertainment" that is incompatible with a democratic order' (p. 9).

McChesney and Herman proposed what can be termed the *global media monopoly* thesis, which has also been put forward by other critical political economists (McChesney, 1999, 2008, 2013; Schiller, 2000; Foster & McChesney, 2003; McChesney & Schiller, 2003). The global media monopoly thesis draws upon the argument of political economists that the media industries, like other branches of capitalist industry, have an innate tendency towards concentration of ownership and control, and that this in turn reduces the level of competition in media markets. Building upon the work of the monopoly capital school of economists associated with the journal *Monthly Review* (Baran & Sweezy, 1968; Foster & McChesney, 2003), they view capitalism as a system that becomes less competitive over time as a result of the concentration of ownership and control. With regard to the media, the dominant image is that of 'the media industries as a giant pyramid, with power concentrated at the top' (Winseck, 2011, p. 23).

It was argued that prior to the 1980s, media systems were predominantly national in terms of ownership, even if they imported significant amounts of media content, with the US being by far the major media exporter. Since the 1980s, however, 'there has been a dramatic restructuring of national media markets, along with the emergence of a genuinely global commercial media market' (McChesney & Herman, 1997, p. 1). The trend towards a global media oligopoly arose from a combination of media firms expanding internationally in order to capture new media markets, mergers and takeovers that have furthered concentration of ownership within media industries, and the rise of multinational, cross-media conglomerates such as Disney, Time Warner, News Corporation, Sony and Viacom. The corporate mega-mergers of the late 1990s and 2000s, such as the Viacom-CBS merger and the AOL-Time Warner merger, featured prominently in this narrative.

As a result, 'a transnational corporate-commercial communication began to be crafted and a new structural logic put in place ... [as] communications ... became subject to transnational corporate-commercial development' (McChesney & Schiller, 2003, p. 6). It is argued that there is a 'feedback loop' between the concentration and conglomeration of media industries and the regime of monopoly capitalism on a global scale, since 'global media giants are the quintessential multinational firms, with shareholders, headquarters, and operations scattered across the globe' (McChesney, 2001a, p. 16). As such, they are in the front line of advocacy for globalization, and implacably opposed to interests or values that are at odds with global corporate and commercial interests. They are not only able to lobby effectively to promote their own corporate interests, but can use the media they control to present images which can in turn influence political behaviour at both elite and mass-popular levels (McChesney, 2001a, p. 11). While this can sometimes manifest itself in support for progressive political causes such as popular-democratic movements against authoritarian rule, or social causes such as campaigns for same-sex marriage, the general tenor of such media is argued to be pro-corporate. Echoing the earlier debates about cultural imperialism, McChesney and Herman argued that such media promote individualism and materialism, displace 'hard news' with entertainment, strengthen conservative and pro-Western political forces (and demonize socialists and radical nationalists), and contribute to the erosion of distinctive local and national cultures (McChesney & Herman, 1997, pp. 152–155).

Political economy of the global internet

A consistent feature of critical political economy has been a degree of scepticism about claims made concerning the internet. Political economists have tended to view the internet as marking a technological change in media but not a more significant social change. They point to the continued dominant place of corporations as the key players on the internet, the centrality of commercial activity on digital platforms and the need for revenues derived from advertising, direct sales and subscriptions as evidence that the internet marks the latest phase in the development of capitalist media, rather than a platform that transcends the constraints of twentieth-century mass communication media.

In his 2000 book *Digital Capitalism: Networking the Global Market System*, Dan Schiller presented the critical perspective on the emergent internet in the following way:

> Far from delivering us into a high-tech Eden, in fact, cyberspace itself is being rapidly colonized by the familiar workings of the market system. Across their breadth and depth, computer networks link with existing capitalism to massively broaden the effective reach of the marketplace. Indeed, the Internet comprises nothing less than the central production and control apparatus of an increasingly supranational market system. (Schiller, 2000, p. xiv)

In a similar vein, Robin Mansell argued the need for a critical political economy approach to the study of new media that would:

> make issues of power explicit in the analysis of mediated experience ... [and] foster an understanding of pressures towards the commodification of new media and its consequences for the way in which power is distributed through the material conditions of the capitalist system. (2004, p. 102)

Eugenia Siapera proposed that even if the internet and digital media have been reshaping capitalism from 'industrial' to 'informational' forms (a topic to be explored in more depth in the next chapter), it remained the case that 'the exploitative nature of capitalism reducing everything to profit and loss is still the dominant logic' (2012, p. 60). Curran *et al.* argued that there has been a persistent tendency, in both the popular and scholarly literature, to misunderstand the internet because 'the impact of the Internet does not follow a single direction dictated by its technology. Instead, the influence of the Internet is filtered through the structures and processes of society' (Curran *et al.*, 2012, p. 9).

In *Digital Disconnect*, Robert McChesney (2013, pp. 63–95) proposes six key themes from the political economy of communication that he saw as being central to understanding the internet:

1. There is a need for a normative or ethical perspective on evaluating the impact of the internet. McChesney proposed that *public sphere* theory (Habermas, 1974) with its question about whether new media technologies are enhancing civic participation and democratic discourse, provides such a normative framework;
2. The question of *affordances* associated with new media technologies, or what they enable people to do and how they enable people to act in new ways, needs to be considered alongside questions of *access*, or how widely such a technology is available throughout societies. This raises the issue of the *digital divide*, or inequalities of access between information 'haves' and 'have-nots', at both the national and global levels;
3. Like mass media such as broadcasting, internet content providers and service platforms remain largely dependent upon advertising revenue, direct sales and subscriptions, and this leads them to privilege content that drives traffic to websites in order to maximise commercial returns;
4. In contrast to claims that the internet would herald a new era of free market capitalism, there remains a range of ways in which monopoly profits are accrued online including: copyright restrictions on the re-use of content; attempts to circumvent 'Net neutrality' and direct users towards content from which the service provider derives commercial benefit, and the 'first mover' advantages that accrue from being the best-known provider of a service (e.g. Google with search, Amazon with e-commerce, Uber with ride services);
5. The greater diversity of voices potentially enabled by the low barriers to online participation in practice come up against the difficulty of developing sustainable business models for new news and information providers, while traditional journalism is hit hard by the migration of advertising and classified revenues from traditional news sites;
6. Public policy continues to play a vitally important role in shaping the internet's development (cf. Curran *et al.*, 2012, pp. 12–17), and the unequal power of corporations and business lobbyists compared to citizens remains a constraining influence upon the democratizing potential of the internet.

On a global scale, one would also note the unequal nature of access to internet governance forums, the dominance of US-based corporate and government interests, and the difficulties in getting issues on the agenda that would open up internet governance to greater public scrutiny and democratize access to online communication resources (Hamelink, 2015, pp. 226–227).

It is important to note that this does not entail a root-and-branch rejection of the possibilities of the internet to radically expand the scope of participatory democratic politics. The political economist Christian Fuchs, for instance, identifies the potential of social media to promote new forms of radical political networks and to revivify the public sphere, but argues that such endeavours are in contradiction with the commercial demands of social media platform providers (Google, Facebook etc.) to commodify big data and sell user information to advertisers, as well as state agencies accessing personal data for purposes of political surveillance (Fuchs, 2015, pp. 357–365). Similarly, McChesney observes the new potential created by the internet to promote community self-government through measures such as participatory budgeting, to improve the quality of journalism by enabling non-corporate alternative media, and to mobilise people as part of political movements for social change at all levels, from the local to the national to the global (McChesney, 2013, pp. 231–232). But these political economists argue that 'the democratization of the Internet is integrally related to the democratization of the political economy' (McChesney, 2013, p. 22), and that entails addressing powerful corporate interests who dominate internet technologies and platforms.

Debating critical political economy

In the conclusion to this chapter, I want to note three areas of continuing debate in critical political economy. First, there is the understanding of markets and competition that informs the field. The argument that markets and competition have become less important over time as media giants have been able to control and 'tame' the market through monopoly power has been a dominant one in critical political economy, but this claim has not gone uncontested. Second, there is the relationship between power and ideology, and particularly the proposition that economic power automatically equates to political and cultural-ideological power. This has particularly crystallized in recent years around the claim that neoliberalism has constituted a global dominant ideology central to the reshaping of global media and communication in the interests of dominant fractions of capital. Finally, there will be some discussion of the political implications of critical political economy, with particular reference to nationalism and internationalism and the ideologies of neoliberalism and globalism.

Changing media industry dynamics

Both 'first generation' dependency theorists and contemporary critical global political economists have been strongly influenced by the *monopoly capital* school of neo-Marxist political economy. Marxist theories of monopoly capitalism held that the concentration of capital (expansion of the scale of production) and the centralization of capital (concentration of ownership and rise of large corporations) promoted the rise of monopolies and cartels. Neo-Marxists, such as the *Monthly Review* school of political economists, updated this thesis to argue that large corporations were now able to 'tame' the capitalist market and insulate themselves from competitive forces, particularly through the management of consumer demand through marketing and advertising strategies (Baran & Sweezy, 1968). In a contemporary restatement of the monopoly capitalism thesis, John Bellamy Foster identified the resulting modifications in corporate behaviour in the context of monopoly in these terms:

> With the rise of the giant firm, price competition ceased to take place in any significant sense within mature monopolistic industries ... In this strange, semi-regulated world of monopoly capital, there is no longer a life-or-death competition threatening the survival of the mature capitalist enterprise ... Rather, the giant corporations that dominate the contemporary economy engage primarily in struggles over market share. (Foster, 2000, pp. 6–7)

Applying the monopoly capital thesis to contemporary media, McChesney argued that 'the simple truth is that for those atop our economy success is based in large part on *eliminating* competition ... All investors and firms desire to be in as monopolistic a position as possible' (McChesney, 1999, p. 138). In the media industries, this has meant that 'a small number of firms ... thoroughly dominate the market's output and maintain barriers to entry that effectively keep new market entrants at bay' (McChesney, 1999, p. 138). For McChesney and other critical political economists, 'the prevalence of oligopoly – or in more popular parlance, corporate power – undermines the case for the marriage of capitalism to democracy' (McChesney, 2013, p. 40).

The question of whether the media industries have become more or less competitive over time has been the subject of considerable debate. The claims of McChesney and other media monopoly theorists such as Ben Bagdikian (2000) that 'there are now fewer and larger companies controlling more and more' (McChesney, 2001b), were challenged by the MIT media economist Benjamin Compaine (Compaine, 2001; cf. Compaine and Gomery, 2001). Compaine argued that critical media scholars underestimated the extent of movement within the 'league table' of top media companies and the extent to which the internet has introduced new forms of competition to traditional media giants. It was also noted that the competitive advantages that are associated with conglomeration needed to be weighed against new forms of risk and possibilities to accrue losses as a result of such expansionary activities. While there are examples of successes of expansion across sectors in order to create new synergies – such as Disney's acquisition of Pixar and Google's acquisition of YouTube – the history of such expansions is also replete with instances of overreach and failure (e.g. AOL-Time Warner, News Corporation and MySpace) (Flew, 2011).

Assessing these debates, Winseck (2011) observed that while the monopoly capital school provided important insights into the behaviour of those media companies and owners 'at the top' of the ownership pyramid, 'not enough attention is paid to the details of the key players, markets, and the dynamics and diversity that exist among all the elements that make up the media' (Winseck, 2011, p. 23). For instance, one of the reasons why there are a large number of mergers and acquisitions in the media sector is because of the dynamism and innovation that exists among smaller, more emergent players in the media ecosystem, and to solely focus upon how competition and innovation is suppressed at the top provides a one-sided account of the sector's overall dynamics (Cunningham *et al.*, 2015, pp. 60–62). In his massive empirical account of trends in media concentration in the United States, Noam (2009) found evidence that supported arguments for both an increase and a lessening of competition, concluding that technological and policy changes led to reduced barriers to entry and more competition in many media industries for much of the 1980s and 1990s, but that there was a trend towards consolidation in the digital media industries in the 2000s (pp. 34–39). For Noam (2009, p. 39) what we find in the media industries are a combination of:

1. *Giants*: firms that become both ever-larger, in both absolute terms and relative to their competitors;
2. *Mavericks and innovators*: smaller participants who benefit from lower entry barriers with new products and services (sometimes subsequently acquired by the industry giants);
3. *Specialists*: smaller firms that carve out significant market niches.

Importantly, Noam finds that the definition of a media industry is becoming increasingly blurry, as the power of the traditional media giants such as Time Warner, Disney, News Corporation, Viacom, etc. has been profoundly challenged by the new ICT-based *integrator* forms such as Google, Apple, Microsoft, Netflix, Amazon and others (Noam, 2009, pp. 436–446). The market power that the latter companies have comes from their control over digital distribution *platforms* rather than over copyright-protected *content*. Such fluidity in media markets suggests the need for some caution in using size itself as the proxy for market dominance, associated with the influence of the all-powerful media mogul. Indeed, a reading over time of

McChesney's work supports such a conclusion. When the media giants are discussed in his earlier works (McChesney & Herman, 1997), it is the 'big six' of Time Warner, Disney, News Corporation, Viacom, Bertelsmann and Sony that controlled copyright-based industries such as film, broadcasting, music and publishing. By 2012, however, these firms have fallen down the league table of the largest US corporations, and the list is now dominated by Apple, Google, Microsoft, Amazon, AT&T and IBM, meaning that 'the Internet monopolists sit at the commanding heights of U.S. and world capitalism' (McChesney, 2013, p. 131). In other words, market power has mutated in media industries over recent decades, and a political economy approach needs to be able to capture those changing industry and market dynamics.

Economic power and cultural power: the neoliberalism debate

It was noted in this chapter that there are two major approaches to the question of ideology among critical political economists. The first, associated with authors such as Herman and Chomsky (1988), tends to see the translation of economic power, or the ability of monopolists to control markets, as being readily translatable into political power, or influence over the state and the political process, and cultural power, or the ability to gain popular consent to a dominant ideology that serves corporate interests. The second, associated with cultural studies theorists such as Hall (1986) but also political economists such as Murdock and Golding (2005), identifies these relationships as more complex, multi-layered and contradictory. Rather than seeing the media industries straightforwardly as disseminators of corporate propaganda that serves their own material interests, these theorists point to forces of contestation, such as the professional ideologies of media professionals and the dissenting perspectives of audiences, as well as sources of conflict and contestation among business owners themselves (e.g. differences between traditional media content industries and digital platform providers about the appropriate scope and reach of copyright laws).

These can be seen as debates about how readily economic power determines cultural power. It will be noted in the next chapter that globalization theorists have tended to identify significant disjunctures between economic power and cultural power that render globalization more of a mosaic of intercultural differences and proliferating identities than the top-down imposition of Western knowledge systems backed up by ideology and force. In recent years, many political economists have argued that *neoliberalism* has become the dominant ideology of global capitalism, used to promote the interests of the largest transnational corporations and to ensure the compliance of nation-state governments with global agendas. In his highly influential *A Short History of Neoliberalism*, David Harvey defined neoliberalism as:

> A theory of political economic practices that proposes that human well being can best be advanced by liberating individual entrepreneurial freedoms and skills within an institutional framework characterized by strong private property rights, free markets, and free trade. The role of the state is to create and preserve an institutional framework appropriate to such practices. (Harvey, 2005, p. 2)

Dan Schiller (2000) argued that the current shape of the global internet was formed through an alliance of dominant US computing and telecommunications interests with the largest transnational companies around a 'shared political axiom: that corporate capital's ownership and control of networks should be put beyond dispute ... [and] the neoliberal freedom to fashion networks into instruments of enterprise should remain unalloyed' (p. 1). Miller *et al.* (2005, p. 57) referred to the 'prevailing neoliberal "Washington Consensus"' that is 'animated by neoliberalism's mantra of individual freedom, the marketplace and minimal government involvement in economic matters'. Boyd-Barrett (2015, p. 134) has argued that in spite of criticisms of the media imperialism thesis, it is still the case that 'the officially enshrined values of the largest economies in the world' are 'associated with the philosophy of neoliberalism: a philosophy of the "free" market executed through unregulated monopolistic or oligopolistic capitalist production and exchange, consumerism and individualism'. Hesmondhalgh (2013, p. 40) argued that there has been a dominant 'neoliberal approach to culture' that has shaped domestic and international media policies since the 1980s. This entails 'assuming that the production of efficient markets should be the primary goal of public policy ... [and] downplaying or marginalizing the specificity of media and culture' on the basis of non-economic criteria. Hardy concluded his account of trends in global communication policy making with the proposition that 'neoliberalism has become a dominant force in supranational and national communications policy [as] corporations have also increased their influence to unprecedented levels' (Hardy, 2014, p. 192).

Such arguments are squarely within the Marxist tradition of a dominant ideology, where the dominant economic interests can assert hegemony over the dominant ideas projected through the media and other cultural institutions, and can control the political process. Theorists of neoliberalism identify its origins as lying with the Reagan administration in the US and the Thatcher government in the UK in the 1980s, but extending its global reach through international policies adopted by entities such as the World Bank and the International Monetary

Fund – the so-called 'Washington Consensus' – and through the adoption of more market-friendly positions by so-called 'Third Way' governments such as the US Democrats under President Bill Clinton and the UK Labour Party led by Tony Blair (Harvey, 2005, pp. 90–98; cf. Giddens, 2001).

Nationalism and globalism

There are a number of difficulties with the term 'neoliberalism' as it has been used in academic debates, including the tendency for there to be as many definitions as there are authors, a propensity for it to be ascribed to multiple disparate phenomena, and the overwhelmingly pejorative understanding that exists of the term (Boas & Gans-Morse, 2009; Flew, 2012a, 2014b). At the same time, it seeks to capture (however imperfectly) a concern that had been growing worldwide during the 2000s about the influence of unchecked corporate power, rising inequalities and the sense that an unaccountable global elite had usurped power from local citizens. This concern manifested itself in movements such as Occupy in the United States and the *Indignados* in Spain, and the rise of left-populist movements such as SYRIZA in Greece and the Bernie Sanders presidential campaign in the US. The dominant ideology has gone under different names. Steger (2005, p. ix) referred to *globalism*, as 'a political ideology that endows the concept of globalization with market-oriented norms, values, and meanings'. Sklair (1998, p. 297) defined the dominant culture-ideology of globalization as *consumerism*, which 'proclaims … that the meaning of life is to be found in the things that we possess'.

What arises is a potentially bifurcated set of political responses to globalization and global capitalism. There has been a growing right-populist movement throughout the 2000s and 2010s to counterpose nationalism with globalism, arguing that capitalist globalization leaves behind the traditional working classes of nation-states, and weakens national cultures and institutions by shifting power to supranational institutions and multicultural elites. The rise of politicians such as Donald Trump in the United States and Marine Le Pen in France, and the vote in Great Britain to leave the European Union ('Brexit'), have owed something to these sentiments. Critics on the left tend to favour multicultural citizenship and cosmopolitan identities, seeing this 'new nationalism' as essentially racist and backward-looking. Sklair (1997, p. 48) argues that 'the global capitalist system uses the myth of the nation-state … to deflect criticism and opposition to its hegemonic control of the global system'.

What I will argue in later chapters is that this does not really resolve the question of the relationship between nation-states and globalization, and stems from an inadequate understanding of global media and its relationship to cultures. It overstates the weakness of the nation-state, and underestimates the degree to which national cultures and identities are rooted in institutional forms. At the same time, it does raise the familiar question of the extent to which critical political economists have an investment in how global media and cultural institutions operate, and how forms of global media and communications policy interact with national media systems. For example, if there is opposition to multilateral trade agreements, are there alternative measures being proposed or is the intention to reduce the overall level of global trade and investment? A retreat into various forms of economic protectionism and ethno-nationalism potentially creates new problems greater than those identified with capitalist globalization. The policy field that presents itself to those seeking to transform the global media system is, therefore, a complex one to negotiate.

Note

1   The term 'first generation' is used with caution, not least because authors such as Kaarle Nordenstreng, Oliver Boyd-Barrett and Cees Hamelink are very active in the political economy of global media, having all recently published books (Boyd-Barrett, 2015; Hamelink, 2015; Nordenstreng & Thussu, 2015). What I want to capture with the term is the extent to which dependency theory, the NWICO and the Cold War were all shaping forces on the critical political economy of the 1970s and 1980s. By contrast, work in the late 1990s and 2000s was more shaped by theories of neoliberalism, global capitalism and the rise of global media production networks. Also, the studies of the 1970s and 1980s were, by necessity, largely focused upon film and television, whereas twenty-first-century critical political economy needs to engage with the global internet.

CHAPTER 4

Globalization theories

Globalization: definitions and clarifications

Globalization has been one of the key concepts of social theory in recent years, and one that has had significant influence upon thinking about media and communication. Globalization theories have parallels with modernization theories in that both see communications media as one of the key ways through which people and societies are increasingly exposed to one another through technologies that carry messages at speed across great distances. Marshall McLuhan's famous thesis that broadcast technologies would give rise to a *global village*, where 'electric circuitry has overthrown the regime of "time" and "space" and pours upon us instantly and continuously the concerns of all other men [*sic*]' (McLuhan & Fiore, 1967, p. 16), is a concept rooted in modernization discourses, yet it anticipates globalization theories, particularly in its perception of the autonomous impact of media upon social identities.

Similarly, globalization theories also intersect with political economy theories of global media, particularly in their understanding of capitalism as an integrated yet unequal world-system, where commerce, investment and trade flows bind people and nations ever more tightly together. Karl Marx and Friedrich Engels were arguably the first major modern theorists of globalization, with their observations in *The Communist Manifesto* (first published in 1848), that 'the need of a constantly expanding market for its products chases the bourgeoisie over the whole surface of the globe', and 'the bourgeoisie has through its exploitation of the world-market given a cosmopolitan character to production and consumption in every country' (Marx & Engels, 1983 [1848], p. 22). Theories of global capitalism, dependency and world-systems theory clearly mark out this relationship between globalization and critical political economy (Wallerstein, 1974; Brewer, 1980).

A common feature of globalization theories is the observation that globalization has become the central defining reality of our times. Benyon and Dunkerley (2002, p. 2) argued that 'what is undeniable is that globalization, in one form or another, is impacting on the lives of everyone on the planet ... It is changing consciousness, too, as everyone everywhere becomes more globally aware and oriented'. The sociologist Anthony Giddens, in his 2002 BBC Reith Lectures, argued: 'Globalization is not incidental to our lives today. It is a shift in our very life circumstances. It is the way we now live.' (Giddens, 2002, p. 19) Ulrich Beck observed that 'globality is an unavoidable condition of human intercourse at the close of the twentieth century' (Beck, 2000, p. 15). Thomas Friedman identified globalization as arising from the 'inexorable integration of markets, nation-states and technologies' (Friedman, 2005, p. 9), while Malcolm Waters identified globalization as 'a social process in which the constraints of geography on economic, political, social and cultural arrangements recede' (Waters, 2000, p. 5).

A variety of definitions of globalization have been offered, even if, as Held *et al.* observed, 'no single coherent theory of globalization exists' (Held *et al.*, 1999, p. 436). Four influential definitions of globalization are provided below:

> Globalization as a concept refers both to the compression of the world and the intensification of consciousness of the world as a whole ... both concrete global interdependence and consciousness of the global whole. (Robertson, 1992, p. 8)

> Globalization can ... be defined as the intensification of worldwide social relations which link distant localities in such a way that local happenings are shaped by events occurring many miles away and vice versa ... Local transformation is as much a part of globalization as the lateral extension of social connections across time and space. (Giddens, 1990, p. 64)

> Globalization ... denotes the expanding scale, growing magnitude, speeding up and deepening impact of transcontinental flows and patterns of social interaction. It refers to a shift or transformation in the scale of human organization that links distant communities and expands the reach of power relations across the world's regions and continents. (Held & McGrew, 2002, p. 1)

> Globalization refers to the expansion and intensification of social relations and consciousness across world-time and world-space. (Steger, 2009, p. 15)

Robertson (1992) provides a means of comprehending how globalization occurs according to such definitions. Social theory posits a relationship of individuals to societies, which increasingly take a national form, and of individual selves to humankind more generally, or the relationship of membership of one culture to that of other cultures. But as Figure 4.1 shows, there is a fourth element to these relationships, which is the

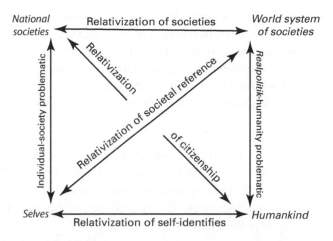

Figure 4.1 The global field

Source: Robertson (1992, p. 27). Reprinted with permission of SAGE Publications.

relationship that all have to the world system of societies. Globalization theories posit that while such links and interconnections have long existed – the poet John Donne wrote that 'No man is an island' in 1624 – a range of economic, technological, political, social and cultural processes have intensified such connections over the last 30–50 years in particular.

This figure is revealing since it indicates that the impact of global forces on local identities is by no means a new thing. If we think about great trading routes such as the Silk Road that linked China, Central Asia, the Middle East and Europe, or the extent of the Roman Empire in the first century AD, or Columbus's voyage to the Americas in 1492, it is apparent that a transnational dimension has existed to commerce and trade, and to cultural and intellectual flows, for many centuries. Globalization thus needs to be given a historical dimension, lest it be seen as a universal feature of human civilizations, where growing contact with other societies and cultures is the inevitable consequence of continuous improvements in transport and communications. Alternatively, globalization could be seen simply as a synonym for *global capitalism*, with its relentless tendency towards the expansion of markets, and the global expansion of capital accumulation in order to exploit new sources of wealth and labour-power, as described by Marx and others long before globalization theories made distinctive claims. Arif Dirlik, for instance, argued that 'if globalization means anything, it is the incorporation of societies globally into a capitalist modernity, with all the implications of the latter – economic, social, political, and cultural' (Dirlik, 2003, p. 275).

The proposition that globalization marks a *qualitatively new* feature of economies, polities, societies and cultures, and hence requires new approaches to social theory, is the distinctive perspective of globalization theorists. To take one influential example, Ulrich Beck argued that modern sociology was framed around 'a territorial definition of modern society, and thus a model of society centered on the national state' (Beck, 2000, p. 25). For Beck, such:

> 'methodological nationalism' ... collapses in the course of economic, political, ecological, cultural and biographical globalization. World society means the emergence of new power opportunities and new social spaces for action, living and perception, which break up and muddle the nation-state orthodoxy of politics and society. (2000, p. 65)

Held *et al.* (1999, p. 17) proposed three reasonably discrete historical epochs in the development of globalization:

1. The *early modern* phase from the fourteenth to late eighteenth centuries, marked by the emergence on the one hand of the modern nation-state in Europe and the United States, and on the other by European expansion across the globe to establish territorial empires. This is a period where the first major trading companies emerge, and colonialism is linked to trade, but where imported goods are largely luxury items, and most people of the world consume goods that are produced in reasonable geographical proximity to where they live;

2. The *modern* phase, from the early nineteenth century to the end of World War II in 1945. This period was marked by a dramatic growth in foreign trade and investment, and a massive increase in the international movement of people, as well as the expansion and consolidation of colonial empires. It is during this period that an integrated international division of labour begins to emerge, but it remains within colonial empires, with the colonies typically being providers of primary products to the industrializing core nations of Europe;

3. The *contemporary* phase from 1945 to the present, which sees the consolidation of a global system of states, particularly with the decolonization of much of Africa, Asia, the Middle East, Latin America and the Caribbean, and which entails a substantial intensification of economic globalization in all of its forms: trade, investment and production.

A number of globalization theorists, such as Robertson (1992), Waters (2000), Castells (1996, 2009), Held (2004) and Kaldor (2003), would propose a fourth stage, emerging in the 1970s and flourishing from the 1980s onwards, marked by the globalization of media and communications technologies, the rise of global social movements and a global civil society, and the breaking up of the Soviet Union and the communist states of Eastern Europe in 1989–1990.

Strong globalization?

Many of the arguments presented can be described as *strong globalization* theories. Strong globalization theories argue that the process of globalization has marked a shift in the economic, political and cultural dynamics of societies that is of such a scale that the analytical tools by which we understand social processes in the twenty-first century are fundamentally different to those which were applicable to twentieth-century societies. Ulrich Beck's statement on 'methodological nationalism' above would be an example of such a strong globalization argument. In a similar vein, the international relations theorist Martin Shaw argued that 'the idea of a national society in the old sense has declined as the ideas of a global society ... have grown' (Shaw, 1997, p. 29). Such a global society is, for Shaw:

> No more or less than the entire complex of social relations between human beings on a world scale ... Global society can be said to exist, in the sense that global relationships are sufficiently strong and established to be defined as the largest context of social relations as a whole. (1997, pp. 31–32)

Among the core propositions of strong globalization theories, which we will encounter with regards to global media production, global culture and the relationship to nation-states, are:

1. Markets increasingly operate on a global scale, and are dominated by a diminishing number of transnational corporations (TNCs);
2. These TNCs organize their activities on a global scale, and are less constrained by the policies and regulations of nation-states;
3. The power of nation-states is in decline, with many of their core operations being superseded by the laws and regulations established by supranational governmental institutions;
4. As a result, political activity that focuses upon incremental reforms within the framework of nation-states is misplaced, as real decision-making power increasingly resides outside of their territorial boundaries;
5. Globalization generates a global cultural experience where subjective identities are defined less by the relationship of individuals to geographically defined spaces and the 'imagined community' of the nation-state, and more by their relationship to complex and interconnected global media and communications flows;

6. This twenty-first-century global condition is unprecedented, for while capitalism has been an international system since its inception, it is only now that global networks of technology and communication enable it to function as a fully integrated global system.

It is important to note that globalization theories differ in their focus from world-systems theories, discussed in Chapter 3. Immanuel Wallerstein (1974, 1990, 1997, 2000) argued that the development of a world economy connected by trading relations and an emergent international division of labour was accompanied by the extension of political power by Europe (and, later, the United States) over large parts of the rest of the world through colonialism and imperialism, leading to an integrated capitalist world-system. For Wallerstein, these unequal political relations operated in the service of economic power, enabling the construction of a capitalist world system with three tiers of states: the core, the semi-periphery, and the periphery. Unequal economic relations, reinforced by the exercise of political power, enabled the ongoing transfer of surplus from the periphery to the core, further developing the core states while 'under-developing' the periphery. World-systems theories generally endorse theories of media and cultural imperialism, particularly in the construction of the relationship between Western cultural influence and the formation of transnational elites in the non-Western periphery (Brewer, 1980, pp. 165–167; Wallerstein, 1997; Sklair, 2002, pp. 40–42).

Globalization theorists have generally distanced themselves from world-systems theory, and the differences provide important insights into the different ways in which the two approaches identify the relationship between economic, political and cultural power. Anthony Giddens (1990, 1997) saw world-systems theory as one-dimensional in its focus on the world capitalist economy as the primary 'institution of modernity' to be globalized, arguing that the nation-state system, the international division of labour and the world military order also needed to be considered as dynamic shaping influences in their own right (Giddens, 1997, pp. 22–24). Moreover, the relationship between these institutions and the wider global system needed to be understood reflexively: nation-states are 'pulled' in certain directions by global forces, but they also 'push' their own agendas on the global stage. For Giddens, world-systems theory too readily represents nation-states – particularly those of the periphery – as the passive 'victims' of globalizing capitalist modernity. Malcolm Waters (2000) argued that the economic determinism of Wallerstein's world-system theory missed the importance of cultural drivers of globalization. Waters argued that symbolic exchanges (of cultural forms, money, digital information etc.) are more readily globalized than material exchanges (labour, physical goods and services), meaning that the world economy becomes increasingly globalized to the extent that it is increasingly a cultural economy. As Waters describes his framework, 'material exchanges localize; political exchanges internationalize; symbolic exchanges globalize' (2000, p. 6).

Globalization, culture and power

In order to better apprehend the distinctiveness of globalization theories, as compared with other theories of global media such as modernization theories, critical political economy and world-systems theory, we can note how theorists have approached two key concepts: culture and power. In order to do this, the section will focus upon four key theorists of globalization: Anthony Giddens, Arjun Appadurai, Manuel Castells and John Tomlinson. All of these authors consider the cultural as well as the economic and political dimensions of globalization, lay stress upon its systemic nature and its uniqueness as a stage of capitalist modernity, and seek to draw out the relatively unpredictable and contingent nature of globalization's influences and effects on people and cultures. A distinction is thus being made between those theorists who understand globalization as essentially the spread of global capitalism, more or less explicable using tools and theories associated with political economy (as outlined in Chapter 3), and those who have proposed that it requires new theories and concepts, as is argued in different ways by Giddens, Appadurai, Castells and Tomlinson.[1]

It was noted in Chapter 1 that power can be identified as existing in four forms: economic, political, military, and cultural or symbolic. The critical question that arises is the relationship between these four forms. For some critical political economists, as was noted in Chapter 3, the four are essentially synonymous, part of an integrated media-propaganda system enforced by a relatively unified global ruling class. Globalization theorists, by contrast, argue that the relations between the four forms are relatively complex, multi-layered and indeterminate in their final outcomes. In *The Consequences of Modernity*, Anthony Giddens (1990) argued that modernity is characterized by the rise of four distinct institutions:

1. Capitalism, as an economic system based upon commodity production, private ownership of capital, and a class system based upon ownership/ non-ownership of the means of production;
2. Industrialism, involving the growing application of technology to production, and the greater use of energy and physical machinery to produce goods;
3. Surveillance, and the growing use of information as a means of social control and administrative power;
4. Military power, and the state monopoly over the means of violence.

From this perspective, capitalism is a globalizing force that shapes economic life but cannot constitute a 'society' in its own right: control over military power and the means of surveillance is increasingly the domain of the nation-state, which 'must be explained and analysed separately from discussion of the nature of capitalism or industrialism' (Giddens, 1990, p. 57). Giddens' focus on the distinctiveness of the institutions of the nation-state, which draws some inspiration from the work of Max Weber, distinguishes his analysis of global modernity from that of world-systems theory, which sees globalization as largely an outgrowth of capitalism. Giddens' approach is shown in Figure 4.2. At the same time, it shares with modernization theories – also strongly influenced by Weber – the dualistic or 'great divide' approach that demarcates the traditional or pre-modern from the modern, and largely identifies modernity with the technologies and institutions of the industrial capitalist West (Holton, 1998, p. 42).

For Giddens, the dominant social force has been the transformation from traditional societies to modernity, as 'the modes of life brought into being by modernity have swept us away from *all* traditional types of social order, in quite unprecedented fashion' (1990, p. 4). Modernity is viewed by Giddens as an inherently globalizing and dynamic system that has three core features:

1. The separation of time and space, and the dislocation of space as social category from place as the site of lived experience;
2. The disembedding or 'lifting out' of social relations from local contexts of interaction, characteristic of money-based economies and the growing importance of expert systems to practices of government and rule;
3. The growing reflexivity of knowledge systems and agents within them, which entails perpetual questioning of forms of knowledge and social practice.

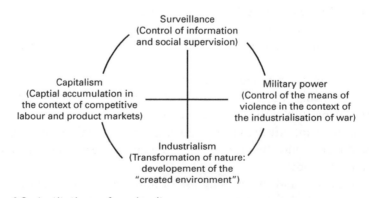

Figure 4.2 Institutions of modernity

Source: Giddens (1990, p. 59). Reprinted with permission of Polity and Stanford University Press.

Giddens describes contemporary globalization as a 'radicalization' of modernity. It is part of what he refers to as an intensification or 'stretching' of social and personal relations, meaning that 'the modes of connection between different social contexts or regions become networked across the earth's surface as a whole' (1990, p. 64). The rise of global media is tied up with industrialism insofar as it has entailed 'the transformation of the technologies of communication' (1990, p. 77) and processes of cultural globalization and global information flows. Stressing the continuity between earlier and contemporary globalization processes, Giddens made the point that 'the global extension of the institutions of modernity would be impossible were it not for the pooling of knowledge that is represented by the "news"' (1990, p. 77), although the media does not otherwise feature prominently in his account of globalization.

While Giddens' account of global modernity stresses its institutional forms, particularly the relationship between globalization and nation-states, Manuel Castells' work on communications power and the network society has argued that the institutions of industrial capitalism are being increasingly displaced by a 'new, informational mode of development [where] the source of productivity lies in the technology of knowledge generation, information processing, and symbol communication' (Castells, 1996, p. 17). The informational economy is tied to the rise of the network society, where 'presence or absence in the network and the dynamics of each network *vis-à-vis* others are critical sources of domination and change in our society' (1996, p. 469). For Castells:

> Networks constitute the new social morphology of our societies, and the diffusion of networking logic substantially modifies the operation and outcomes in processes of production, experience, power, and culture. While the networking form of social organization has existed in other times and spaces, the new information technology paradigm provides the material basis for its pervasive expansion throughout the entire social structure. (1996, p. 469)

The network society is linked to a new economic regime that he terms the *information technology paradigm*, where information, networking, flexibility and convergence are inherent outcomes of the pervasive impacts of new ICTs upon all aspects of economy, politics, society and culture. Castells' metaphor of the network as the core element of the information technology paradigm is developed in the context of a *new economy* that is based on ICTs, and has three fundamental characteristics:

1. It is *informational*, in the sense that 'the capacity of generating knowledge and processing/managing information determine the productivity

and competitiveness of all kinds of economic units, be they firms, regions, or countries' (Castells, 2000, p. 10);

2. It is *global*, since 'its core strategic activities have the capacity to work as a unit on a planetary scale in real time or chosen time' (Castells, 2000, p. 10);

3. It is *networked*, as it is based upon both information networks such as the internet and the networked enterprise as the dominant form of economic organization, driven by global financial markets, strategic alliances and partnerships, and electronic commerce that consolidates 'the internet-based, interactive, networked connection between producers, consumers, and service providers' (Castells, 2001, p. 75).

Castells proposed that cultures are primarily defined through the dominant communication technologies of a particular historical era, meaning that 'because culture is mediated and enacted through communication, cultures themselves, that is our historically produced systems of beliefs and codes, become fundamentally transformed, and will be more so over time, by the new technological system' (1996, p. 328). He presented global cultures as being in a period of transition, from the mass media culture of broadcasting technologies, where societies could be organized around shared images and messages disseminated through television, to new media cultures where consumers are increasingly the producers of culture, where power shifts from control over content and messages to control over platforms and services, and where there will be growing differentiation among audience-users at the national level and new forms of segmentation at a global level. In terms of the relationship between place and space, Castells concluded that with internet-based media 'localities become disembodied from their cultural, historical, geographical meaning, and reintegrated into functional networks ... inducing a *space of flows* that substitutes for the space of places' (1996, p. 375).

In *Communication Power*, he elaborated upon the latter concept, arguing that the cultural dimension of networked communication generated two contradictory trends: the parallel development of a global culture and multiple identity cultures; and the simultaneous rise of mediated individualism, or *mass self-communication*, and new cultures of collective ownership and sharing of digital content by the *creative audience* (Castells, 2009, pp. 116–135). The global network society, then, is one where cultural power, as with other forms of power, is shifting from the territorially based institutions of the nation-state to globally integrated networks, or what Saskia Sassen (2006) has termed 'global assemblages'. Castells summarizes this argument as follows:

> If power relations exist within specific social structures that are constituted on the basis of spatio-temporal formations, and these spatio-temporal formations are no longer primarily located at the national level, but are

global and local at the same time, the boundary of society changes, and so does the frame of reference of power relationships that transcend the national ... under the conditions of multilayered globalization, the state becomes just a node (however important) of a particular network, the political, institutional, and military network that overlaps with other significant networks in the construction of social practice. (2009, pp. 18–19)

This theme of the decline of nation-states in an era of global modernity is also characteristic of the work of Arjun Appadurai (1990, 1996). For Appadurai, the two key elements that make the current era of globalization a culturally distinctive one are the relationship between globalization of electronic media on the one hand and mass migration on the other. Global media flows insert themselves opportunistically into 'this fertile ground of deterritorialization, in which money, commodities and persons are involved in ceaselessly chasing each other around the world' (Appadurai, 1990, p. 303). At the same time, migration and the diasporic experience compel those involved to construct new identities as they 'seek to annex the global into their own practices of the modern' (Appadurai, 1996, p. 4). In combination, global media and mass migration 'create diasporic public spheres ... that confound theories that depend upon the continued sallence of the nation-state as the key arbiter of important social changes' (p. 4). As a consequence, he argues that 'nation-states, as a complex interactive system, are not very likely to be the long-term arbiters of the relationship between globality and modernity' (p. 19).

Appadurai's work has also provided conceptual underpinnings for theories of globalization and global culture that point to *cultural hybridization*, rather than cultural domination, as being its *raison d'être*. He argued that the *global cultural economy* was based upon a series of recurring tensions between those forces which promote a common global culture (cultural homogenization) and those promoting cultural difference (cultural heterogenization). He proposed that global cultural flows operated across five planes:

1. *ethnoscapes* – movements of people across the world, as tourists, immigrants, refugees, exiles, guest workers, students and so on;
2. *technoscapes* – the movement of complex technologies around the world, and associated capital and skilled labour linked to investment projects;
3. *finanscapes* – the dramatic and unprecedented global movements of financial capital through currency markets, financial institutions, stock exchanges and commodity markets;
4. *mediascapes* – the global flows of images, narratives, media content and so on through print, broadcast, film and video and, increasingly, the internet and digital media;

5. *ideoscapes* – the global circulation of ideas, concepts, values and 'keywords', such as democracy, human rights, environmental consciousness and so on.

For Appadurai, what is distinctive about the current phase of global culture is the growing disjuncture between these flows, meaning:

> this new set of global disjunctures is not a simple one-way street in which the terms of global cultural politics are set wholly by ... the vicissitudes of international flows of technology, labor and finance, demanding only a modest modification of existing neo-Marxist models of uneven development and state formation. (Appadurai, 1990, p. 306)

It also points towards an increasingly transnational cultural politics, where cultures are constituted as geographically dispersed group identities based upon situated difference, that can use global media technologies to engage in 'the conscious mobilization of cultural differences in the service of a larger national or transnational politics' (Appadurai, 1996, p. 15).

Globalization and cultural identities: beyond cultural imperialism

Associated with globalization theories has been a strong critique of cultural imperialism, associated with the critical political economy perspective, and a championing of cultural hybridity and cosmopolitan, post-national forms of cultural identity. John Tomlinson observed that a tendency exists to 'imagine globalization as pushing us towards an all-encompassing "global culture"', and that this is understood by critics as constituting cultural imperialism, or 'the spread of Western – particularly American – culture to every part of the globe, and the consequent threat of a loss of distinct non-Western cultural traditions' (Tomlinson, 2007, p. 355). In his detailed critique of theories of cultural imperialism, Tomlinson (1991) observed that in theories of cultural imperialism and media imperialism developed by Herbert Schiller, Oliver Boyd-Barrett and others, there is often a conflation of media and culture, meaning that patterns of media consumption in different parts of the world are taken to effectively stand in for culture as lived experience. It also loses sight of the diverse ways in which cultural meaning is attached to such global media texts in multiple cross-cultural contexts, and the insights of audience studies that 'audiences are more active, complex and critically aware in their readings than the theorists of media imperialism have allowed' (Tomlinson, 1991, p. 57).

Tomlinson argued that there was an underlying nationalist premise in discourses on cultural imperialism, as it typically presumed 'the domination of one national culture by another' (1991, p. 68). The problems identified were that nations themselves are increasingly multicultural, and the most significant forms of domination within nations are often those of one cultural group over another. Subordinate cultural groups within nations may consciously prefer imported or 'Western' media content over that produced within their own national culture, as it is less reflective of the values and preferences of the dominant national-cultural group or groups (Tomlinson, 1991, pp. 70–84). The construction of national identities, then, is not itself a given or something that is independent of politics, and appeals to the threat of 'cultural imperialism' from outside the nation-state may act to mask forms of inequality and cultural domination within nation-states. It can also serve to mask other forms of imperialism that do not necessarily involve the dominant Western powers; as Appadurai famously observed, 'one man's [sic] imagined community is another man's political prison' (1990, p. 295).

Central to globalization theories, then, is both significant doubt about the possibility of cultural imperialism resulting from global media, and a more conceptually grounded suspicion of cultural nationalism and about claims that the nation-state can be a territorial 'container' of national identities. While political economists point to the economic influence of global media, corporations and brands, there are doubts that this equates to significant cultural influence, and indeed the spread of Western cultural forms and values generates its own forms of cultural opposition or resistance. As a result, 'the vision of Western-liberal-capitalist consumer culture sweeping all before it is severely chastened by this cultural opposition ... what globalization is clearly *not* doing ... is effortlessly installing Western culture as global culture' (Tomlinson, 2007, p. 356). At the same time, and perhaps paradoxically, the global media is seen as one of the cultural forces that is weakening national cultures, or what Néstor García Canclini (1995, p. 229) referred to a 'the loss of the "natural" relation of culture to geographical and social territories'.

Following García Canclini, as well as Giddens' notion of time-space distanciation, Tomlinson (2007) refers to this as a process of *deterritorialization*, whereby:

> the significance of the geographical location of a culture – not only the physical, environmental and climatic location, but all the self-definitions, ethnic boundaries and delimiting practices that have accrued around this – is eroding. No longer is culture so 'tied' to the constraints of local circumstances. (Tomlinson, 2007, p. 360)

Global media are a central part of the cultural forces that contribute to such deterritorialization, as they both enhance awareness of the impact of distant global events on local circumstances (e.g. the impact of fluctuations in Chinese share prices on the Australian property market, or enrolments at the nearby school or university) and greatly enhance the capacity to become more aware of distant others and to make connections with them.

An important consequence is that, rather than globalization leading to the diminution of cultural identities in the face of an ever-expanding *ersatz* global consumer culture, it is instead the case that 'globalization has been perhaps the most significant force in *creating* and *proliferating* cultural identity' (Tomlinson, 2007, p. 364). But the corollary is that identities may be multiple and may be expressed with differing degrees of groundedness and/ or contingency. It becomes possible 'to hold a repertoire of identities – to be at the same time female, Chinese, a Beijinger, a political dissident, a patriot, a Buddhist, and an admirer of Western liberalism ... [and] to hold rights which are ... *transferable* across different contexts' (Tomlinson, 2007, p. 365). The paradox of radical Islamic movements such as ISIS, which make extensive use of the global internet to recruit worldwide in the cause of a pre-modern caliphate, can be understood in the context of identities that can be multiple, fluid and proliferating. The possibility of cosmopolitan or post-national cultural identities, that could constitute a new form of political and cultural citizenship that runs in parallel to the experience of globalization and the declining powers of the nation-state, is a recurring debate in the globalization literature (Hannerz, 1990; Tomlinson, 1997, pp. 181–207; Held, 2004, pp. 170–178), and will be returned to in later chapters.

Globalization and media production: the rise of the regions

The discussion thus far has tended to focus upon the circulation of global media content and upon questions about how it is received by local audiences. In particular, globalization theorists have questioned what Miller *et al.* (2005) termed a 'Global Effects Model' associated with the concept of cultural imperialism, whereby Western media impart values to people in the rest of the world that lead them to adopt views on culture and life that are against their own material interests. Moreover, the attention that the dependency model gives to the relationship between global media and national cultures can lose sight of the internal racial/ethnic and demographic differentiation and unequal power relations that exist within nation-states, which globalization theorists suggest is increasing over time. Joseph Straubhaar has observed:

> very few nations are ethnically homogeneous ... [and] most have fairly large minorities. If language is a primary characteristic of culture, then

most nations are multilingual and not homogeneous nation-states. This opens up a large area of interest in media ... which address media audiences of smaller than national scope. (Straubhaar, 1997, p. 286)

Such critiques of the cultural imperialism thesis typically draw upon cultural studies, postcolonial theories and theories of the 'active audience' (Ang, 1996; Tomlinson, 1999; McMillin, 2007), to question claims about there being relatively predictable consequences among local audiences resulting from exposure to global media content. But there were also important empirical limitations to the claim that such media content was dominant around the world. With particular reference to television, Sinclair *et al.* (1996, 1998) argued that there had been a rise of *geolinguistic regions*, largely outside of the dominant Western metropolitan centres, as 'the Western optic through which the cultural imperialism thesis was developed literally did not see these non-Western systems of regional exchange, nor understand what they represented' (Sinclair *et al.*, 1998, p. 179). Drawing upon extensive case studies of Latin American television, Straubhaar identified 'a qualitative change in world media relations' from the models of one-way media flow that had dominated the political economy of global media, arguing that 'although the United States still dominates world media sales and flows, national and regional cultural industries are consolidating a relatively more interdependent position in the world television market' (1997, p. 296).

Such work draws attention to the fuzziness around terms such as American, Western and capitalist in critical theories of global media. It is also apparent that the US can dominate global media in terms of particular models, genres and formats for media content, yet the actual content itself may be locally developed. National media producers, very often supported by their national governments, have become adept at adapting such models to local contexts and audience expectations, and indeed developing significant regional export markets. While the media sociologist Jeremy Tunstall had previously observed (Tunstall, 1978) that 'the media are American', insofar as the commercially driven, entertainment-based mode of media had become the *de facto* global standard, by 2008 he was arguing that 'the media were American' (Tunstall, 2008), as other parts of the world had learned how to emulate these formats and more effectively package them for their own audiences.

Arising from his extensive work on Latin American audiovisual media, Joseph Straubhaar has argued that, contrary to theories that globalization weakens distinctive national cultures, media have been important forces for strengthening national identities and cultures, and that this role has strengthened, rather than weakened, in the face of globalization. In the case of television in particular, he argues that 'national cultures, national markets supported by national governments, and national television networks still dominate the television viewing reality of most audiences' (Straubhaar, 2007, p. 7). He argued that, in contrast to modernization theorists, dependency theorists were right to draw attention to how media cultures in the Third World were shaped by dominant US and other Western influences, particularly in the spread of advertiser-funded commercial media models, the promotion of Western consumer culture and products, and the unbalanced flow of media content between the First World and the Third World. But what had been neglected was the role played by national commercial interests and government elites in promoting national media and creative industries, whether through establishing national public service broadcasters, setting local content quotas, negotiating technology transfer arrangements with multinational investors, or other forms of national media and cultural policy. This created the conditions for powerful national media conglomerates to emerge, such as Globo in Brazil, Clarín in Argentina, Televisa in Mexico, and others who could take advantage of both their strong awareness of local conditions and their connections to nation-state agencies and political elites to be strong competitors to global and regional media players.

Analysing trends in television programming between 1962 and 2001, Straubhaar identified a decline in the presence of US programming in prime-time schedules in a number of countries, notably Brazil, Colombia, Mexico in Latin America, Australia, Hong Kong, Japan, South Korea and Taiwan in Asia, and Nigeria in Africa. It must be noted that this is not an iron law of a shift to local programming: there are key variables including market size, the relative wealth of a nation, competition among domestic producers, government policies, relationship to other industries (e.g. film, advertising), the behaviour of local entrepreneurs and audience preferences (Straubhaar, 2007, pp. 72–73). Extending this work to a 20-nation study over the 1962–2001 period, Xu et al. (2013) found that there was a clear positive relationship between the size and GDP of a nation, the maturity of its broadcast media system, and the amount of locally produced programming, and that this was particularly marked in those nations where factors such as language meant that there was a high 'cultural discount' attached to US programming as the dominant global television exporter.

The resilience of national media in the face of globalization is partly a consequence of government policies designed to secure some kind of dynamic equilibrium over time between locally produced media content and material sourced from overseas. It is also reflective of what Straubhaar has termed *asymmetrical interdependence* between these emergent national content providers and the powerful global media players with whom they compete. As Straubhaar points out, the television systems of countries such as Brazil were developed under the close tutelage of the United States, with

Time-Life being the financial backers and key advisors of TV Globo during the 1960s, a time when the military dictatorship ruling the nation enjoyed US political support (Sinclair, 1999; Waisbord, 2000). The subsequent success of TV Globo did not rest upon a nationalist media policy of le défi Américain, but rather upon a combination of selective incorporation of international best practice and a restless search to develop programme types that tapped into local cultural desires and dynamics, such as the telenovela.

The concept of asymmetrical interdependence recognizes that, even in a multichannel and networked media environment where there is growing and seemingly limitless access to imported media content, there remains a strong attachment, which is by no means residual, to locally produced material (cf. Tracey, 1988). There are, however, no universal tendencies here, as some national media systems increase their degree of import dependency over time, while others reduce it. For those who succeed, however, the global expansion of media and the associated rise in demand for content of all forms has opened up new opportunities for international expansion. Sinclair et al. (1996, 1998) observed that globalization, rather than simply involving the spread of US-led media monoculture, had 'forced the West to confront the television cultures of the more "peripheral" regions of the world' (Sinclair et al., 1998, p. 177). Particular regional centres became known for their capacity to capture particular geographical and/or linguistic sub-markets: examples included Mexican TV in the Spanish-speaking world, Brazilian telenovelas in the Lusophone words, Hong Kong action cinema among the Chinese diaspora, Egyptian and Lebanese dramas in the Arab-speaking world, Indian 'Bollywood' cinema among the global Indian diaspora, and 'Nollywood' films from Nigeria among the African nations and the large African diaspora. The processes that favoured such regional centres included their capacity to learn from and adapt US and other generic models while better tailoring them to local tastes and preferences, as well as the cultural proximity of such content to people in nations with the same language and/or equivalent cultural experiences.

There are also instances, such as what Iwabuchi (2002) referred to as 'Japanization' of global culture, and the more recent 'Korean Wave' (Kuwahara, 2014) where international success has deliberately downplayed particular cultural elements in content meant for international markets while also proving adept at adapting or 'glocalizing' imported formats to better fit within local cultures.[2] The question of whether media content can consciously efface its national origins and benefit from its 'cultural odorlessness' (to use Iwabuchi's (2002) term) is a pressing one in an age of access to media from around the world. For example, Korean content can be successful in China as there is not the history of adverse historical relations that marks the China–Japan relationship.

In many respects, Hollywood has pioneered the media content that disguises its cultural roots. Films such as *The 300*, *Avatar* and the *Fast and the Furious* franchise have benefited from their seeming disconnect from an identifiable place, even if their narrative and other conventions as films mark them out as Hollywood products (Cubitt, 2012). In an age of complex global co-production arrangements, where production, post-production, distribution and financing are often highly dispersed, this ability to project beyond a particular national culture or identity is highly valued.

The importance of regional markets, and places that produce media content that has strong regional or geolinguistic uptake, is also explored through Michael Curtin's concept of *media capitals* (Curtin, 2009, 2010). Curtin defines media capitals as 'cities ... [that] function less as centers of national media than as central nodes in the transnational flow of culture, talent and resources' (2009, p. 111), with some leading examples worldwide including Mumbai, Hong Kong, Cairo, Beirut, Seoul and Miami. Moreover, there need be no necessary correspondence between cities as production centres and the nations they are a part of. In the case of Miami, for instance, production is far more likely to be distributed in Spanish-speaking Latin American countries than it is in the United States (Sinclair, 2003). Such cities have become global media production centres by benefiting from some of the dynamics that made Hollywood the world's leading global media capital, such as the concentration of production resources, distributional clout and creative talent, but have also benefited from supportive government policies as well as the capacity to identify 'niche' opportunities for access to international audiences for their products through territorially and linguistically related regions.

Critically assessing globalization theories

One of the difficulties in assessing globalization theories is the absence of a relatively unifying single set of assumptions or framing discourses among those theorists associated with its key arguments. Colin Sparks (2007, p. 126) has made the point that 'there is no single theory of globalization that commands common assent' while, in his collection of essays on the subject, George Ritzer observed that 'everything in globalization studies seems to be up-for-grabs ... [and] the field seems to be up for debates of all sorts' (Ritzer, 2007, p. 4). Another difficulty is that globalization arguments are often tied up with different conceptual claims, including the global spread of modernity (Giddens, 1990), the globalization of the capitalist world-system (Sklair, 2002), the rise of a network society (Castells, 1996, 2009) and critiques of 'methodological nationalism' (Beck, 2000). There is also the question of how strong the claims are surrounding globalization that it constitutes a new epoch in human history. No one would deny that global forces impact upon the everyday lives of people, and are an important part of what shapes nations and culture; it is obviously apparent when one considers global media, communications technologies or the global internet. Even nations that claim to have cut themselves off from such forces, such as North Korea, are clearly implicated in globalization processes, as indicated in November 2014 when confidential data belonging to Sony Pictures Entertainment was illegally acquired and released into the public domain by North Korean hackers in an apparent response to the planned release of the film *The Interview*, a comedy about a plot to assassinate North Korean leader Kim Jong-un (Locker, 2014). The question is one of how significant the shift has been, which in this chapter has been associated with strong globalization theories.

Globalization theories have clearly made some important advances to knowledge in relation to global media and communication. In their critique of theories of cultural imperialism, they have raised the question of how can one know how globally circulated texts are received by those within diverse local cultures. They have also questioned the claims about distinct and discrete national cultures, observing that there has always been a degree to which such cultural nationalisms are 'imagined' through dominant symbolic representations, as well as the extent to which hegemonic constructions of national identity may suppress minority cultures and be less tenable as nations become more demographically diverse and multicultural. Such theories have drawn attention to the degree that space-binding communications technologies such as cable, satellite and the internet have greatly expanded the global *repertoire* of media content available to people throughout the world, while also stimulating the growth of regional production centres and media capitals that challenge notions of a one-way flow of media content from the dominant metropolitan centres to the Third World. Finally, they have questioned claims that there is a straightforward correspondence between economic, political and cultural power, noting that the significance of the latter arises at least in part from the observation that it is not simply reflective of the dominant economic forces. There is no simple one-to-one relationship between control over the means of communication and the capacity to shape global consciousness and cognitive processes.

Economic geographers have also strongly contested the claim that TNCs have risen to such a level of pre-eminence that they have flattened the complex terrain of working in different national economies, and that the expansionary dynamic of TNCs has been such as to overwhelm points of distinction between national economies. Using the UNCTAD *transnationality index* (TNI – to be discussed in detail in Chapter 5 with regard to media companies), the degree of transnationality of the world's 100 largest non-financial TNCs increased from 47 per cent in 1993 to 55.8 per cent in 2003, which is an increase but not a substantial shift in the scale of global operations of these largest corporations who would be expected to be at the forefront of globalization (UNCTAD, 2007). It indicates that, on average, most of the world's largest non-financial TNCs tend to be national corporations with international operations, rather than truly transnational corporations.[3]

The claim that contemporary globalization is without historical precedent has been questioned, most notably by Hirst *et al.* (2009). They argued that while there has been a sustained and significant increase in international integration since 1970, it followed the historical period 1945–1970 where international integration was relatively low, and the period 1914–1945 where it actually declined. They make the historical point that, as measured in levels of international trade, investment, and indeed the movement of populations, the volumes of international transactions in the period from 1970 to the mid-1990s were in fact less than those of the *la belle époque* period of international capitalism from 1890 to 1914.

It has also been argued that much of what is presented as globalization through raw figures on global trade and investment flows may in fact be regionalization, or expansion of corporate operations within well-established potential regions of operation. Rugman (2000) has argued that much of the empirical data that is taken as evidence of globalization in fact points to *regionalization* – the expansion of international trade and investment within defined geo-regional zones such as the NAFTA region of North America (US/Canada/Mexico), the European Union and the East Asian regional zone, increasingly led by China, but with Japan and South Korea constituting powerful centres. There is certainly a need for caution in equating overseas expansion with globalization, as the entry of a US-based corporation into Canada, a Korean company into China or a German corporation into Britain does not necessarily indicate their repositioning as a fully fledged transnational corporation.

Perhaps the most telling criticisms of globalization theories have related to the claim that globalization is associated with the declining role and powers of the nation-state, and an associated decline in national identity and culture. While the powers and capacities of nation-states have undoubtedly been reshaped and reconfigured as a result of global transformations, particularly in the field of media and communications, they nonetheless retain considerable powers over terrestrial broadcasting systems and indeed over digital networks. Regulation at many levels, including content regulations, copyright and intellectual property laws, ownership, surveillance, geo-blocking and managing trade relations remain important features of twenty-first-century media. Indeed, the Edward Snowden revelations in 2012 concerning the activities of the National Security Agency revealed close, ongoing and secretive relations between the US government and the world's largest internet companies, in the nation and in the sector most commonly associated with the relative decline of state regulation. Such developments would support Sparks' observation that:

> The argument for the weakening of the system of states 'from above' by international forces and 'from below' by the rise of different classes of local concern seems unconvincing ... The evidence from this strand of the globalization paradigm thus does not seem to support the view that we are living in a radically new epoch with a different social dynamic to that of preceding periods. (2007, pp. 169–170)

It is important to recognize that the responses of nation-states to globalization need not be only protectionist ones. In the East Asian context, to take one example, the 'developmental states' of South Korea, Taiwan and Singapore sought to foster the development of 'national champions' in the global communications economy as they became more outward facing. The growth in state-funded 24-hour news broadcasting services as vehicles for the exercise of cultural 'soft power' globally (the BBC, Deutsche Welle, France24, Russia Today, China Global Television Network (formerly CCTV International), Singapore's Channel News Asia and others) are one manifestation of nation-states seeking to actively shape the global media environment, rather than being passive and disempowered in the face of it (Sparks, 2016). Waisbord (2016) has argued that, contrary to claims about declining nation-states, South America in the 2000s saw substantial media reforms in nations throughout the continent, and a major wave of 'state-centred policy activism' triggered by 'the coming to power of populist and centre-left coalitions that decided to use state mechanisms to drive change' (p. 43).

Globalization theories point to a global/local nexus that is increasingly displacing the power of the nation-state. But the idea that supranational institutions and agreements have superseded nation-state sovereignty ignores the extent to which the viability and effectiveness of such supranational institutions are dependent upon the continued support of nation-states, particularly the economically and politically most powerful ones (Hirst et al., 2009, pp. 190–196). Indeed, the possibility of a 'global federalism', where 'politics ... would relocate to the global level' (Rodrik, 2011, p. 203), may have receded in the twenty-first century as compared to the late twentieth century, with the relative weakening of US economic power, the rise of China and the difficulties faced by the European Union. This will be returned to with reference to global media policy in Chapter 7 of this book.

The claims of a turn towards localism are also somewhat unclear. In some cases, the relative weakening of the nation-state is associated with rival nationalist claims within those states. The rise of Scottish nationalism within the United Kingdom, and Catalan and Basque nationalism in Spain, are cases in point. Neither involves a rejection of nation-states or national cultures per se; rather, they propose their own nation-states and national identities as an alternative to the UK or Spanish nation-state. As Sparks (2007, p. 166) points out, this is neither new historically – the boundaries of nations, and the incorporation of diverse and competing racial, ethnic and linguistic groups within such nations, has many historical precedents – nor is it 'leading to the erosion of the state as such'. If the claim is that there has been a turn away from national media towards more locally based forms, the evidence is certainly mixed. There has been a growth in community media that are closer to particular communities than to national systems (Rennie, 2006; Forde, 2011), but there has also been a decline in the circulation of local newspapers and the demise of many locally based titles, leading to a greater consolidation of the position of national titles and leading brands. There are very active media that cater to global diasporas (see e.g. Karim, 2003; Siapera, 2010), but again these may be contemporary variants of more longstanding phenomena. Indeed, the famous Chicago sociologist Robert Park identified over 2000 newspapers catering to the various language groups in the United States at the end of the First World War (cited in Sparks, 2007, p. 169).

We thus get conflicting messages from globalization theorists about the continuing significance of nations and nation-states. On the one hand, globalization is seen as deterritorializing production, power and culture to such a degree that it no longer makes sense to focus on the national level, and that substantive engagement requires a turn to supranational or even global forms of governance. On the other hand, the continuing, and possibly growing, strength of national media systems, and the proliferation of new media capitals around the globe suggest that globalism per se is a less power-ful force than is being sometimes assumed, and that the international expansion of media is driven more by regional or geolinguistic dynamics than by those of an omnipotent global culture. It is important to note that movements that have challenged the power of nation-states have themselves been nationalistic, as with Scottish, Catalan and Basque nationalism. Also, resistance to globalization can itself take a nationalist form, and this tendency has arguably been growing in the 2010s with the vote in the UK to leave the European Union (the 'Brexit' referendum) and the election of overtly nationalistic leaders such as Donald Trump in the US, Erdoğan in Turkey, Orbán in Hungary and Kaczyński in Poland. In other words, the dialectical relationship that globalization theorists attribute to challengers to global capitalism may take the form of nationalism as much as it does localism.

Notes

1 A fuller treatment may also include authors such as sociologists Ulrich Beck and Zygmunt Bauman, neo-Marxists such as Michael Hardt and Antonio Negri, popular critics such as Naomi Klein and postcolonial theorists such as Gayatri Chakravorty Spivak. An overview can be found in Coleman & Sajed (2012).

2 Unlike other countries considered, Japan and South Korea do not have particularly multicultural populations, and their national languages are not widely spoken in other countries. Moreover, in the case of Japan, there continue to be sensitivities about its conduct as a colonial power in Asia in the period up to the end of World War II in 1945. This is particularly an issue in China, but it also resonates in South Korea.

3 Dicken (2003) used the example of the retail giant Walmart to illustrate this point. Walmart is the world's largest private employer, with over 2.2 million employees in 2014, working in 11,000 stores in 28 countries. Its sales outside of the US, however, account for only 28 per cent of total sales, and the majority of its workforce is employed in the US (Walmart, 2016). While Walmart is significant in other aspects of globalization, most notably in how it globally sources the items that it stocks but perhaps also in how it encourages thinking about 'mega-marts' as a way of organizing retail activities, it is not a transnational corporation in terms of the bulk of its sales activities, the significance of its overseas investments, or where the majority of its workforce are located. Indeed, in a number of countries in which it operates, it does so under other banners, such as ASDA in the UK and Seiyu in Japan.

CHAPTER 5

The changing geography of global media production

Media geography, space and power

Each of the theories of global media that have been considered so far has an implicit history and an implicit geography. Modernization theories are underpinned by a diffusionist logic, where modernity is taken to be a normative ideal state, and media plays a role in enabling developing nations to acquire the technological, institutional and attitudinal features associated with an (implicitly Western) notion of what it is to have a modern economy, society and culture. In the development communication paradigms of the 1960s it was radio and television that were looked to as agents of modernization, whereas in contemporary accounts it is more likely to be the internet and mobile phones. Critical political economy understands capitalism as a mode of production that has a rapacious tendency towards global expansion. In this framework, media are both conduits for the spread of capitalism and key institutional and ideological players in its expansion and reproduction, including the unequal economic relations and distribution of power resources that political economists see as an inherent feature of the capitalist system.

The history of media in critical political economy is linked to the stages of capitalism, with print media associated with the formation of nation-states and national capitalisms, broadcasting with monopoly capitalism and cultural imperialism, and the internet age with a highly integrated – but also contradictory and contested – system of global capitalism (Schiller, 2000). Globalization theories argue that there has been a fundamental spatial shift in the world-system since the 1980s from a world based upon nation-states, national economies and national cultures that prevailed from the nineteenth century onwards to one where there has been a thorough intermixing of cultures, greater global political interdependence, and an integrated global capitalist market economy driven by the instantaneous flows of data and information enabled by digital media technologies. In relation to media, this requires a shift from what has been termed the 'methodological nationalism' associated with comparative media studies (Hallin & Mancini, 2004) to a deeper understanding of the dialectic between global media and local cultures (Couldry & Hepp, 2009). It also entails an awareness of the growing centrality of communication networks to economic life, cultural awareness and systems of power, as the same networks that circulate global media are also those involved with the circulation of resources, money and information (Castells, 2009).

Media history is a well-established field in media and communication studies. There is an extensive literature on the relationship between media technologies and social change, including the relationship of print media to the rise of nationalism and the modern nation-state (Anderson, 1991; Eisenstein, 1993), the role played by broadcast media in unifying populations through media events that transcend spatial boundaries (Gellner, 1983; Dayan & Katz, 1994), and the relationship of the internet to a globalized 'network society' (Castells, 1996; Barney, 2004).

Media geography has been less well developed, although media history has often worked with an implicit notion of its relationship to place and space. The Canadian communications historian Harold Innis (1991 [1951]) associated different media technologies with forms of rule and empire, arguing that print technologies had a temporal bias (i.e. they promoted continuity over time through the codification of laws) while broadcast media had a spatial bias (i.e. it promoted simultaneous messaging to multiple receivers across vast distances). In his book *No Sense of Place*, Joshua Meyrowitz (1985) argued that one of the consequences of pervasive broadcast media was the blurring of a relationship between personal identity and a geographically defined sense of place, and such media enabled people to feel connected to distant others. This concept has also been central to globalization theories, as seen with Giddens' notions of time-space distanciation and disembedding, Appadurai's concept of global mediascapes and Tomlinson's understanding of deterritorialized identities (Giddens, 1990; Appadurai, 1990; Tomlinson, 1999). Some critical political economists have also drawn upon such concepts. Kevin Robins and David Morley (1995) considered the relationship between media, culture and identity, posing the question of whether the global restructuring of media was creating new forms of community and identity, with particular reference to the expanding political and economic role of the European Union and the question of whether a post-national 'Euroculture' was emerging. In his overview of the political economy tradition, Vincent Mosco (2009) identified spatialization (restructuring of spatial relations) as being one of the three core social dynamics of contemporary media, along with processes of commodification (strengthening of market relations) and structuration (shaping/re-shaping of power relations), and all of these have important spatial dimensions.

Amin has argued that globalization is an 'intrinsically spatial' concept that 'centrally invokes geography', due to its concerns with 'the rise of world-scale processes and phenomena, the intensification of linkage between distant places and cultures, and the associated unmaking and remaking of territorial boundaries and identities' (Amin, 2001, p. 6271). Coe *et al.* (2007, pp. 11–15) identify space as having four interrelated elements:

1. *Territoriality*: spaces are defined both graphically (through maps, charts etc.) and juridically – they are spatially bound by the exercise of particular forms of authority within that space (laws, government etc.);
2. *Location*: a space will have particular environmental, topographical and physical features (mountains, rivers, heat or cold, near oceans or deserts, population density, agricultural activities, mineral resources, etc.), as well as the significance that arises from its location relative to other locations, e.g. its significance in global geopolitics;
3. *Flows across space*: the ways in which resources, wealth, people, information, ideas move from one location to another, both within and between countries;
4. *Uneven spatial relations*: both historical factors and contemporary political-economic forces render some spaces more or less wealthy, politically significant, attractive to visitors etc. than others, and the issue arises of the extent to which this unevenness is the result of systemic factors.

It follows that space is therefore understood as a dynamic concept that is structured and restructured through social relations and human interaction. Doreen Massey summarized the relationship between the spatial and the social, and between geography and other fields of social enquiry, with the observation that 'space is a social construct ... but social relations are also constructed over space, and that makes a difference' (Massey, 1985, p. 12). In *The Condition of Postmodernity*, David Harvey (1989) identifies continuous spatial restructuring as being central to capitalist modernity, since 'the production of new spaces' (Harvey, 1989, p. 183) has been one of the critical ways in which endemic crises in the capitalist economy are dealt with. In *The Rise of the Network Society*, Manuel Castells (1996) identified the core spatial dynamic of the network society as being between 'the new spatial logic that I label the *space of flows*' and 'the historically rooted spatial organization of our common experience: *the space of places*'

(Castells, 1996, p. 378). The space of flows as the 'material form of support of dominant processes and functions' is composed of three elements: (1) the electronic and technological infrastructure which enables digital content to move across space through communication networks; (2) the cities, and particularly the 'global cities' and megacities, that are the core locational 'nodes' of such global networks; and (3) the spatial location and patterns of movement of the dominant managerial elites (Castells, 1996, pp. 412–415). While the dominant elites are integrated into the global space of flows, the mass of the population are tied to places. For Castells, this duality between:

> articulation of the elites [and] segmentation and disorganization of the masses seem to be the twin mechanisms of social domination of our societies ... In short: elites are cosmopolitan, people are local. The space of power is projected throughout the world, while people's life and experience is rooted in places, in their culture. (1996, p. 415)

The challenge that is presented by a complex and dynamic understanding of space and the geographical dimensions of social relations is that the processes of spatial change are not simply territorial but also relational. In other words, as changes occur at one spatial level (e.g. corporations establish international branch offices, digital networks make it easier for media content to move across territorial boundaries, there is large-scale movement of people from one nation to another), they create new relations between spatial levels. Amin (2002, p. 387) has described this as a 'relativization of spatial scales', where the very ontology of place and territoriality – or how people think about the cities, regions and nations within which they are located – shifts in the context of changes associated with globalization, so that the very notions of 'in-here' local relations and 'out-there' global relations are being transformed. A key implication of thinking about spaces in a relational sense, rather than in terms of global forces simply being imposed upon otherwise clearly defined local or national places, is that our definitions of 'the local' and 'the national' are always in a process of being collectively redefined, and being contested. It also raises the point that, in some instances, people may feel closer to people and cultures experiences at a distance than those to which they are most geographically proximate. By enabling the establishment of such global networks through digital communications technologies, global media are likely to be a part of this 'deterritorialization' of cultures and identities, even if we also find parallel evidence of media being critical to the maintenance of territorially defined local and national identities.

How the media became national

It was noted in Chapter 2 that the media have played a central role in the formation of national identities and the development of nationalism. Modern nationalism has relied upon the formation of a sense of collective cultural identity, and the nation became a form of what Anderson (1991) termed 'imagined community' that developed in parallel with forms of political community, whereby people became citizens of a territorially defined nation-state. National culture is understood in nationalist discourses as shared language, customs, history and possibly ethnic or religious identity. Thompson (1995, p. 51) has made the point that:

> The creation of a sense of national identity had advantages for political rulers: it could help to consolidate the nation-state, to counter tendencies towards fragmentation and to mobilize support for military and other aims ... The emergence of a sense of national identity – and indeed of nationalism ... was closely linked to the development of new means of communication which enabled symbols and ideas to be expressed and diffused in a common language.

Claims about the centrality of national cultures to a sense of identity are, however, problematic for two reasons. First, people can identify with a diverse array of institutions on the basis of a shared culture. Sociologists have argued that institutions are 'not only formal rules, procedures or norms, but also the symbol systems, cognitive scripts, and moral templates that provide the "frames of meaning" guiding human action' (Hall & Taylor, 1996, p. 947). The institutions of the nation-state are not the only institutions with which individuals can identify. People can identify with political institutions, religious institutions, global causes, their work organizations, etc. in ways that are no less intense, and often more intense, than their relationship to nation-states.

The history of modern nationalism and nation-states also tells us that, while there may be a 'striving to make culture and polity congruent [and] to endow a culture with its own political roof' (Gellner, 1983, p. 43), this is an exercise that entails risks. Forms of genocide, 'ethnic cleansing', religiously and racially inspired purges and civil wars have arisen from the desire to ensure that a dominant culture prevails within nation-states. Thompson (1995, p. 50) has made the point that, historically, 'the establishment of a strong state generally preceded the formation in a strong sense of national identity within its boundaries'; moreover, national identity has in any case 'remained an elusive and deeply contested feature of modern political life' (p. 50). Moreover, as nation-states have frequently been formed through 'the forceful incorporation of diverse populations into discrete territorial units' (p. 51), attempts to forge national identity through a common culture or history – i.e. a shared past – have often proved to be fraught with danger. Nationalism may be promoted as an ideology and a primary source of identity, but it can also repel people, particularly if it is associated with forms of injustice.

Two distinctive approaches can be identified in how nation-states managed the introduction of broadcast media (van Cuilenburg & McQuail, 2003). The first gave primacy to the development of commercial media, and looked to government to engage in regulation of these media in the public interest. The second focused upon public service broadcasting or state-run media. In many countries, national media systems evolved as a hybrid of these two influences. But both have, until recently, tended to predominantly focus upon national media systems.

A dominant role for the commercial media was the path most obviously followed in United States broadcasting from the 1920s onwards, although the significance of the commercial model has grown greatly worldwide since the 1980s (McChesney, 1999; McChesney & Schiller, 2003). Newspapers have until very recently circulated overwhelmingly within spaces that are primarily national (e.g. *The Times*, *Le Monde*, *El País*, *Der Spiegel*) or even local: while we may think about *The New York Times*, *The Wall Street Journal* and *The Washington Post* as US or even global newspapers, their titles indicate their strong local roots. It was not until *USA Today* was launched in 1982 that a US newspaper claimed to be explicitly for a national market, and it has only been with the move to online publishing that titles such as *The Guardian*, *Daily Mail* and *The Wall Street Journal* have been able to significantly expand beyond their countries of origin.

The capacity of broadcasting services to reach across territorial boundaries has long been balanced against what Philip Schlesinger (1991a, p. 162) has referred to as the desire of nation-states to engage in 'communicative boundary maintenance' through media and communications policies. Recognizing that 'in the modern world ... social spaces are also communicative spaces' (Schlesinger, 1991b, p. 299), national governments have sought to manage media flows within national territories, through measures that have ranged from banning ownership of satellite dishes to setting local content quotas to promoting local ownership and setting controls over foreign control of media. They have also engaged in more pro-active measures to stimulate local media production, including subsidies and other incentives (e.g. tax incentives) to support local cultural production, particularly in high-cost media such as film and, more recently, games (Grant & Wood, 2004; cf. Murphy *et al.*, 2014; Ho & Fung, 2016 on games).

There has also been a history of media owners gaining highly beneficial terms on which to rise to prominence in national media systems, on the basis of close ties to national governments. In Latin America, media entrepreneurs such as Goar Mestre (Cuba until the 1959 revolution, and then Argentina), Emilio Azcárraga Jean and Rómulo O'Farrill (Mexico), and Roberto Marinho (Brazil) were able to cultivate close relationships with national governments that enabled them to develop powerful media empires. Networks such as Televisa in Mexico, Brazil's TV Globo, Argentina's Clarín and Colombia's Caracol TV became dominant national media players, and significant exporters of TV content through the Spanish-speaking and Portuguese-speaking worlds, on the basis of their powerful connections to government (Sinclair & Straubhaar, 2013). While these Latin American commercial media barons benefited at various times from connections to major US media companies, including CBS, NBC and Time Warner, it has been the case that 'the major private, commercial television networks have tended to have close relationships to government' (Sinclair & Straubhaar, 2013, p. 20).

The second pathway to developing national broadcasting systems has been that of public or state-funded broadcasting. It is important at the outset to make a distinction between the model of public service broadcasting (PSB) pioneered by the British Broadcasting Corporation (BBC) upon its establishment in the UK in 1927, and that of state-run broadcast media. In many parts of the world, media that was financially supported by the state also functioned as a propaganda arm of the state, with strict government control over media content. The Chinese case is interesting, in that the post-1978 reforms under Deng Xiaoping and his successors saw Chinese television become increasingly commercialized, but this has occurred under continuing conditions of strict censorship, where mass media outlets such as China Central Television (CCTV) are seen as having a particular role in upholding the cardinal principles of the Chinese communist party-state (Zhao, 2008; Keane, 2015). In Western Europe, Hallin and Mancini (2004) identified the relationship between broadcasters and government as a key factor in differentiating media systems, contrasting countries with a strong history of political control over broadcasters, such as Greece, with those where more pluralistic and independent models had evolved, such as Germany.

The BBC model of public service broadcasting has had great international influence. It provided the template for PSB in nations of the British Commonwealth, such as Australia, Canada and South Africa, as well as being influential in countries such as Germany and Sweden (Gorman & McLean, 2009, pp. 142–146). Even Japan, as a nation where other British influences are relatively minor, operated its NHK service along lines similar to those of the BBC. Features of the PSB model typically include: universal reach and accessibility; a mandate to educate as well as entertain the public; statutory independence from the government of the day; the obligation to represent conflicting points of view in a fair and impartial manner; the need for inclusivity in programming; and an ethos of professionalism and creativity within the organization (Hendy, 2013). It is important to note that the community which PSBs serve is a national community. When Hendy (2013, p. 3) refers to 'the value of a strong public dimension to media ... mindful of the value to be found in collective experiences and in nurturing our collective potential', he is referring to a national collectivity that is coterminous with the nation-state through which such a service is funded. Similarly, with regards to the notion of media committed to the principles of citizenship, rather than that of consumerism, it is primarily a national citizenship that is being developed, which engages with a national polity and public sphere.

Approaches to media globalization

While print and broadcast media may have a spatial bias towards the national, technologies such as the internet, cable, satellite and wireless media readily provide media content from around the globe, often through the globally ubiquitous platforms and services provided by Google, Apple, Facebook, Microsoft, Amazon, Netflix and others. In 2016, 3.4 billion people, or 47 per cent of the world's population, were accessing news, information, movies, games and entertainment through the internet, of whom 2.5 billion were in the developing world (ITU, 2016).

The period since the 1970s saw an intensification of trends promoting economic globalization. Led by the rapid globalization of financial markets in the 1970s, triggered by the breakdown of the Bretton Woods monetary system and the oil price shocks of the early 1970s (Held *et al.*, 1999, pp. 199–205), the growth in foreign trade, foreign investment and foreign exchange transactions substantially exceeded growth in world GDP from the 1970s to the 2000s. Data from the United Nations Commission for Trade, Aid and Development (UNCTAD) (see Table 5.1) shows rapid growth in foreign direct investment (FDI), cross-border mergers and acquisitions (M&As), and the sales, output, assets and employment rates of foreign affiliates, considerably exceeding overall growth in global gross domestic product (GDP), fixed capital formation and exports. These are proxy measures for a globalizing economy.

Table 5.1 Selected indicators of foreign direct investment and international production, 1982-2015

	Value at current prices ($US billion)				
	1982	1990	2002	2007	2015
FDI inflows	59	209	651	1418	962
FDI inward stock	802	1954	7123	14500	24,983
Cross-border M&As	...	151	370	729	721
Sales of foreign affiliates	2737	5675	17,685	20,335	36,668
Gross product of foreign affiliates	640	1458	3437	4720	7903
Total assets of foreign affiliates	1091	5899	26,543	40,924	105,778
Exports of foreign affiliates	722	1197	2613	4976	7803
Employment of foreign affiliates (thousands)	19,375	24,262	53,094	49,565	79,505
GDP (in current prices)	10,805	21,672	32,227	51,228	73,152
Gross fixed capital formation	2286	4819	6422	11,801	18,200
Exports of goods and non-factor services	2053	4300	7838	15,034	20,861

Source: UNCTAD (2003, 2006, 2016). Reprinted with the permission of the United Nations.

This trend can be seen clearly if we note rates of growth in these indicators from 1990 to 2015. Taking 1990 as a base year, we can see (Figure 5.1) that the rate of growth of 'globalization' indicators such as FDI and FDI capital stock, exports of foreign affiliates, and sales of foreign affiliates far exceeded rates of growth of GDP, direct investment (gross fixed capital formation) and exports more generally. This is reflective of an almost continuous process of global expansion of capitalism from 1990 to the present, interrupted by the global financial downturn of 2007-2008 and reduced rates of foreign direct investment subsequent to then.

Dunning (2015) argued that capitalism since the 1990s has become an increasingly global system since:

1. Cross-border transactions are deeper, more extensive and more intercon-nected;
2. Resources, capabilities, goods and services are more spatially mobile;
3. Multinational corporations (MNCs) have become more central to wealth creation and distribution, and they originate from, and produce in, a wider range of countries;
4. There is a much greater volume of transactions, and resulting volatility, in global capital and financial markets;

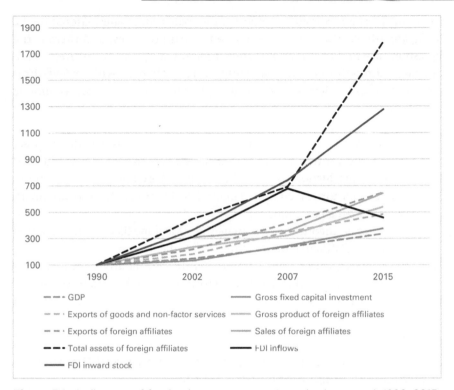

Figure 5.1 Indicators of foreign investment, assets and sales growth 1990–2015
Source: UNCTAD (2003, 2006, 2016). Reprinted with the permission of the United Nations.

5. ICTs and electronic commerce have transformed the nature of cross-border transactions, particularly in services.

Dunning (2015, p. 17) identified a series of attracting, enabling and threatening factors that promoted an expansion of global capitalism. *Attracting* factors include market liberalization policies, growing markets in emerging economies and the geographical dispersal of both created assets and entrepreneurial activity. *Enabling* factors include the development of the global internet, the lowering of barriers to cross-border transactions, the globalization of capital and financial markets, and advances in global transport and communication. *Threatening* factors include intensified global competition, the need to manage currency and financial risk, geographical diversification of risk and accelerating rates of technological obsolescence.

Media have particularly relevance as enabling factors for economic globalization, providing the technological and communications infrastructure of global capitalism and, in the accounts of some critical political economists, the ideological support for globalist ideologies. Global media companies have also played a key role in such processes, and there is the question of whether such companies promote a 'globalist' or 'neoliberal' ideology through their media content. This chapter will review three approaches to understanding media globalization from an economic perspective:

1. *Critical political economy* theories, which identify global media corporations as the central drivers of media systems around the world, and see media production as being increasingly based around a new international division of cultural labour (NICL) driven by the dominant US-based media corporations;
2. *'Glocalization'* theories, which argue that global media corporations need to adapt to distinctive national markets and cultures;
3. *Media capital* theories, which argue that the central drivers of media are increasingly clustered in particular cities and regions around the world, and that there is less a single dominant media system than a series of competing media systems.

Critical political economy: global media giants and the new international division of cultural labour

It was noted in Chapter 3 that the critical political economy approach has long focused upon the global dimensions of media, and how they articulate to wider structures of power, inequality and domination. Early work by Herbert Schiller, Oliver Boyd-Barrett and others connected the rise of the entertainment-communication-information (ECI) industries to US dominance in the global capitalist world-system, and to cultural imperialism. Miller *et al.* (2005) have advanced this agenda, and have associated global media production with an NICL and a division of jobs between a controlling 'core' and a low-wage periphery with much of the world's creative workers being in competition for global capital investment. We will consider this perspective in the context of transitions within the global media industries, and the rise of the global ICT-based giants and networked digital media platforms.

The critical political economy perspective has pointed towards growing domination of the world's media by a small, and diminishing, number of commercial media giants. McChesney and Herman argued that 'the ... global media system is dominated by three or four dozen large transnational corporations (TNCs) with fewer than ten mostly U.S.-based media conglomerates towering over the global market' (1997, p. 1). Steger (2009, p. 76) placed global media corporations at the centre of his account of globalization, arguing:

> the global cultural flows of our time are generated and directed by global media empires that rely on powerful communication technologies to spread their message ... a small group of very large TNCs have come to dominate the global market for entertainment, news, television and film.

Held *et al.* (1999) concluded that, at least where the media are concerned, 'there can be little doubt that ... a group of around 20–30 very large MNCs dominate global markets for entertainment, news, television, etc., and they have acquired a very significant cultural and economic presence on nearly every continent' (p. 347).

McChesney and Herman (1997) argued that the period since the 1980s had seen a 'new structural logic' in global communications, whereby national media systems came to be increasingly dominated by global corporations who were themselves expanding their corporate reach and control over markets through takeovers, mergers and conglomerate expansion. In doing so, they have been aided and abetted by nation-state policies of deregulation and privatization that have been proposed under the general ideological rubric of neoliberalism (McChesney & Schiller, 2003; McChesney, 2008). Such tendencies towards global media monopolies are also seen to characterize the internet-based and ICT industries. Dan Schiller (2000, p. xiv) argued that 'the Internet comprises nothing less than the central production and control apparatus of an increasingly supranational market system', and subsequent work on the internet from a critical political economy perspective (Siapera, 2012; McChesney, 2013; Hardy, 2014, Chapter 5) has tended to view these industries, as with the media industries generally, 'as a giant pyramid, with power concentrated at the top' (Winseck, 2011, p. 23).

The questions raised around global media concentration and domination can be approached from two angles. The first considers how big are media companies compared to the world's largest companies generally, while the second asks how transnational are the largest companies. A measure of the relative size of media and media-related companies can be made using *Fortune* magazine's 'Global 500' index (Fortune, 2016). This index measures the world's 500 largest companies on the basis of sales revenue, and has been undertaken annually in its current form since 1995. Among the world's highest ranked companies are technology giants such as Apple (ranked at 9), Samsung (13), Amazon (40), Microsoft (82) and Alphabet (the parent company of Google, 94). The number of companies that are unequivocally in the media business and are among the world's largest 500 companies is now quite small. It includes Disney (164), Twenty-First Century Fox (360) and Time Warner (374), with Comcast (96) and Sony (113) also holding significant media assets in their conglomerate structure. This is very different to the situation in the 2000s where the traditional media companies were dominant. It has been noted by commentators such as McChesney (2013) as marking a shift from the content- or copyright-based industries to the digital platform/service industries.

It is also worth noting that, measured on assets rather than sales, companies such as Apple, Samsung, Microsoft, Sony and Alphabet/Google rank considerably more highly. This suggests that, while we do find concentration of media ownership and the dominance of large companies in different media markets, they are not necessarily the same companies. This means that consideration of competition in media markets needs to account not only for established firms, but also for those who can disrupt these industries, as Apple, Google, Facebook, Amazon, Netflix and others have done for traditional print, broadcast, music and publishing industries (Cunningham *et al.*, 2015, pp. 29–33). This is at odds with claims that the rise of monopoly means the negation of competition, even if the forms of competition are not necessarily price-based.

The second question is the extent to which these are companies that operate primarily on a global scale. There is an important distinction to be made between media corporations which operate on a truly global scale and those which are primarily nationally based corporations with overseas operations. Forms of media globalization that revolve around media exports have existed at least since the expansionary strategies of the Hollywood majors into Europe and Latin America in the 1920s. They are not synonymous with the development of a geographically dispersed global assets base, arising from foreign direct investment, strategic partnerships, and mergers and acquisitions. Peter Dicken (2003, p. 30) has defined a global corporation as:

> a firm that has the power to co-ordinate and control operations in a large number of countries (even if it does not own them), but whose *geographically-dispersed operations are functionally integrated*, and not merely a diverse portfolio of activities. (Emphasis in original)

This definition of a global corporation is contrasted to that of 'national corporations with international operations (i.e. foreign subsidiaries)' (Dicken, 2007, p. 225).

One measure of the 'transnationality' of corporations on the basis of such definitions is the *transnationality index* developed by UNCTAD. The transnationality index (TNI) measures the percentage of a company's assets, sales and employees that are outside of the country's home base, and divides this figure by three. One useful feature of the TNI is that it does not rely upon a single measure of transnationality, such as foreign sales or assets, but aligns this to other indicators of the globalization of corporate operations, such as international employment. This controls for the tendency for some industries to be inherently global according to just one indicator: oil, gas and extractive mining companies, for example, tend to have a highly diversified geographical asset base by virtue of where they find resources in the ground. A company with a high TNI is also more likely to have a more 'globalized' corporate culture and be diverse in terms of its cultural influences; by contrast, a predominantly 'national' company will tend to be strongly shaped by dominant cultural traits of its home country (Doremus *et al.*, 1998).

On the basis of the TNI, we find that media companies are generally less transnational than those in industries such as electronic equipment, software and telecommunications (see Table 5.2). The UNCTAD TNI shows that the most transnational companies in the world tend to be in mining, oil and gas,

Table 5.2 Transnational index (TNI) indicators for major media and related corporations, 2015)

Company	Home Country	Industry	Total Assets ($USbn)	Foreign assets as % of total	Revenues outside of home country/ region (%) *	TNI**
Vodafone	UK	Telecoms	202	90	85	88.9
Deutsche Telekom	Germany	Telecoms	162	74	63	61.9
Telefonica	Spain	Telecoms	163	53	77	63.6
Apple	US	Electronics	207	58	61	59.6
Sony	Japan	Electronics	149	28	71	54.8
Microsoft	US	Software	142	40	47	42.8
Google	US	Software	110	36	56	41.9
Disney	US	Media	69	22	23	–
Time Warner	US	Media	63	***	27	–
21st Century Fox	US	Media	50	9	35	–

Source: UNCTAD (2016); company annual reports. Reprinted with the permission of the United Nations.

*For US-based companies, the United States and Canada are taken to be the North American region in their annual reports.
**TNI could not be calculated for Disney, Time Warner and Fox as there was insufficient detail in their annual reports.
***Foreign assets cannot be identified from Time Warner balance sheets.

and advanced manufacturing industries such as motor vehicles. In the media sector, the broad pattern is that telecommunications companies tend to be the most transnational, followed by those engaged in electronic hardware, then those in computing software, with media and entertainment companies being the least transnational.

This evidence would support the arguments of globalization sceptics such as Glyn and Sutcliffe (1999), who argued that barriers to the international tradability of services remained significant. This generates a problem for 'strong globalization' arguments, as it is service industries that are growing most rapidly in terms of percentage of sales and employment worldwide. Given the extent of media convergence occurring, it is difficult to generalize: Apple is clearly in the software as well as hardware industries, and Microsoft and Google are increasingly engaged in ICT hardware industries. But it does provide a note of caution for claims that a small number of companies are increasingly dominating the global media landscape, at least if media firms are defined in a more traditional sense of producers and distributors of copyrighted and professional information and entertainment content. It would also indicate that, to use Dicken's distinction, most of these companies are best thought of as national corporations with international operations, rather than as truly global corporations.[1]

A key feature of the contemporary global media landscape is the rise of global production networks and increased international competition for media production activity. In their analysis of the political economy of 'Global Hollywood', Toby Miller and his colleagues (Miller *et al.*, 2001, 2005) proposed that these developments constituted a *new international division of labour (NIDL)* in media and cultural production, arguing that a *new international division of cultural labour (NICL)* has been taking shape with regard to global media production. They drew upon work by the German economists Frobel *et al.* (1980), who had observed the trend since the 1970s for MNCs to invest in industrial production in developing countries, primarily to take advantage of lower wages. The flip side of this was often the closure of factories and 'de-industrialization' in the advanced, higher wage economies of Europe and North America. While some developing nations established an industrial base through these free-trade zones (FTZs) – the FTZs developed in China under Deng Xiaoping in Shenzhen, Pudong and elsewhere being perhaps the most famous – critics at the time wondered whether this was converting 'banana republics' into 'pyjama republics', or places once reliant upon primary exports to centres for low-wage sweatshop manufacturing (Adam, 1975).

Miller *et al.* use the NICL concept to argue that the Hollywood majors have been engineering a new international distribution of labour tasks and production processes, through differentiation of cultural labour and the globalization of production processes. Hollywood has long operated as a global system in terms of its markets and its capacity to attract talent from other national media systems into their orbit, but the current phase of global production is seen as redistributing work globally in order both to reduce overall costs and to 'discipline' US cultural workers by demonstrating their capacity to shift large-scale media production around the globe. In such a strategy, they argue, 'MNCs can discipline both labor and the state, such that the latter is reluctant to impose new taxes, constraints or pro-worker policies in the face of possible declining investment' (Miller *et al.*, 2001, p. 52). This is similar to the process envisaged by the NIDL theorists that MNCs would exploit the opportunities provided by low-wage labour in developing nations, using advances in transport and communications technologies and various tax incentives and fewer regulations to trigger a global 'race to the bottom' in labour and environmental standards (Frobel *et al.*, 1980; Crotty *et al.*, 1998; Klein, 2000).

Miller *et al.* proposed that Hollywood majors have constructed the world of audiovisual media production into three zones: (1) the US as the global centre, where knowledge, finance and decision making remain concentrated; (2) a semi-periphery or intermediate zone of (predominantly English-language) countries – including Canada, Britain, Australia and New Zealand – where production can be transferred to take advantage of cost advantages relative to foreign exchange rates; and (3) the rest of the world, which is completely subordinate to the centre and is drawn upon opportunistically for one-off productions (Miller *et al.*, 2005, p. 127). These three zones echo the core/semi-periphery/periphery demarcation of the globe associated with the world-systems theory of Immanuel Wallerstein and other dependency theorists, but the centre increasingly exerts its power through control over copyright and intellectual property, while production activities are increasingly dispersed globally (Miller *et al.*, 2005, Chapter 4).

The NICL presents an account of the globalization of media production as primarily a top-down, industry-driven process, whereby cost advantages accrue from playing off one location against another and relying upon the propensity of governments worldwide – at local, state and national levels – to offer very generous incentives to attract footloose media-related investment capital. Mirrlees (2013, p. 173) identifies such a 'race to the bottom' as 'the unintended consequence of integration with global Hollywood'.

In their account of Hollywood productions in Australia, Goldsmith *et al.* (2010) question whether such accounts are one-sided and overly pessimistic. They argue that it underestimates the capacity of the host locations to shape the terms of engagement with big media producers, and the degree to which locational decisions are driven not only by cost factors but by the attributes of different locations themselves. Such factors are what they term 'bottom-up' influences that need to be seen as coexisting with the 'top-down' strategies of the major global media corporations. Discussing the rise of Vancouver as a 'Hollywood North' for film and television production that had relocated from the US to Canada, Tinic (2005) makes the point that while the initial impetus for such locational shifts may have been economic, the 'stickiness' (Markusen, 1996) of such locations for ongoing production activity hinges upon the skills of the local workforce, the quality of infrastructure and the support of governments and other key decision makers. In this way, locations such as Sydney's Fox Studios, the Gold Coast, Wellington in New Zealand, and Vancouver and Toronto in Canada can become flourishing second-tier production locations. Figure 5.2 shows the complex range of factors that influence production location decisions in the audiovisual media industries, and the degree to which purely cost-related factors are one component of a complex array of factors shaping such decisions.

Globalization or glocalization?

While globalization theories, as discussed in Chapter 4, see the process of economic globalization as being a pervasive and dominant force in contemporary societies, they do not necessarily see this in terms of the dominance of Western-based media giants over the rest of the world. Part of the reason for this relates to the concept of cultural hybridity, and the idea that globalization is associated with greater cultural inter-mixing, which is not synonymous with cultural imperialism or cultural domination: this will be discussed in Chapter 6. But it also relates to the possibility that the growing dispersal of media production across a wide range of geographical locations is associated with the centres of media production becoming more dispersed over time. Scott has argued that 'the steady opening up of global trade in cultural products is now making it possible for various audiovisual production centers around the world to establish durable competitive advantage and to attack new markets' (2004, p. 474). Rather than media globalization accelerating the disintegration of national media production companies and locations, Scott proposed that these same global forces are in fact promoting the rise of new production centres that challenge the hegemony of 'Global Hollywood':

> Although Hollywood's supremacy is unlikely to be broken at any time in the foreseeable future, at least some of these other centers will conceivably carve out stable niches for themselves in world markets, and all the more so as they develop more effective marketing and distribution capacities ... This argument, if correct, points toward a much more polycentric and polyphonic global audiovisual production system than has been the case in the recent past. (2004, p. 475)

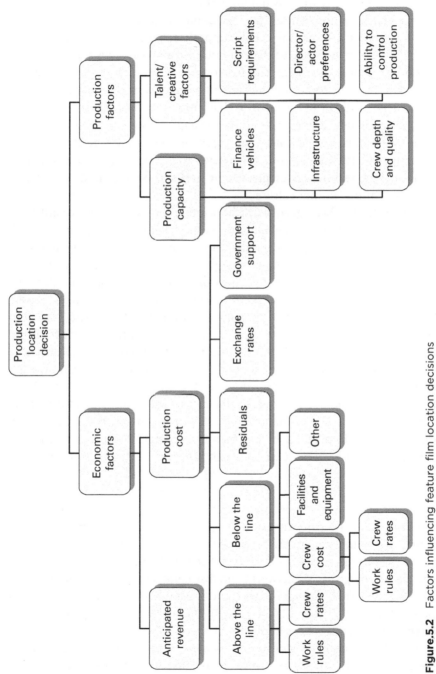

Figure.5.2 Factors influencing feature film location decisions

Source: Ausfilm (2000, p. 13) (in Flew, 2007, p. 133). Reprinted with permission of Ausfilm.

One way in which the global-local dynamic can be read as being more complex than simply top-down domination is through the concept of *glocalization*. Robertson and White (2007, p. 62) have argued that if we think about the global and the local, not as polar opposites, but rather as 'different sides of the same coin', we can see that 'in order to produce goods for a market of diverse consumers, it is necessary for any producer, large or small, to adapt his/her product in some way to particular features of the envisaged set of consumers'. In this respect, then, globalization is a 'self-limiting process … in so far as all ideas and practices have to adapt to contexts and niches, then in the sense of it being a homogenizing force, globalization really makes no sense' (p. 63). Their point is that, whatever the global origins of a particular idea, product, technology or practice, it needs to be 'localized' in order to take root within another culture.

Sinclair (2012) has argued that glocalization has been an important force shaping the global advertising industry. While global advertising agencies work with MNCs to develop global brands – with media and digital companies such as Apple, Google, Microsoft, Amazon and Disney being among the world's top global brands (Interbrand, 2016) – they often find it necessary to adapt the global product to local circumstances. Sinclair argues that such strategies were led in the 1990s by Japanese companies in Asia such as Sony, who wanted to strategically downplay their national roots when operating in other countries in the region (Sinclair, 2012, p. 118). Another instance of such glocalization, or cultural adaptation, has been around television formats. Programmes such as *Millionaire, Survivor, The Apprentice, So You Think You Can Dance, The X Factor, The Voice* and many others screen in many countries around the world, but have slight national variations in each country in which they are broadcast. Television format can be understood as templates, or a 'set of invariable elements in a program out of which the variable elements of individual episodes are produced' (Moran, 2004, p. 5). In what Moran (2004) has referred to as 'the pie and the crust' framework, there are a set of original elements to the format that are invariable and are indeed the intellectual property of the production company that developed them (the 'crust'), within which a variety of unique elements are developed for local markets and audience tastes and preferences (the 'filling' of the pie). Such content is produced locally, but has the advantage for TV networks and distributors of being content that has already been tested in other markets, and is seen as 'the ultimate risk minimization strategy' (Waisbord, 2004, p. 365). It is also typically experienced and interpreted by audiences as local content.

The phenomenon of glocalization can be seen as providing a critique, yet paradoxically also a confirmation, of globalization theories. It points to the limits of understanding globalization as a simple process of cultural homogenization, since there are clearly processes of local cultural adaptation taking place around global products and global media and cultural texts. At the same time, the fact that global media companies have such confidence that their global brands can be adapted to multiple local markets can be read as a sign of their power in those markets, particularly when they can work effectively with local partners. Mirrlees (2013, p. 201) has argued:

> while these entertainment forms depart from the 'Americanist' texts and culturally monolithic commodity representations of previous periods, they also highlight a transnational corporate strategy set on overturning the remaining barriers to capitalist accumulation posed by territorial expressions of cultural nationalism and translocal cultural particularisms.

Media capitals

One feature of both academic and policy discourse in the 2000s has been a growing interest in the role played by cities and regions as catalysts of creativity and innovation. A number of factors have lain behind what Scott (2008) has termed the 'global resurgence' of interest in cities, and their relationship to media and the broader creative economy. One has been the rise of creative industries' academic and policy discourse, which has given particular attention to the question of what makes a creative city (Hall, 2000; Landry, 2000; Florida, 2002, 2008; Currid, 2007; Evans, 2009). A second factor has been the search among urban policy makers for the settings that would enable them to develop a 'Local Hollywood' (Goldsmith et al., 2010) or 'the next Silicon Valley'. Of particular importance here has been the role played by urban amenity in what is perceived as a 'global competition for talent' (Storper & Scott, 2009).

A third factor has been growing academic interest in the concept of *clusters*, which were first identified by the British economist Alfred Marshall (1980) and have long been a core concept in economic geography (Amin, 2000, 2003). The work of business management theorist Michael Porter saw renewed interest in clusters, defined as 'a geographically proximate group of interconnected companies and associated institutions in a particular field, linked by commonalities and complementarities' (Porter, 2000, p. 254). In his work on competitive advantage, Porter (1998, 2000) proposed that the location of firms in related and supporting industries in a particular cluster generated spillover benefits, including productivity gains arising from access to specialist inputs and skilled labour, innovation opportunities arising from sustained interaction with others in the industry, and opportunities for new business formation resulting from better access to resources required by start-ups, such as access to venture capital, creative talent and a high appetite for risk. Internationally, successful clusters include the 'Silicon Valley' high-tech industry in in northern California, the film and television industries in southern California, the fashion industry in Milan, jewelry makers in Paris, financial services in London, wine making in northern California and country music in Nashville.

Finally, there has been discussion about whether cities, and particularly those 'global cities' that are at the core of global networks, have been displacing nation-states as the core power centres of contemporary globalization. Scott *et al.* (2008, p. 15) argued that city-regions had increasingly become the 'motors of the global economy', and that 'with the internationalization of markets, the economies of global city-regions have grown accordingly' (p. 14). In the cultural sphere, Isar *et al.* have argued that:

> Cities ... have become the 'mixing bowls' in which all the combined and uneven processes of globalization play out, particularly in the cultural field. Cities are becoming the protagonists in cultural policy and politics whose importance equals and sometimes exceeds that of national governments. (2012, p. 3)

While it was thought that the global proliferation of the internet and digital media technologies would see location becoming less important, as the same tasks could be performed from virtually anywhere in the world that had technical infrastructure of sufficient quality, there has in recent years been an energetic search among artists, entrepreneurs, investors, policy makers, journalists, cultural *animateurs* and many others to uncover the wellsprings of creativity and its relationship to place. This was associated with the underlying assumption, found most strongly in the creative cities writings of authors such as Charles Landry (2000) and Richard Florida (2002), that creativity as a distinct human talent had to be nurtured in supportive communities characterized by high degrees of social tolerance and an underlying 'soft infrastructure' of dense networks of trust and mutual support. In discussing the centrality of New York City in the global creative economy, Currid (2007, pp. 85–86) argued:

> people find success in creative industries by casting a wide net through their networks of weak ties, and by being open to the structured randomness that such ties bring ... By engaging their networks, creative people instigate the dynamics that propel their careers and bring them some measure of economic success.

Internationally successful cities and regions often derive benefit from what Michael Storper (1997) has termed *untraded interdependencies*, or 'the conventions, informal rules, and habits that coordinate economic actors under conditions of uncertainty ... [and] constitute region-specific assets' (Storper, 1997, pp. 4–5). Successful city-regions or clusters are typically characterized by: dense networks of small firms coexisting with industry giants; well-established relations of trust and reciprocity among buyers and suppliers; strong movements of skilled people into the city or region; access to sources of finance, technical expertise and business services; and a supportive institutional infrastructure that promotes knowledge sharing among participants, and often includes universities in key roles. With regard to the latter, one can think of the relationship of universities such as Stanford, Harvard and MIT to the technology industries of Silicon Valley and Boston, or the role played by the University of California Los Angeles and the University of Southern California in developing talent and connections for the Hollywood film industry.

Hollywood represents the archetypal creative media cluster, even in a global media industry 'characterized ... by a heavy concentration in a limited number of cities, where large media clusters have emerged' (Karlsson & Picard, 2011, p. 3). In his historical geography of Hollywood, Scott (2005) argued that its rise as the world's pre-eminent audiovisual media cluster was by no means inevitable: New York was the dominant media centre of the early twentieth century, followed by Chicago. But those who did establish their production bases in Hollywood developed superior business strategies, based around feature films and the star system, which ensured that by the 1920s Hollywood had developed a superior community of producers that in turn formed the basis for the further concentration of resources in the region. The break-up of the studio system after the Paramount anti-trust decision of 1948 paradoxically strengthened Hollywood as a production centre, as it led to new competition between the big studios and smaller independent producers, the rise of complex inter-firm networks, and new competition for talent and resources arising from the expansion of the television industry (de Propris & Hypponen, 2008; Christopherson, 2011).

As an industrial district, Hollywood is not only a cluster of producers and creative talent, but also of specialist services and supply firms, agents and specialist business services (legal, financial etc.), and government agencies and institutional actors who support the industry's development in various ways. It has developed dynamic and distinct local labour markets, with a large number of potential employees and a diverse array of skills being clustered in the greater Los Angeles area. It is also an intensive learning region, characterized by massive amounts of tacit knowledge, the fast diffusion of new ideas and information (Cooke, 2002) and serendipitous interpersonal exchanges that generate what Storper and Venables (2004) term 'buzz'. Finally, the efficient production base of Hollywood is matched by effective marketing and distribution strategies that generate tendencies towards industry concentration and oligopoly within the domestic industry, while making it a formidable force in international markets (Wasko, 2003; Grainge, 2008).

The concept of *media capitals* is a variant of creative cluster theories developed by media theorist Michel Curtin (2007, 2009, 2010). Curtin argues that media capitals are:

> Cities ... [that] function less as centers of national media than as central nodes in the transnational flow of culture, talent and resources. Rather than asking about relations among and between nations, we should explore the ways in which media industries based in particular cities are participating in the restructuring of spatial and cultural relations worldwide. (2009, p. 111)

In proposing media capitals as an alternative framework to that of media or cultural imperialism, Curtin posits its value as 'a concept that at once acknowledges the *spatial* logics of capital, creativity, culture, and policy without privileging one among them' (2009, p. 117). His framework identifies three key variables that shape the spatial dimensions of media and the emergence of media capitals. First, there is the *logic of accumulation*, which generates competing pressures towards the concentration of production resources on the one hand and extension of markets on the other, in order to realize the greatest possible returns on investment in the shortest period of time. There are thus centralizing (centripetal) tendencies in the sphere of production and decentralizing (centrifugal) tendencies in distribution, that promote the rise of production clusters on the one hand and relentless pressures for geographical expansion on the other. Such dynamics are central to the rise of Hollywood as the quintessential media and creative cluster whose cultural products have global reach but can be identified with second-tier media capitals such as Mumbai, Cairo, Miami and Hong Kong, which have developed distributional reach through privileged access for their products through territorially and linguistically related regions. Singapore has also sought to become a media capital, trading off its small population, history of heavy state cultural management and relative lack of cultural influence against its reputation for effective project management, a highly skilled workforce and a relatively cosmopolitan cultural identity (Lee, 2016).

Second, there are *trajectories of creative migration*. The clustering of media production into media capitals means that these urban locations act as 'talent magnets' for particular types of creative workers. Third, there are *forces of sociocultural variation*, which include the legal, institutional and policy frameworks within which media firms and industries operate, which have for the most part been nationally based even if also strongly influenced by international developments. Contrary to claims about the end of the nation-state, Govil (2009, p. 140) has argued that that 'the national remains a powerful mode for engaging the spatial and temporal practices that organize the contemporary media industries across varied economies of scale'. At the same time, as Sarakakis (2012) has pointed out, it is cities more than nations that become linked into global circuits of cultural production, as they offer distinctive attractions to globally mobile creative workers, and they become the focus for foreign private investment when such capital dwarfs the funds and resources being made available through national media and cultural policies.

The frameworks compared

The three frameworks for understanding global media production outlined in this chapter are not necessarily in opposition to one another. One could acknowledge, for instance, that there is an unequal global distribution of cultural power and resources as the critical political economists do, but also identify the capacity for nation-states to respond proactively to capture more power and resources within this system by adopting strategies along the lines of media capital approaches. Similarly, the capacity of local cultures to resist and transform globalization that is presented by the idea of glocalization does not in itself deny the point that there are dominant global corporations and global brands: a KFC with Chinese or Indian items on the menu is still a KFC, and hence a part of the dominant global culture.

There are, however, important differences in focus and scale between the three approaches, as shown in Table 5.3 below. The critical political economy framework is the most 'macro', in that its object of analysis of the global media system, as part of the global capitalist system as a totality. As this system is seen as being unequal and exploitative at a global level, the capacity for those operating at a local or national scale is relatively constrained by broader structural power relations.

The glocalization framework understands globalization as a more dialectical process, where there are strong 'top-down' global forces shaping national media and cultural systems, such as the role played by global media corporations, but there are also 'bottom-up' elements of local cultures and local and national institutions, that force important strategic accommodations on the part of these powerful global economic interests. Such an approach aligns strongly with concepts of cultural hybridity and the idea that cultural identities are becoming less geographically and territorially defined as a consequence of globalization.

The media capitals framework identifies strong opportunities for local authorities and nation-states to shape the 'terms of trade' through which they engage with global media production networks. Drawing upon the concept of clusters that has a long history in economic geography, this work identifies the degree to which, as Michael Storper has put it, the inter-action between new digital technologies, organizational changes such as networking, and competition among cities and regions to capture economic rents produces a global economy where:

> Certain key regions are at the heart of generating important kinds of economic rents in contemporary capitalism ... [and] the image of the global economy as a sort of delocalized 'space of flows' of human, physical and financial capital controlled from major corporate headquarters manifestly fails to grasp the nature of the new competition. (Storper, 1997, p. 218)

The media capitals framework has elements of the globalization paradigm, particularly insofar as authors such as Curtin (2009) distance themselves from theories of media imperialism. But it also refers back to the significance of local and particularly national institutions in shaping the global media economy. In that respect, it is a more state-centric approach than typically characterizes globalization theories.

Table 5.3 Comparison of theories of global media production

		Focus	Primary dynamic	Capacity for local adaptation
Critical political economy	New international division of cultural labour (NICL)	Macro (global capitalism/world systems)	Top-down – led by MNCs	Low due to unequal power resources
Globalization Theories	Glocalization	Macro/micro (global/local dialectic)	Top-down and bottom-up (MNC and local actors)	Variable – depends in part on local actors
	Media capitals	Micro (local and nation-state actors)	Bottom-up (driven by local and nation-state actors)	High due to importance of local institutions

US-China film co-productions as a case study

There has been astonishing growth in film audiences in China over recent years. It is estimated that ticket sales for films grew tenfold between 2005 and 2015, and that box office revenues increased by 2200 per cent over this period, from 2 billion yuan (about $US300m) in 2005 to 44 billion yuan ($US6.8bn) in 2015 (Brzeski, 2015). As a result, China is overtaking the United States as the world's largest film market. Associated with this rapid audience growth have been significant changes in the positioning of

Chinese films globally. In the 1980s and 1990s, there was a distinction to be made between the films of 'Fifth Generation' filmmakers such as Chen Kaige and Zhang Yimou, whose films, such as *Raise the Red Lantern* (1991) and *Farewell My Concubine* (1993), reached international audiences through the 'art house' cinema circuit, and the 'main melody' dramas that dominated Chinese screens, with officially sanctioned topics and themes. In this environment, Hollywood films were keenly sought after by Chinese audiences. Even though quota restrictions limiting the number of foreign films able to be distributed in China to 20 meant that there was a flourishing black market in copied DVDs of Hollywood products, it was still the case that Hollywood films dominated the Chinese film market, accounting for as much as 60 per cent of box office revenues (Chu, 2002).

The situation changed quickly in China in the 2000s. The international success of films such as *Crouching Tiger, Hidden Dragon* (2000), *Hero* (2002) and *House of Flying Daggers* (2004) established pan-China co-productions as a global phenomenon (Yeh, 2010), even if such films were also criticized within China for pandering to Hollywood conventions while also avoiding content or themes that could alarm Chinese censors. Critics such as Zhao (2010, p. 176) argued that 'although *Hero* appears triumphant in China ... [it] testifies to the triumph of the Hollywood-style commercial mode of film production in China'. The signing of the Closer Economic Partnership Agreement (CEPA) between China and Hong Kong in 2003 was a major catalyst to pan-China co-productions, as it enabled the highly regarded filmmakers of Hong Kong to have greater access to China's vast and growing film market. At the same time, as Yeh (2010) has argued, accommodation to the censorship demands of Chinese state agencies such as the State Administration of Press, Publication, Radio, Film and Television (SAPPRFT, formerly known as the State Administration of Radio, Film and Television, or SARFT) has undercut moves towards a more innovative pan-Asian cinema, as filmmakers are continually second guessing the Chinese regulators and taking a more cautious approach to the content and themes of their films. At the same time, leading Chinese filmmakers such as Zhang Yimou were frustrated that their big budget films such as *The Flowers of War* (2011) received only limited release in the US, despite their success in China and the presence of Hollywood lead actors such as Christian Bale.

The 2010s saw a surge in US-China film co-productions. Films such as *Iron Man 3* (2013), *Transformers: Age of Extinction* (2014), *Jurassic World* (2015), *Furious 7* (2015), *Avengers: Age of Ultron* (2015), *Kung Fu Panda 3* (2016), *Warcraft* (2016) and *The Great Wall* (2016) were co-productions between the leading Hollywood studios and Chinese partners, and grossed high box office internationally, including in both the US and China. Often based on comics or games and/or sequels to successful blockbusters, these films provided popular fare that did not trouble the Chinese censors, while also taking advantage of the incentives offered by Chinese government agencies such as the China Film Co-Production Company (CFCC). On the China Hollywood Society website, advantages of such co-production arrangements are identified as including access to abundant human and natural resources at low cost, access to the world's largest film market (noting that there was, as of 2016, a quota of 34 foreign films per year that could be distributed in China, excluding authorized co-productions) and increased awareness of Chinese culture (China Hollywood Society, 2014). It notes two types of co-production: *assisted production*, where the foreign party provides the capital and the Chinese party provides assistance in regard to equipment, facilities, location, labour, etc. in return for a fee, but where full ownership rights reside with the foreign party; and *joint production*, where the Chinese and foreign parties jointly invest in and produce the film, and share the copyright subsisting in the film and risks and profits from the project. A joint production is considered to be a Chinese domestic film for the purposes of quotas, and has a requirement that Chinese actors constitute one-third of the film's cast (China Hollywood Society, 2014; cf. Kokas, 2016). The latter is intended to be a counter to the doubtful claims of films such as *Furious 7* to contain significant 'Chinese elements'.

The advantages of these co-productions to the Hollywood studios are fairly straightforward. Co-productions provide unique access to Chinese investment capital, while also enabling entry into the fast-growing Chinese film market. Dealing with agencies such as the SARFT and the adverse consequneces of censorship or films being banned from release in China are risks, but are seen as the necessary conditions of doing business with China. The motivations on China's part are more complex, and are a mix of economic, political and cultural factors. Economically, there is a desire to boost cultural exports in order to redress the cultural trade deficit (Keane, 2016), and Chinese filmmakers have become increasingly aware of the need to collaborate with Hollywood in order to both get access to global distribution networks and to acquire the 'soft skills' associated with producing popular media content with broad audience appeal. But there is also the political motivation of expanding China's global cultural influence in a manner that its leaders see as commensurate with its growing economic influence. In what has been a recurring theme of China's leaders and major policy think tanks, former President Hu Jintao observed that 'the overall strength of China's culture and its international influence is not commensurate with China's international status' (quoted in Flew, 2016c, p. 34). Xi Jinping evoked similar concerns in late 2014 when he argued that:

To strengthen our cultural soft power, we should disseminate the values of modern China ... More work should be done to refine and explain our ideas, and extend the platform for overseas publicity, so as to make our culture known through international communication and dissemination. (Xi, 2015, p. 179)

From the three perspectives on global media production considered in this chapter, we could deduce the following predictions about the future of US-China film co-productions. For critical political economists, they may simply be seen as a means of Global Hollywood expanding its market reach into the world's largest market, without changing in any significant way the types of films that it makes or the values that the films embody. Such an argument sees the Chinese interests being essentially co-opted into the hegemonic Hollywood model; that will benefit a small number of Chinese investors, but do little to shift the balance of global cultural power.

For glocalization theorists, these co-productions present a fascinating case study in cultural hybridization, and the possibility of generating new forms of global media content that has appeal in both North American and Chinese popular culture. The economics of the co-productions have the potential to be win–win for both parties, but the risk is that such films become overly hybridized, and lack appeal to Western or Chinese audiences.

For media capital theorists, it could be China that ultimately benefits from these co-production models, or at least its major production centres such as the Hengdian World Studios in Zhejiang Province, the world's largest film production centre. From this perspective, involvement with the big budget Hollywood blockbusters marks a stage in the local industry's evolution, from being a national industry to one that can compete on the global stage through the cultural technology transfer that arises from the interaction between international investors, local capital and the emergent networks of local producers who can enable the transfer of technology, knowledge and 'soft skills' that arise from the adaptation of global best practices to local environments. From this perspective, the major new media interests such as the Dalian Film Group are at an early stage in their global development, as they look to follow the path established in the ICT industries by such global brands as Huawei and Lenovo.

One unanswered question in these debates is the extent to which US-China film co-production opportunities are framed within a wider global political economy of US-China relations. The two countries have been increasingly seen as rivals for global leadership, and their significant political and ideological differences remain, even if trade and investment relations between the two countries have boomed since the 1990s. In the more uncertain global political environment of the late 2010s, there may be pressure on both the US and Chinese sides to curtail partnerships in the media space, particularly if there were to be significant diplomatic or even military conflict over issues such as the future of Taiwan or territorial claims in the South China Sea.

Conclusion

The development of global media production networks draws attention to both the similarities and differences between media and other industries. Global capitalism has since the 1970s been characterized by intensification of an international division of labour, facilitated by technological advances in transport and communication, the global internet and state incentives to relocate capital and production to their own national territories. Critical political economists have identified similar trends in the global media industries, with theories such as the new international division of cultural labour (NICL). As with the literature on transnational corporations more generally, however, it is possible to overstate the degree to which media networks have become truly global, disconnected from the influence of national cultures and nation-state governments. There are also counter-tendencies occurring, such as glocalization and the rise of media capital among 'second tier' cities, that have the potential to challenge the hegemony of Global Hollywood. It is notable that one of the enduring influences of Hollywood, over and above the media content it produces, is the idea that successful media and creative industries can be developed through the geographical clustering of creative talent, media companies and associated infrastructure and supporting institutions. Moreover, countries that seek to usurp US cultural influence, such as China, have nonetheless been keen to take lessons from the dominant players, seen most notably in the flurry of film co-productions that were such a feature of the late 2000s and 2010s.

Note

1 Twenty-First Century Fox is somewhat anomalous here. Now a US-based media conglomerate, it was until 2011 News Corporation, founded and led by the Australian Rupert Murdoch. Murdoch expanded News Corporation from its Australian roots in the 1970s and 1980s, with significant newspaper acquisitions in the UK and the US. The acquisition of a 50 per cent share in the Twentieth-Century Fox film group in 1985, and the subsequent creation of the Fox Television Network in 1987, saw News Corporation become one of the world's biggest media companies. But it did not relocate its head office from Australia to the United States until 2004, by which time 55 per cent of its revenues came from North America, and over 90 per cent of its assets were held outside of Australia.

CHAPTER 6

Global media cultures

Five definitions of culture

The previous chapter focused on the changing dimensions of media production, and the question of whether the rise of global production networks and the shifting spatial relations of media marked the emergence of a new international division of cultural labour (NICL), a turn towards 'glocalization' and cultural hybridity, and the rise of new media capitals that challenge the dominance of the dominant US and Western metropolitan media centres. In this chapter, we will consider global media from the perspectives of culture and consumption, and how the products of global media are consumed in different local and national contexts.

This chapter will begin with a discussion of the various ways in which the concept of culture is understood. Raymond Williams observed that 'culture is one of the two or three most difficult to define words in the English language' (Williams, 1976, p. 87). The term 'culture' is multifaceted and can have several distinct and competing meanings. Indeed, the field of cultural studies, which authors such as Williams, Stuart Hall and others established in the British context in the first instance, has long wrestled with the significance of these various competing meanings. This matters for three reasons. First, it is apparent when a term such as 'media culture' is used that there are different levels of significance attached to it depending upon the ways in which culture is being understood. If we see the media as a significant shaper of culture, and take a more media-centric approach, then the possibility of a global media culture, whether viewed positively as a 'global village' or negatively as 'cultural imperialism', can be better comprehended. Second, there is the question of the extent to which culture can be shaped by governmental institutions, through cultural policies or related strategies such as creative industries policies. Finally, there is the relationship of culture to globalization, and the question of whether cultures are increasingly hybridized or whether distinct national cultures remain important. Needless to say, how all of these issues are addressed has major implications for how we think about global media, and the cultural implications of increasingly globalized media production networks.

One of the challenges of defining culture is that its dominant meanings have changed over time, as well as between societies. As Bocock (1992, p. 231) has observed, 'the meaning of the term "culture" has changed over time, especially in the period of the transition from traditional social formations to modernity'. The first definition of the term referred to the tending of crops or animals, as seen today when we talk of 'agriculture' or 'horticulture'. From the sixteenth century onwards, it began to acquire a second definition, and to be used to refer to the cultivation of minds, and the idea that some people could be more or less 'cultured', based on the acquisition of particular forms of tastes or manners. An associated development from this period was that some societies were also more 'cultured' or 'civilized' than others; this is the origin of the idea of 'Western civilization' as a particular – and, for its champions, superior – form of sociocultural order.

The acquisition of culture, then, was associated with a secular process of human development. Such arguments would become influential in post-World War II theories of modernization as applied to the developing world. Drawing loosely upon the sociological work of Max Weber, and particularly his notion that modernization was associated with the emergence of a 'modern mental type', authors such as de Sola Pool (1963), Schramm (1964), Lerner (1968), Rogers (1969) and others invested considerable significance in the capacity of communications media to transform beliefs, values and attitudes towards those they saw as being associated with the more economically advanced Western societies (Sparks, 2007, pp. 21–28). Schramm (1964, p. 114) saw the role of the mass media in development as being one of enabling 'the transition to new customs and practices and, in some cases, to different social relationships. Behind such changes in behaviour must necessarily lie substantial changes in attitudes, beliefs, skills and social norms'. The social psychologist David McClelland (1961) proposed that the difference between societies in economic performance could be attributed primarily to their 'need for achievement', and the way in which this psychological drive manifested itself in entrepreneurial behaviour. In these instances, culture is being identified as something that can and should be changed through conscious action, whether through the media, by governments, by development communication specialists, by political movements or by other institutional or social actors.

Williams (1976, p. 87) argued that it was not until the eighteenth century that culture came to be more specifically associated with a third definition, that of 'intellectual and especially artistic activity ... [where] culture is music, literature, painting and sculpture, theatre and film'. It is in this period that culture came to acquire particular class overtones:

> Only the wealthy classes of Europe could aspire to such a high level of refinement. The modern meaning of the term 'culture', which associates it with 'the arts' is also closely related to this definition, since it refers not only to the actual work of artists and intellectuals, but to the general state of civilization associated with the pursuit of the arts by a cultivated elite. (Bocock, 1992, p. 231)

For Williams, the struggle to enable culture to become part of the shared patrimony of a whole society, without class barriers and other forms of distinction, was part of what he termed the 'long revolution' for a democratic culture, a struggle he saw as being on a par with the demands for political democracy, and a historical transformation equivalent to that of living in an industrial economy (Williams, 1965).

The fourth definition is the *social* definition of culture as 'a particular way of life, whether of a people, a period [or] a group' (Williams, 1976, p. 18). This is often referred to as the social or anthropological definition of culture: it is descriptive rather than judgemental; it incorporates both 'high' and 'popular' culture; and it refers to 'meanings and values not only in art and learning but also in institutions and ordinary behavior' (Williams, 1965, p. 57). From this perspective, we refer to cultures in the plural, whether of groups, societies or social classes, as 'the meanings, values and ideas embodied in institutions, in social relations, in systems of belief, in mores and customs, [and] in the uses of objects and material life' (Hall & Jefferson, 1976, p. 10). Its roots lie in anthropological accounts of 'primitive' societies by authors such as E. B. Tylor and Ambrose Evans-Pritchard (Inglis, 2004 pp. 56–60). It was adopted in sociology by Talcott Parsons (1951), who interpreted culture as something that is transmitted as heritage, learned within a social context and shared within a social order. For Parsons, 'culture ... is on the one hand the product of, [and] on the other hand a determinant of, systems of human social interaction' (1951, p. 15).

A fifth conception of culture understands it as primarily a *symbolic* system through which people in a society interact with one another. This is known as the *structuralist* conception of culture, first proposed by the French anthropologist Claude Lévi-Strauss. From this perspective the interest is in what culture *does*, rather than what culture *is*, and particularly how it integrates individuals into a symbolic system, so that 'social action in the formation, reproduction and even adaptation of actual cultures is ... a surface manifestation of a series of deeply internalized master patterns at the deep structural level of cognition' (Jenks, 1993, p. 63). Critical to such cognition is the capacity to communicate, and this led to theorists of language identifying culture as primarily a linguistic or signifying system, with communication at its centre. In *A Theory of Semiotics*, Umberto Eco observed that 'every act of communication ... presupposes a signification system as its necessary condition' (Eco, 1976, p. 9). This understanding of culture as a symbolic system based around signification, through which individuals are incorporated into social formations through social, linguistic and psychological relationships, has been highly influential within cultural studies. Hall and Jefferson pointed out how culture refers not only to ways of life, but also to the '"maps of meaning" which make things intelligible ... and through which the individual becomes a "social individual"' (1976, p. 11). Frow and Morris observed that 'every aspect of social life' is shaped by 'a network of representations – texts, images, talk, codes of behavior, and the narrative structures organizing these' (1996, p. 345).

Cultural studies and cultural policy

One characteristic of changing definitions of culture has been that, over time, they have tended to become more inclusive of a wider range of phenomena. This is particularly the case with those definitions that understand culture in terms of 'ways of life'. In seeking to understand and interpret culture as something broader than the arts and literature, Raymond Williams proposed that:

> Culture is the description of a particular way of life, which expresses certain meanings and values not only in art and learning but also in institutions and ordinary behavior ... Such analysis will ... include elements in the way of life that to followers of the other definitions are not 'culture' at all: the organization of production, the structure of the family, the structure of institutions which express or govern social relationships, [and] the characteristic forms through which members of the society communicate. (Williams, 1965, pp. 57–58)

From this perspective, culture can only be defined and understood through its complex interplay with other aspects of a society, including its economic relations, political institutions, social structures and belief systems. This broad and inclusive definition of culture has been central to the development of *cultural studies*, defined in one influential account as 'an interdisciplinary field ... committed to the study of the entire range of a society's arts, beliefs, institutions and communicative practices' (Grossberg *et al.*, 1992, p. 4).

Cultural studies academics have drawn attention to the multiple ways in which cultural institutions, relations and practices are infused with elements of power, conflict, control and resistance, and how these intersect with broader social divisions based upon class, gender, race, ethnicity, sexuality and (dis)ability (see, for example, Storey, 1996). At the same time, the relationship between cultural studies and cultural policy is a complex one. Some cultural studies academics, such as Tony Bennett (1998) have argued that culture needs to be viewed as 'intrinsically governmental', meaning that 'an engagement with policy issues needs to be seen as a central component of the practical concerns of cultural studies', necessitating 'the development of effective and productive relationships with intellectual workers in policy bureaux and agencies and cultural institutions' (Bennett, 1998, p. 4). Others

have criticized a policy orientation for narrowing the focus of cultural studies, downplaying elements of conflict and contestation, and subordinating
the field to 'bureaucratic statism' (During, 1993, p. 20; cf. McGuigan, 2004).

The historical roots of cultural policy lie in the French Revolution of
1789, when the Revolutionary government transferred the royal art collec-
tions from the Palace of Versailles to the Louvre, and moved other historically significant art works from the palaces of the nobility to the new public
museums and galleries. This set in train the idea that art works belonged to
the people, made available through the institutions of the nation-state as the
guardians of a common cultural heritage. The establishment of museums,
galleries, libraries and other public institutions for the display of cultural
heritage has been a feature of all nation-states, and in the post-World War II
period international agencies such as UNESCO played a key role in advising
newly independent nations on the development of a national cultural policy
(UNESCO, 2004).

Cultural policy in its contemporary form took shape in the second half of
the twentieth century. In Britain, the Arts Council of Great Britain was established in 1946, chaired by the economist John Maynard Keynes. For Keynes,
the principal purpose of an arts policy was to promote creative excellence,
with government having a role in providing financial and infrastructural
scaffolding that is both critical and limited: the key balancing act is to keep
the government of the day at 'arm's length' from decisions about the content
of artistic and cultural output (Skidelsky, 2003, pp. 728–729). In France, the
formation of the Fifth Republic in 1958 was a catalyst for cultural policy
development (Looseley, 1995). The first Ministry of Culture was headed by
the writer André Malraux, who saw cultural policy as having three critical
tasks:

1. The maintenance of cultural *heritage*, with the state distributing the
    'eternal products of the imagination' among the national population
    through museums, galleries, libraries and other public exhibition spaces;
2. Promoting the *creation* of new artistic and cultural works through public
    support for artists and cultural workers;
3. The *democratization* of culture, with an activist role for cultural policy in
    redressing socio-economic inequalities by cultural means.

The appropriate scope and breadth of cultural policy is a subject of ongoing
debate, because it is both a set of policies specifically aimed at the arts, and
a series of measures to shape culture more broadly. The cultural economist
David Throsby (2010) identified cultural policy as being a form of public
policy that is applied to the production, distribution, consumption and
trade in cultural goods and services, but also acknowledged that this is an

insufficient definition as it only refers to *explicit* cultural policies. Policies in a vast range of other fields have cultural dimensions and impacts, including economic policy, trade policy, urban and regional development policies, education policy, and policies towards copyright and intellectual property. Ruth Towse (2010) has argued that the point that the traditional concern of cultural economics with market failure, or the inadequacies of commercial firms in the creative industries as cultural providers, is self-limiting, since an ever-growing range of cultural goods and services are provided through the commercial cultural sectors, and the interface that governments have – or should have – with these commercial media and creative industries warrants detailed consideration.

From a policy perspective, debates about the range of activities deemed to be cultural raise the issue of the appropriate scope and instruments of cultural policy. As Bell and Oakley (2015, p. 17) observe, 'the issues raised by using a very broad definition of culture as way of life is ... that it is difficult to know where "culture" ends and "everything else" begins'. Similarly, as the scope of cultural policy is broadened beyond the arts, the range of objectives associated with it is similarly expanded, along with the range of agencies and ministries involved in its development and implementation. While this includes notionally 'non-cultural' fields such as education, urban and regional planning, tourism, immigration and other fields, the most contentious relationship has been that between cultural development and economic development, as it draws attention to the complexities of relationships between 'culture' and 'economy' at an analytical level, and publicly supported and commercially funded cultural institutions and activities at the more practical level (Flew, 2012b; Bell & Oakley, 2015, pp. 29–34).

Three perspectives on global culture: modernization, global capitalism and cultural hybridity

The rise of global media raises the question of whether it is possible, or desirable, to move towards a single global culture. If we work from the anthropological conception of culture, and the idea that cultures are unique and historically grounded forms of lived and shared experience, passed down as customs and traditions across generations, then the concept of global culture is a definitional impossibility. In a debate on the possibility of global culture in the academic journal *Theory, Culture and Society*, Anthony Smith made this argument:

> If by 'culture' is meant a collective mode of life, or a repertoire of beliefs, styles, values and symbols, then we can only speak of cultures, never just culture; for a collective mode of life, or a repertoire of beliefs, etc.

presupposes different modes and repertoires in a universe of modes and repertoires. Hence, the idea of a 'global culture' is a practical impossibility ... Even if the concept is predicated of *homo sapiens*, as opposed to other species, the differences between segments of humanity in terms of lifestyle and belief-repertoire are too great, and the common elements too generalized, to permit us to even conceive of a globalized culture. (Smith, 1991, p. 171)

By contrast, authors who focus upon the more communications driven dimensions of culture, and the role played by symbolic representation through media in social imagining and meaning-making, can envisage a more global culture arising as an offshoot of global media. In his historical account of the media and modernity, John Thompson argued that there has been a strong connection between the technologies and institutions of communications media and the globalization of modernity:

If we focus in the first instance not on values, attitudes and beliefs, but rather on symbolic forms and their modes of production and circulation in the social world, then we shall see that, with the advent of modern societies ... a systematic cultural transformation began to take hold. By virtue of a series of technical innovations associated with printing and, subsequently, with the electronic codification of information, symbolic forms were produced, reproduced and circulated on a scale that was unprecedented. Patterns of communication and interaction began to change in profound and irreversible ways. The changes ... comprise what can loosely be called the 'mediatization of culture'. (Thompson, 1995, p. 46)

Modernization theories

Early modernization theories were explicit in arguing the need for the mass media to enable cultural transformation as a means of modernizing developing countries, and promote what Max Weber referred to as the 'modern mental type', whether as urban entrepreneurs, political leaders or other societal change agents. Everett Rogers (1976, p. 126) defined the dominant modernization paradigm in development communication as being one where 'continuing underdevelopment was attributed to "traditional" ways of thinking and acting ... the route to modernization was to transform the people, to implant new values and beliefs'. One of the core features of the participatory turn in development communication has been to reject such accounts as being Eurocentric and neo-colonial in their orientation to traditional cultures. Authors such as Servaes (1999, p. 88) argued the need for approaches that focus upon 'the importance of the cultural identity of local communities', and the need for dialogue and reciprocity between local cultures and the researchers and practitioners engaging with them. What also typically follows is what Melkote (2010) termed 'epistemological plurality', recognizing the multiplicity of forms of knowledge, and the limitations of modernization theories based upon 'universal truths and our notions of objective social reality' (p. 118).

Participatory communication approaches have, as noted in Chapter 2, radically transformed development communication, challenging the perceived ethnocentricity and underlying assumptions of the superiority of 'Western' culture that underpinned the modernization paradigm. But three issues have arisen in the wake of such discussions. The first is concern that aspects of 'traditional' culture can be reified, even if they are at odds with other development principles, such as those derived from universal understanding of human rights. Structural inequalities deriving from class, caste, race, religion, ethnicity and gender are challenged in principle by the concept of universal human rights, as enunciated in statements such as the United Nations' *Universal Declaration on Human Rights* (UN, 1948). International development agencies have often played a critical role in promoting universal human rights, as they have been in a position to link development aid to action to address human rights abuses, or promote more equitable access to vital social resources such as education or health care. At the same time, 'liberal' interpretations of human rights, based on universalist values, frequently come up against local cultures and traditions, particularly around questions of gender equality, but also in areas such as LGBT (Lesbian, Gay, Bisexual and Transgender) rights, and the rights of religious, ethnic and other minorities. Kurlantzick (2012) has observed that:

> Nations continue to dispute the importance of civil and political versus economic, social, and cultural rights. National governments sometimes resist adhering to international norms they perceive as contradicting local cultural or social values. Western countries – especially the United States – resist international rights cooperation from a concern that it might harm business, infringe on autonomy, or limit freedom of speech. The world struggles to balance democracy's promise of human rights protection against its historically Western identification.

Second, there is the tendency to reify cultures through *civilizational* discourses, where cultures are seen as singular, monolithic, and inevitably in conflict with one another. The culture-as-civilization argument was presented most forcefully by the US political scientist Samuel Huntington (1993), who proposed that civilizations are 'the highest cultural grouping of people and the broadest level of cultural identity people have ... defined both by common objective elements, such as language, history, religion, customs, and by the subjective self-identification of people' (Huntington, 1993, p. 24). Huntington believed that there were only a small number of core civilizations in the world, including the Western, Islamic, Confucian, Hindu, Slavic-Orthodox and other civilizations. He saw a coming 'clash of civilizations' as inevitable, since 'Civilizations are differentiated from each other by history, language, culture, tradition and, most important, religion ... These differences ... are far more fundamental than differences among political ideologies and political regimes' (1993, p. 25). Globalization increased the likelihood of civilizational conflict for Huntington, since 'increasing interactions intensify civilization consciousness and awareness of differences between civilizations and commonalities within civilizations' (1993, p. 26). Huntington's argument is the dark side of Marshall McLuhan's 'Global Village' thesis. Globalization and modernity, driven by communications technologies, bring cultures closer together, but rather than promoting enhanced mutual understanding, they bring conflicting values, beliefs and ideas into greater proximity with one another. Moreover, as globalization weakens the power of nation-states and modernization undermines more traditional sources of social identity, it also promotes the rise of religion, often in fundamentalist or highly doctrinal forms, as an alternative source of social identity to that of civic nationalism.

The third question that arises from the debate between modernization theories and participatory communications approaches is around questions of power and political economy. Fundamental to the critique of modernization theories has been the claim that they focus upon individual and/or cultural pathologies rather than upon unequal power relations and access to social and economic resources. A corollary of this has been that, in the absence of acknowledging such structural inequalities and choosing to act on behalf of the poor and disadvantaged, development communication practitioners risk becoming the unwitting tools of local, national and transnational state and corporate elites. Melkote (2010, p. 119) argues that the reality of the social and political situation in most developing countries is such that the urban and rural poor, women, and other people at the grassroots are trapped in a dependency situation in highly stratified and unequal social and economic structures'. Addressing such systems of domination cannot occur simply at the level of ideas, such as the promotion of more participatory and community-centric knowledges, but starts to point in the direction of critical political economy and its structural critique of global media and communication.

Critical political economy

The relationship between culture and political economy has been a complex one, with many different approaches taken to articulating the connection between the two. Sum and Jessop (2015, pp. 18–19) have identified at least 13 distinct approaches. These have included: the study of cultural economics and cultural production (Best & Paterson, 2010); analyses of economics from the perspective of cultural studies (Ruccio, 2008; Grossberg, 2010); arguments that the economy is becoming increasingly 'culturalized' (du Gay & Pryke, 2002); and applications of policy studies to cultural theory that draw out strategies for developing cultural policy (Bennett, 1998) and the creative industries (Cunningham, 2013).

The key debate, however, has related to the ambiguous legacy of Marxism to the study of culture (Williams, 1973; Hall, 1986, 1996a; Barrett, 1991). At one level, the legacy of Marxism to the study of culture is relatively straightforward. It is proposed that the realm of culture cannot be understood independently of the economic and political forces that shape and constrain it. The concept of *ideology* is central to the Marxist theory of culture, as it is proposed that in class societies it is control over the production and distribution of ideas that is central to the maintenance of power, and that these 'means of mental production', which include the media in all of its forms, are controlled by the same class that controls other economic resources, as discussed in Chapter 3. The 'ruling class = ruling ideology' equation, which has also been referred to as the instrumentalist (Murdock & Golding, 2005, pp. 61–62) and radical functionalist approach (Hardy, 2014, pp. 41–44), has had an important, if problematic, influence on critical political economy approaches to media and culture, with the *propaganda model* of media developed by Noam Chomsky and Edward Herman (Herman & Chomsky, 1988) being a highly influential example.

Several problems have been identified with this conceptualization of the media and culture under capitalism. It raises the question of why the working classes and other dominated groups appear to consent to forms of rule under capitalism, given the notable lack of success of Marxist political parties in Western capitalist democracies. Hall argued that:

> while the economic aspect of capitalist production processes has real limiting and constraining effects ... the determinacy of the economic for the ideological can only be in terms of the former setting limits for defining the terrain of operations ... of thought. (1996a, p. 44)

As a result, political-economic and cultural-ideological forces need to be seen as 'mutually determining', and possessing a 'relative openness or relative indeterminacy' (Hall, 1996a, p. 45). Applied more specifically to the media,

Murdock and Golding critiqued the propaganda model as 'overlook[ing] the contradictions in the system', and the degree to which 'owners, advertisers and key political personnel cannot always do as they wish. They operate within structures that constrain as well as facilitate, imposing limits as well as offering opportunities' (2005, p. 63).

A second Marxist approach to the relationship between political economy and culture identifies culture and ideology as existing as a level in a social formation where economic relations are in a dominant, but not necessarily determinant, relationship to the political and ideological 'levels' through which social relations are largely understood and contested. This is what is known as the 'base-superstructure' model, but, following Williams (1973), Hall (1996a) and others, the relationships proposed between culture, ideology, politics and economics are complex and mutually determinant. This is in contrast to a one-way transmission model, where cultural and media institutions and practices simply provide mechanisms through which economic and political power translates into cultural and ideological domination.

In his overview of the critical political economy of media approach to these questions, Hardy (2014) proposed that models such as the propaganda model are partly right in their focus on how powerful economic and political forces shape and set limits to the flow of culture and ideas in capitalist societies, but that there needs to be systematic analysis of countervailing forces to such elements of structural domination. He identifies forces that promote dominant class interests as including concentration of ownership, state censorship, commercial pressures to maximize audiences, the higher spending power of more affluent consumers, and advertiser influence over content. At the same time, he emphasizes that there are countervailing forces that models such as the propaganda model do not adequately encapsulate. These include state media regulations, policy or financial support for alternative media, the ability of consumers or community groups to collectively organize around unfavourable media coverage, and the values and power of media producers themselves, particularly through collective organizations such as trade unions (Hardy, 2014, p. 55). The balance of forces in any particular society at any given time will vary, and countervailing forces are stronger in some national contexts than others. For example, the Scandinavian countries have a history of press subsidies for alternative media that is reflective of an ongoing commitment to structural pluralism (Karppinen, 2012).

With regards to the global system, it was observed in Chapter 3 that the critical political economy approach was aligned with theories of cultural and media imperialism, notably in the work of authors such as Herbert Schiller and Oliver Boyd-Barrett. It was argued that such theories have tended to underestimate the significance of local and national cultural preferences as a continuing determinant of media audience behaviour, and have overestimated the extent to which the ideas of people outside of the dominant Western nations are influenced by the cultural content of the West, most notably the United States (cf. Tunstall, 2008).

At a more conceptual level, it can be seen that the base/superstructure framework has had a strong influence on theories of the capitalist world-system. This has perhaps been most noted with regards to the work of the world-systems theorist Immanuel Wallerstein. Robertson and Lechner (1985) argued that Wallerstein's world-systems theory treated culture as epiphenomenal, existing only as either a consequence of economic changes or as a barrier to the logic of expansion of the world-system. They argue that in a variety of ways capitalism has been shaped by cultural – and particularly religious – attempts to give it meaning, ranging from the relationship between Protestantism and economic individualism, the role of families in Confucian cultures, to communalist elements in a variety of the world's religions, from Catholicism to Islam.

In more recent work, Wallerstein (1990, 1997) has sought to more explicitly foreground culture in world-systems theory, but has done so in ways that stress the role played by culture in either maintaining systems of political-economic power or in enabling the contradictions inherent in the capitalist world economy as a system to be better managed. Critics argue that this is still an overly functionalist account of global culture, as cultural developments remain largely determined by political and economic forces that operate autonomously of such cultural elements (Boyne, 1990; Giddens, 1990; Robertson, 1992; Tomlinson, 1997).

In an argument strongly influenced by world-systems theories, Sklair (1998, 2002) has argued that the missing element in Wallerstein's work is a conception of how a *transnational capitalist class* (TCC) forms, and what constitutes its dominant culture-ideology. Sklair proposed that while the dominant economic entity is the transnational corporation (TNC), its dominance can only be secured through transnational practices, defined as 'the effects of what people do when they are acting within specific institutional contexts that cross state borders.... [and] create globalizing processes (Sklair, 2002, p. 84).

For Sklair, the key political fractions of the TCC are:

- TNC executives and their local affiliates (corporate fraction);
- Globalizing state and inter-state bureaucrats and politicians (political fraction);
- Globalizing professionals (technical fraction); and
- Merchants and media (consumerist fraction).

Where these fractions of the TCC have their greatest influence is in the cultural-ideological sphere, where they aim towards the total inclusion of all social classes in the culture-ideology of consumerism, which 'proclaims ... that the meaning of life is to be found in the things that we possess. To consume, therefore, is to be fully alive, and to remain fully alive we must continuously consume' (Sklair, 1998, p. 297). This in turn promotes the accumulation of capital on a global scale. For Sklair, this generates a new politics of globalism and anti-globalization movements:

> Pro-capitalist global system movements are, therefore, those that support the transnational corporations, serve the interests of the transnationaly capitalist class, and promote the culture-ideology of consumerism. Anti-capitalist global system movements, consequently, are those that challenge the TNCs in the economic sphere, oppose the transnational capitalist class and its local affiliates in the political sphere, and promote cultures and ideologies antagonistic to capitalism consumerism. (Sklair, 1998, p. 297)

What we can see here is that culture and ideology are being used interchangeably in Sklair's analysis. This is because culture is being understood as something that can be imposed on subordinate classes by a transnational capitalist class, and indeed does important work in securing consent to such a system of domination. Consumption as an expression of cultural identities is thus incorporated into an account of consumerism as the dominant ideology of global capitalism. In a similar vein, Steger (2005) understands globalism as a variant of neoliberalism, a political ideology whose central tenets include:

> the primacy of economic growth, the importance of free trade to stimulate growth, the unrestricted free market, individual choice, the reduction of government regulation, and the advocacy of an evolutionary model of social development anchored in the Western experience and applicable to the entire world. (pp. 8–9)

Globalism is thus the extension of neoliberalism, as first developed in the US under the Reagan administration and in the UK under the Thatcher government, on a global scale. Steger argued that 'neoliberal globalists were "market fundamentalists" who believed in the creation of a single, global market in goods, services, and capital' (2005, p. 11).[1]

Globalization theories

Globalization theories differ from critical political economy in attaching greater significance to the role played by cultural forces in shaping contemporary globalization. As we noted in Chapter 4, authors such as Anthony

Giddens argued that globalization could be interpreted as a series of mutually reinforcing developments related to the spread of capitalism, modernity, industrial society and the system of nation-states, with none of these having causal or analytical primacy over the others. Arjun Appadurai argued that the global cultural economy was shaped by the interaction between five 'scapes' – ethnoscapes, technoscapes, finanscapes, mediascapes and ideoscapes – and that globalization needed to be understood as the interaction between the global movement of people, culture and ideas as much as by global flows of capital, finance and commodities. Summarizing this perspective, John Tomlinson defined globalization as:

> A multidimensional process, taking place simultaneously within the spheres of the economy, of politics, of technological developments – particularly media and communication technologies – of environmental change and of culture. One simple way of defining globalization, without giving primacy to any one of these developments, is to say that it is a complex, accelerating, integrating process of *global connectivity* ... globalization refers to the rapidly developing and ever-densening network of interconnections and interdependencies that characterize material, social, economic and cultural life in the modern world. (Tomlinson, 2007, p. 352)

Concepts of interconnectedness and interdependence displace those of determination in discussions of the economy–culture relationship in the globalization paradigm.[2] In critiquing the perceived economic determinism of critical theories of global capitalism, Tomlinson (2007) has argued that they rest upon conceptually impoverished notions of both the cultural and the economic. When it is argued that globalization – or global capitalism or global neoliberalism – have impacts on culture, or consequences for culture, the concept of culture 'seems to be a peculiarly inert category: something that people experience or imbibe but do not themselves produce or shape' (Tomlinson, 2007, p. 353). Globalization theorists have insisted that culture is constitutive of globalization, and not simply an effect or reflection of primarily economic processes, since culture is understood as 'the ways in which people make their everyday lives, individually and collectively, meaningful by communicating with each other' (Tomlinson, 1999, p. 19). While this occurs through practices of symbolic representation, in which global media have come to play an important role, and global media may project certain 'worldviews' that can be deemed to be ideological at some level, it is an unduly narrow and reductionist interpretation of culture that reduces the process of making meaning to simply absorbing the dominant system of symbolic representations.

This argument recalls the longstanding debate in media studies about 'dominant ideology' and 'active audience' approaches to the relationship between media texts and audiences (Morley, 1989; Curran, 1990; Allor, 1995). Theories that identify media as the principal source for transmitting a dominant ideology typically start, as Herman and Chomsky do with the propaganda model, by identifying evidence of concentration of media ownership and the dominance of advertising-funded media. One example of such a logic is provided by Kellner and Pierce, who identify the media as playing a central role in disseminating corporate domination and pro-capitalist ideology, or what they term 'globalization from above':

> There is little doubt that from the perspective of political economy, global media outlets are overwhelmingly shaped and determined by transnational corporate interests ... The superstructure created by this global media oligopoly is an example of 'globalization from above', where the flow of information, images, cultural artefacts and entertainment is distributed from a uniform and increasingly unregulated source. The nation-state loses power as the distributor of cultural forms and commodities to transnational corporations where the reproduction of consumer culture attitudes and lifestyles has become one of the consequences of the 'globalization from above' model. (2007, pp. 377–378)

Critics of the dominant ideology perspective have argued, drawing upon media and cultural studies paradigms, that such accounts privilege systems of production and distribution over practices of consumption and processes of making meaning from cultural texts and artefacts. Using Stuart Hall's semiotic account of communication (Hall, 1993b), it is argued that such analyses privilege the encoding of meaning in production practices informed by ownership of the means of cultural production, over practices of decoding, or the 'interpretative work' (Hall, 1993b, p. 99) involved in ascribing meaning to such texts. While one possible outcome is what Hall termed the dominant-hegemonic meaning, where audiences simply accept dominant media narratives, a more common practice is what has been termed 'negotiated reading' which 'contains a mix of adaptive and oppositional elements' (Hall, 1993b, p. 102). Extending this analysis further, it is apparent that reception, or the question of who constitutes 'the audience', cannot be divorced from underlying social relations based around class, gender, race, ethnicity, sexuality or other forms of sociocultural identity. Such negotiated readings are likely to be rendered even more complex when applied on a global scale, where imported media content has to gain acceptance in a range of very different cultural contexts. To the extent that it is successful, it is often because it downplays its roots in a given national culture.

The argument that globalization is as much a cultural process as it is an economic one also relates to the growing centrality of digital communication technologies and networks to the global economic order. The idea that culture is increasingly a part of the productive forces under the conditions of informational capitalism is central to Manuel Castells' theory of the network society. Global communication networks are at the core of the informational mode of development, where 'the source of productivity lies in the technology of knowledge generation, information processing, and symbol communication' (Castells, 1996, p. 17). As a result, 'because informationalism is based on the technology of knowledge and information, there is a specially close linkage between culture and productive forces ... in the informational mode of development' (Castells, 1996, p. 18). More generally, economic practices can also be seen as cultural ones: decisions that we make about what we consume are expressive of our cultural identities, even as they are also purchasing decisions made around the consumption of commodities. The extensive literature on *cultural economy* explores such questions in depth (Lash & Urry, 1994; du Gay & Pryke, 2002; Callon *et al.*, 2004), often linking the growing significance of the cultural dimensions of the economy to the rise of services and knowledge-based and creative industries in advanced capitalist economies (Allen, 2002; Flew, 2005).

Identity, hybridity and deterritorialization

Globalization theorists work with the concept of culture in both of its primary definitional senses, as expressive of communal identities and ways of life, and as mediated forms of symbolic communication. Three concepts are critical to understanding how culture is understood within this framework: identity; hybridity; and deterritorialization. Both modernization theories and critical political economy largely work with dualistic conceptions of identity. For modernization theorists, the polarity is between traditional and modern forms of identity, with the developmental project premised upon promoting the latter at the expense of the former. For critical political economists, global capitalism is seen as promoting congruent 'global', 'transnational' or 'neoliberal' identities, to which there are oppositional forms premised around a defence of localism in various forms, that can run across the political spectrum from conservative ethno-nationalism to populist protectionism, and from radical Islam to grassroots civil society movements (Steger, 2005, pp. 95–126). In both cases, as was noted earlier, identity is presented as something that globalization does things to, and is inherently fragile and at risk in the face of globalizing processes that have 'swept like a flood tide through the world's diverse cultures, destroying stable localities, displacing peoples, bringing a market-driven, "branded" homogenization of cultural experience' (Tomlinson, 2003, p. 68).

Tomlinson (2003) presents the counter-proposition that 'globalization, far from destroying it, has been perhaps the most significant force in *creating and proliferating* cultural identity' (p. 68). Two propositions are critical to this revisionist interpretation. First, if we understand globalization as the globalization of modernity, which includes capitalist economic relations but is not reducible to them, then we can see the powerful connection between modernity and the institutionalization of collective identities. This is most apparent in the case of nationalism and national identities, where nation-states continually work to create a common national culture and set of personal identifications with that culture, with the media playing a particularly critical role. At the same time, nation-states are typically multi-ethnic in their nature, and in many instances were founded upon the subjugation of particular ethnicities or nationalities in the context of colonialism and slavery. The struggles of oppressed and marginalized peoples for recognition within such nation-states are overlaid with the impact of mass migration, often driven by economic imperatives, and the processes of community formation among ethnic and linguistic minorities (Castles & Davidson, 2000).

Second, there is a need to conceive of identities relationally, rather than only as a thing that people possess. This is apparent in how the policies of multiculturalism seek to accommodate the growing cultural diversity of national populations, where historically 'the concept of the nation-state usually implies a close link between ethnicity and political identity' (Castles, 1997, p. 5). As Bennett (1998) has observed, multiculturalism as public policy typically has a strong cultural policy dimension, as governments seek to respond to the growing pluralization of 'ways of life' within nations by demonstrating active support for a plurality of cultures within cultural institutions, including those of the media.[3]

The discussion has thus far focused upon what Scholte (2005) describes as *territorial identities*, where a relationship to culture is defined in terms of a relationship – current or prior – to a defined territory or place. Scholte observes that 'the pluralization of identities under contemporary globalization' needs to be complemented by a discussion of *non-territorial identities*, or attachments and affiliations based upon age, class, disability, gender, race, sexual orientation or other aspects of ascribed behaviour or a common sense of belonging. Scholte observes that 'large-scale globalization since the middle of the twentieth century has spurred unprecedented growth of non-territorial identities and associated networks of solidarity and struggle' (Scholte, 2005, p. 240).

It follows that there are multiple forms of identity related to cultural globalization. With regards to *territorial identities*, there is of course national identity, or a shared sense of culture and belonging within a currently recognized nation-state. There are also those territorial identities associated with places from which one has migrated, ancestral relations and affiliation to what Scholte (2005) terms *micro-nations*. The latter include indigenous peoples whose territories were appropriated by colonial powers, those who strive for recognition and autonomy within nation-states (e.g. Catalans and Basque in Spain, Scots in the United Kingdom, Québécois in Canada, Tibetans and Urghyrs in China) and other ethnic and tribal groupings that have a distinctive identity within nation-states, including a distinctive language (e.g. Cantonese in China). Scholte observes that while there were 193 sovereign nation-states in 2005, there were over 800 micro-nationalist movements at that time (2005, p. 233).

There has also been the view the broad trajectory of modernity is away from terriotorially defined national identities towards non-territorial identities. Stuart Hall observed that 'the great discourses of modernity ... led us to expect ... the gradual disappearance of the nationalist passion ... [and] the subsumption of these particularisms into a more cosmopolitan or internationalist consciousness' (Hall, 1993a, p. 353). Spencer & Wollman (2002) pointed out that for both liberalism and Marxism, nationalism came to be seen as a retrograde ideology: for liberals, it subsumed the sovereign individual within the collectivist imaginary of the nation, whereas for Marxists such as Rosa Luxemburg it promoted 'national prejudices' that 'operated to divide workers on national lines, mobilizing national identity against class identity' (Spencer & Wollman, 2002, p. 11). Global movements such as feminism and the LGBT movement posit identities based upon gender or sexual orientation as transcending the nation. Race, religion and ethnicity have long constituted alternative touchpoints to national identity, and periodically achieve concrete political expression through movements such as the pan-Arab or pan-Africanist movements. Major world religions such as Islam, Judaism and Buddhism are notable for their historical uncoupling from particular nations, although this can be subject to change, as seen with the idea of the state of Israel as a 'Jewish nation' (Spencer & Wollman, 2002, p. 53).

Scholte (2005, p. 232) has argued that globalization has promoted 'the growth of alternative frameworks of collective identity'. These include identities that are adopted by individuals rather than being in some sense ascribed. Commitments to the environment, human rights and peace are examples of 'collective solidarity with fellow human beings anywhere on earth' (Scholte, 2005, p. 242), adopted on the basis of an understanding of shared human and/or planetary fate rather than ascribed personal characteristics or past associations with particular histories, cultures and beliefs. These forms of *cosmopolitan* identity, and the process through which authors such as Ulrich Beck (2006, p. 73) have argued that 'themes of global importance are becoming part of the mundane experience and "moral lifeworlds" of human beings' in the context of greater global interconnectedness through communications media, will be discussed further in Chapter 7.

The notion that globalization would be associated with multiple forms of cultural identity is central to the concept of *hybridity*. With its roots in postcolonial theory, as developed by authors such as Homi Bhabha (1994) and Gayatri Chakravorty Spivak (1990), hybridity has been defined as referring to 'processes of racial, linguistic or cultural mixing that are understood to result in something different from the sum of their discrete parts' (Darling-Wolf, 2009, p. 483). Authors such as García Canclini (1995), Kraidy (2005) and Pieterse (2015) have made the point that while hybridity appears as a new category in dominant narratives of Western modernity – with the shift from largely monocultural to increasingly multicultural societies arising from large-scale migration – it has been a feature of many non-Western cultures for a long time, as one significant impact of colonialism was racial, cultural and linguistic intermixing that has also gone by such names as 'creolization', 'mestizaje' and 'syncretism'.

In communication and media studies, an important element of hybridity has been the manner in which media texts are sufficiently 'open' to be interpreted in various ways by differently culturally situated audiences. An oft-cited example is the way in which American rappers and R&B performers have been able to project a transcultural 'blackness' that sees them identified primarily as 'black' entertainers and secondarily as American ones. This in turn allows a music genre such as rap to be adopted and re-inscribed across multiple local cultural contexts, while retaining a shared set of global norms and conventions. Kraidy (2005) has argued that, when interpreted in this way, hybridity does run the risk of being understood as *corporate transculturalism*, where 'cultural fluidity [is] a tool to make corporations more profitable, consumers more satisfied, and the world generally a better, more connected and more vibrant place' (p. 95).

Hybridity is identified in the literature on cultural globalization as transcending the dualisms that arise between thinking about globalization as entailing an inevitable clash of civilizations or as growing cultural homogenization arising from cultural imperialism (Kraidy, 2005, pp. 39–45). It was noted in Chapter 4 that Arjun Appadurai made a similar call for cultural hybridization as being central to the global cultural economy, based as it was upon a tension between forces promoting a common global culture (cultural homogenization) and those promoting cultural difference (cultural heterogenization).

Jan Nederveen Pieterse (2015) has argued that hybridity is the *leitmotif* of globalization, arguing that:

Globalization or the trend of growing worldwide interconnectedness has been accompanied by several clashing notions of cultural difference. The awareness of the world 'becoming smaller' and cultural difference receding coincides with a growing sensitivity to cultural difference ... Yet it is interesting to note how the notion of cultural difference itself has changed form. It used to take the form of national differences, as in familiar discussions of *national* character or identity. Now different forms of difference have come to the foreground, such as gender and identity politics, ethnic and religious movements, minority rights, and indigenous peoples. (pp. 41–42)

Pieterse contrasts the hybridity paradigm to two other common popular understandings of the cultural impact of globalization. The first draws upon Samuel Huntington's (1993) theory of the 'clash of civilizations', and foresees a hardening of divisions between 'civilizational spheres', defined as a loose admixture of nation-states, geographical regions, religious identities, language groups and cultural practices, and including the Christian-humanist West, the Islamic Middle East and the Confucian cultures of East Asia. Pieterse makes the point that the broader understanding of culture utilized by Huntington rests upon a fixed and discrete understanding of cultural difference, whereas hybridity theories draw attention to their fluidity, open-endedness and interconnectedness.

The second set of theories Pieterse discusses are those concerned with cultural convergence or homogenization, or what Ritzer (2004) and Barber (2000) have termed 'McDonaldization' or 'McWorld'. Ritzer understood 'McDonaldization' as synonymous with the global spread of a particular set of American values associated with that fast-food restaurant, or 'the process whereby the principles of the fast-food restaurant are coming to dominate more and more sectors of American society as well as the rest of the world' (2004, p. 19). Benjamin Barber pointed to a global condition that he described as 'one McWorld tied together by communications, information, entertainment, and commerce' (Barber, 2000, p. 21). Its only effective form of resistance thus far has been the austere, pre-modern ethos of the *jihadists* such as Al-Qaeda and ISIS.

It is in contrast to these approaches that Pieterse presents the alternative of *hybridization* or cultural mixing. For Pieterse:

Hybridization is an antidote to the cultural differentialism of racial and nationalist doctrines because it takes as its point of departure precisely those experiences that have been banished, marginalized, tabooed in cultural differentialism. It subverts nationalism because it privileges border-crossing. It subverts identity politics such as ethnic or other claims to purity or authenticity because it starts out from the fuzziness of boundaries. If modernity stands for an ethos of order and neat separation by tight boundaries, hybridization reflects a postmodern sensibility of cut'n'mix, transgression, subversion. (2015, p. 53)

Pieterse summarizes the different paradigms for the interpretation of cultural difference in the terms set out in Table 6.1.

Table 6.1 Three ways of seeing cultural difference

Dimension	Differentialism	Convergence	Mixing
Cosmologies	Purity	Emanation	Synthesis
Analytics	Territorial culture	Cultural centres and diffusion	Translocal culture
Lineages	Differences in religion, language, region, class or caste	Imperial and religious universalisms	Cultural mixing of technologies, languages, religions
Modern times	Romantic differentialism, Race thinking, chauvinism, Cultural relativism	Rational universalism, Modernization, Coca-colonization	Métissage, creolization, syncretism
Present	'Clash of civilizations', Ethnic cleansing, Ethno-nationalism	McDonaldization, Disneyfication	Postmodern culture, trans-national cultural flows, cut 'n' mix
Futures	Mosaic of immutably different cultures and civilizations	Global cultural homogeneity	Open-ended ongoing mixing

Source: Pieterse (2015, p. 55). Reprinted with permission of Rowman & Littlefield Publishers.

A final key concept in theories of cultural globalization is that of the concept of *deterritorialization*, or what García Canclini described as 'the loss of the "natural" relation of culture to geographical and social territories' (García Canclini, 1995, p. 229). John Tomlinson (1999) argued that:

> The idea that globalized culture is hybrid culture has a strong intuitive appeal which follows directly from the notion of deterritorialization. This is because the increasing traffic between cultures that the globalization process brings suggests that the dissolution of the link between culture and place is accompanied by an intermingling of these disembedded cultural practices producing new complex hybrid forms of culture. (Tomlinson, 1999, p. 141)

Tomlinson's approach to deterritorialization refers to the lack of congruity between particular cultures and the dominant cultural coordinates of the geographical spaces in which they are located. It may refer, for instance, to Sikhs in London, Salvadoreans in Los Angeles, or Vietnamese in Sydney, who live in a location but may struggle to belong to that place in a wider sense, since its forms of belonging as defined by genealogies of cultural meaning and history have been created independently of them. In that respect, a diasporic identity, which is neither that of a place of origin nor of a current locale, but is a new form of 'imagined community', may indeed constitute a form of deterritorialization, or a reconfiguring of the relationship between culture, place and identity. In his account of uses of media in urban Nigeria, Larkin (2008, p. 2) drew attention to the deterritorializing dimensions of shared media consumption practices, observing that 'media ... provide the infrastructure to facilitate and direct transnational flows of cultural goods and the modes of affect, desire, fantasy, and devotion these goods provoke'.

Deterritorialization presents the possibility of reterritorialization, or what Robbins (1998, p. 3) referred to as 'a reality of (re)attachment, multiple attachment, or attachment at a distance'. Authors such as Appadurai (1996) and Tomlinson (1999) saw a strong connection between identities formed through transnational media flows, since the mass migration of people across the globe has promoted diasporic communities that have sought to remain connected with originating cultures by maintaining links through the use of various media. The possibility of 'reterritorialization' has been increased with new media such as the internet and the creative use of household information technology and entertainment equipment. Miller and Slater's (2000) study of internet use in Trinidad found that, rather than the internet being an 'imposed' global technology which 'disrupted' local cultural traditions, the various possibilities of the technology had been taken up in different ways to globally project a 'Trini' identity. In particular, it generated critical linkages between people in Trinidad, the 'Trini diaspora' (e.g. Trinidadian students at North American universities) and wider global communities of interest. Miller and Slater present their findings as an explicit rebuff to those who would argue that the specificities of culture has been lost in the global space of flows, or that the relationship between the local, the national and the global is understood as a form of scalar progression coterminous with shifts from print to broadcast to online media.

Conclusion: how global is culture?

The major theories of globalization and culture point towards homogenization on the one hand and fragmentation on the other. For some critical political economists, it is as if commodities themselves are the bearers of cultural transformation, as people around the world are absorbed into what is variously termed globalism, consumerism or neoliberalism, on the basis of exposure to the media and cultural products of Western TNCs. This is similar to the earlier vision of modernization theorists that exposure to mass media (or, in more contemporary parlance, to iPhones and Facebook) would lead to a cultural transformation towards dominant Western ideologies: the difference being that critical theorists reject that vision of global modernity, whereas modernization theorists – and related theories such as 'soft power' – welcome it (Sparks, 2012).

By contrast, theories of the fluidity of identities, hybridity and deterritorialization associate globalization with the proliferation of identities, and the seemingly endless permutations that can subvert a modernist norm of attachment to a national, ethnic or racial identity. But there may be two notions of hybridity being conflated here – one empirical and one conceptual. One registers empirical realities that the global movement of people, and greater ethnic, cultural and racial inter-mixing means that societies have become increasingly multicultural, and that this in turn challenges notions of a 'dominant culture' derived from particular dominant forms of cultural identity within nation-states. This is undoubtedly true, although it is not historically unprecedented: mass voluntary migration in the period from 1815 to 1914 was proportionately greater than that in the period from 1945 to 2000 (Castles & Miller, 2003). According to the United Nations, about 213 million people were migrants in 2010, and international migrants are typically about 3 per cent of the world's population (Berg & Besharov, 2016). This means that while the international mobility of people around the world is an important feature of contemporary global culture, it is also the case that the vast majority of the world's population remain in the countries in which they were born. Moreover, given that over half of the world's migrants are located in ten countries, it is also the case that large-scale migration has far more influence on some national cultures than others, and these are most typically economically developed nations such as the United States, Canada, Germany, France, the United Kingdom and Australia (Berg & Besharov, 2016, p. 58).

The problem with hybridity in the conceptual sense, as a general condition of the global subject, is that it returns the question of whether identities are essentially a matter of personal choice. This question has featured in debates about postmodernism, with Jean-François Lyotard famously observing in *The Postmodern Condition* that 'eclecticism is the degree zero of contemporary culture' (Lyotard, 1984, p. 76). This is what Mathews (2000) has referred to as the 'cultural supermarket' conception of identity, where the global market offers us an infinite array of possibilities to shape and form cultural identities. Bauman (1996, p. 18) observed that 'if the modern "problem of identity" was how to construct an identity and keep it solid and stable, the postmodern "problem of identity" is primarily how to avoid fixation and keep the options open'. Stuart Hall presented identities as 'points of temporary attachment to the subject positions which discursive practices construct for us' (Hall, 1996b, p. 8). The key again is to avoid fixity, closure, essentialism: the concept of identity is 'a strategic and positional one' (p. 3), and options need to be kept open.

An obvious question to raise in this context is how available are the multiple identities of the 'cultural supermarket' to people around the globe. As with cosmopolitanism, to be discussed in Chapter 7, 'while some people in our globalizing world have the freedom to choose, many more do not' (Mathews, 2000, p. 179). Mathews notes that consideration of the state has been curiously absent from any of the discussions of cultural identity in the context of globalization, even though the literature on nations as 'imagined communities' repeatedly draws attention to the myriad routine forms of 'banal nationalism' (Billig, 1995), of and the role played by national cultural institutions in shaping a relationship between citizens and the state at the levels of the taken-for-granted and everyday life (Mihelj, 2011). There is also a notable gap in the consideration of the relationship of institutions to individual identities. The anthropologist Mary Douglas (1987, p. 112) observed that 'institutions confer identities' by framing situations, defining roles and values, motivating subjects and generating meaning out of a repertoire of available discourses and systems of representation. The sociological literature on institutions also emphasizes their cultural-cognitive function, or the 'influence on the very perception that people have of reality' (Dequech, 2003, p. 464).

The missing part of the equation, in conclusion, is a governmental perspective on culture, as advocated by cultural studies theorists such as Tony Bennett (1998). One interesting feature of multicultural societies is that they require an institutionalization of identities as a condition for engagement with state agencies and national governments. Tomlinson (2003, p. 274) makes the point that 'political subjects can now experience and express, without contradiction, both attachments to the nation, multi-ethnic allegiances *and* cosmopolitan sensibilities', and more forms of identity and attachment could be added to this list, e.g. LGBT campaigns around issues such as marriage equality. So a proliferation of identities in the context of cultural globalization can be consistent with the institutionalization of forms of identity, which entails fixity as well as openness. There is also a need to acknowledge that nation-states can be flexible and reflexive in response to cultural hybridity and deterritorialization; they are not tied to traditional conceptions of national culture and identity.

Notes

1   Neoliberalism is a term that can have several definitions. Critical political economists tend to adopt definitions of the sort outlined by Steger, and most notably by Harvey (2005), as a dominant ideology premised upon variants of

free-market economics. Other definitions, notably those inspired by Foucault (2008), understand neoliberalism as a distinctive mode of governmentality, or a construction of the relationship of citizens to the state, based primarily around competitive behaviour and calculative individualism. For a summary of this literature, see Flew (2014a) and Springer *et al.* (2016).

2   Although the relationship is a complex one in neo-Marxist theories of culture. As was noted above, authors such as Raymond Williams and Stuart Hall, and the cultural studies tradition that they helped to shape and define, saw such relationships as complex and mutually constitutive. However, much of the literature on globalization inspired by Marxist political economy has tended to understand such relationships in economically determinist terms, where globally dominant cultures are understood as the ideological supports of global capitalism, such as neoliberalism, consumerism or globalism.

3   One manifestation of this has been the development of multicultural broadcasting. In Australia, the Special Broadcasting Service (SBS) was established in 1978 to operate alongside the traditional public broadcaster (the ABC), and with an explicit remit to not only programme content in languages other than English, but to ensure that all such content on its television channels was subtitled. In this way, it was intended to 'mainstream multiculturalism' by enabling all Australians to share in a more diverse array of media content. This goes beyond multiculturalism as a kind of proportional representation, towards ensuring greater awareness of cultural diversity throughout the whole of Australian society. On SBS, see Ang *et al.* (2008).

CHAPTER 7

Globalization, nation-states and media policy

Nation-states and the global system of states

While the period since the end of World War II in 1945 is associated with the accelerated development of globalization, it also saw the number of nation-states in the world almost quadruple. As noted in Chapter 2, nation-states are defined geographically and politically by sovereignty, citizenship and internationally recognized territorial boundaries, but are also defined culturally through a sense of shared history, language, beliefs and values, and rituals and ceremonies. With regards to the media, they are central to both the conveying and the contesting of these cultural dimensions of national identity. Government agencies also play a key role in regulating the media, in terms of ownership, content and performance. In some instances, this may involve direct government ownership and financing of media organizations, such as public service broadcasters (PSBs), but it also involves the application of laws, policies and regulations to privately owned and controlled media. In most countries, laws also set limits to government influence over private media, through measures such as constitutional protections of freedom of speech, seen as a hallmark of liberal democracies in particular.

A critical question raised in globalization debates is whether it weakens the power of nation-states. The argument is that for much of the twentieth century, national governments sought to regulate national economies using Keynesian demand management techniques, accompanied by the development of welfare states to provide a social safety net to citizens. The *regulatory state* (Braithwaite, 2006) also developed agencies to manage the conduct of businesses and provided key inputs, that ranged from physical infrastructure to national education systems to generate the workforce human capital and skills required to effectively participate in the national economy. This system, variously termed Fordism (Aglietta, 1987; Harvey, 1989; Murray, 1989), organized capitalism (Lash & Urry, 1987) and the Keynesian welfare state (Esping-Anderson, 1990; Jessop, 2002), was underpinned by a series of political-economic institutions, agreements between competing interest groups (notably business and trade unions, but also civil society institutions such as churches and social movements), and ideas of what constituted a 'good society'.

The post-World War II international economic order was also anchored around a system of states. The defeat of the Axis powers (Germany, Japan, Italy) was associated with a return to the 'Westphalian' order where states agree to be bound by international law and mutual agreements to not interfere in each other's internal affairs, and with decolonization the newly independent nations of the 'Global South' sought similar guarantees of national sovereignty.[1] An architecture of international trade and finance developed around the Bretton Woods system (Gilpin, 1987, pp. 131–134), whose institutions and agreements included the International Monetary Fund (IMF), the General Agreement on Tariffs and Trade (GATT) and the World Bank. The intention was to develop an international economic order based around 'embedded liberalism', and avoid the conflict between domestic autonomy and international agreements through 'the creation of institutions that limited the impact of domestic and external developments on one another ... to solve the problem of simultaneously achieving both international liberalization and domestic stabilization' (Gilpin, 1987, p. 132).

It was in the context of these distinctive national capitalisms (Hall & Soskice, 2001; Clift, 2014) that national media systems emerged, with distinctive mixes of commercial and public service media, differing degrees of state control over media content, different ideas about journalistic autonomy and media professionalization, and varying degrees of openness to imported media content, alongside their own local cultural inflections upon media genres and formats. Media regulations were typically underpinned by a broader vision of a regulatory state, overseeing and managing the conduct and behaviour of media institutions according to 'public interest' criteria on behalf of a national citizenry (van Cuilenberg & McQuail, 2003). Broadcast media emerged in a period when there was a broad political consensus that the state had a central role in managing public institutions, and that the media were 'not just another business', as the 1947 Hutchins Commission on the Press in the United States argued (McQuail, 2005, pp. 170–172). In the US context, Horwitz has referred to a 'progressive' belief that 'democratic governmental power reconciled the tension between the needs of powerless consumers and the productive might of the corporation', and that 'the administrative process [operated] not only to protect powerless consumers, but also to effect rationality and fairness in the economy generally' (Horwitz, 1989, pp. 25, 26). In the context of broadcast media, such regulatory processes sometimes took the form of a *social contract* between commercial broadcasters and government regulators as guardians of the 'public interest' (Flew, 2006). The concept of the 'public interest' in broadcasting arises, as Streeter (1996) observed, from the dual nature of the airwaves (spectrum) as a public resource and as private property, meaning that access to the airwaves was seen as a 'gift' of a public resource for private uses, which broadcasters held as a form of *public trust*, and around which governments could impose reciprocal 'pro-social' regulations around areas such as national content quotas, local programming requirements, children's programmes and complaints-handling procedures.

Globalization is seen as one of the forces, alongside technological change and the adoption of pro-market or 'neoliberal' political ideologies, that has been steadily eroding this 'post-war settlement' since at least the 1980s. In a perceptive early account, Robin Murray (1971) referred to the growing 'territorial non-correspondence' between capitalism as a global economic system and the political regime of territorially defined nation-states. Various accounts exist of this tendency being in play. The author and *New York Times* columnist Thomas Friedman referred to the 'Golden Straitjacket', whereby globalization forces national governments to adopt policies of free trade and openness to private foreign investment as the condition of rising economic prosperity, with the result that, under conditions of economic globalization, 'your economy grows and your politics shrink' (Friedman, 2001, p. 106). From the perspective of globalization theories, David Held argued that under conditions of globalization 'the operation of states, in an ever more complex international system, both limits their autonomy and infringes ever more upon their sovereignty' (Held, 1989, p. 202). From a Marxist perspective, Michael Hardt and Antonio Negri argued in *Empire* that 'Over the past several decades ... we have witnessed an irresistible and irreversible globalization of economic and cultural exchanges ... [and] declining sovereignty of nation-states and their inability to regulated economic and cultural exchanges' (Hardt & Negri, 2000, pp. xi–xii).

Associated claims have been made about the collapse of the system of states as the primary form of governance in the global political-economic system. International political economists have referred to the nation-state being 'diminished' as 'the nation-state has "lost" sovereignty to regional and global institutions' (Cable, 1995, p. 27), and becoming 'hollow, or defective, institutions' as 'state authority has leaked away, upwards, sideways, and downwards' and 'structural forces [are] bringing about the hollowing out of state authority' (Strange, 1995, pp. 56, 57). It has been argued that a *new medievalism* has come to prevail in international relations, marked by the end of national sovereignty and the Westphalian order of a system of states, as a result of globalizing economic and technological changes (Freidrichs, 2001). For proponents of the new medievalism:

> In the era of the internet, governments have lost their monopoly over information and can therefore be successfully challenged by non-government actors ... New medievalists see the once-dominant hierarchic order of nation-states being supplanted by horizontal networks composed of states, non-government organizations and international institutions. (Gilpin, 2002, p. 243)

While such developments are most commonly viewed pessimistically, as equating to a loss of democratic power on the part of citizens that arises from national sovereignty, others have seen the rise of networked global governance as opening up new possibilities for the development of global civil society and cosmopolitan 'post-national' forms of citizenship and identity. As one marker of such developments, there were over 37,000 active international non-governmental organizations (INGOs) in 2015, as compared to less than 200 in 1900 (Held & McGrew, 2002; UIA, 2015).

Media policies and national media systems

Media policy has been central to the development of media in all of its forms. The freedom to communicate has been constrained by general civil and criminal law, as well as by laws and regulations specific to the media. Government institutions have regulated the ownership, production and distribution of media, and seek to manage and shape cultural practices in order to direct media institutions towards particular policy goals. Media organizations are also subject to a series of technical, marketplace and conduct regulations over elements of ownership, content and performance, both as general forms of industry regulation (for example, laws to ensure competitive markets), and regulations that are specific to the media, by virtue of their unique role as an instrument of public communication. Media policy is also frequently articulated to other fields of public policy, including cultural policy, telecommunications policy, policies towards the creative industries, copyright policy and industry development policy.

Rationales for media regulation have included:

- concerns about their potential impact on children and other 'vulnerable' individuals (Hutchison, 2004);
- the ability to use such media for the development of a national cultural identity;

- implied rights of public participation and involvement associated with the significance of media as forms of public communication, and possible tensions between their nature as a common cultural resource and private ownership (Horwitz, 1989; Streeter, 1996);
- 'public good' elements of the media commodity, including non-rivalrous and non-excludable elements of access and consumption, and the costs of production being largely unrelated to the costs of access or consumption (Collins *et al.*, 1988);
- the possibilities of 'market failure' in a commercial media system, including concentration of media ownership due to the prevalence of economies of scale and scope (Doyle, 2013), inadequate provision of 'minority' content that lacks commercial appeal (Davies, 2014), and the potential to avoid producing local content and developing the local production industries when content can be more cheaply imported (Flew, 2006).

In their pioneering analysis of comparative media systems, Daniel Hallin and Paolo Mancini (2004, 2005) sought to develop 'ideal types' to define the media systems of North America and Western Europe, based upon the relationship between media institutions, social systems, political systems and underlying values and ideologies about the role of the media in liberal-democratic societies. They identified four key variables that saw individual nations cluster around three models:

1. *Polarized pluralist* (Greece, Spain, Portugal, Italy and – to a lesser extent – France): strong connections between media outlets and political parties, with weak development of media professionalization and periods of state censorship of the media;
2. *Democratic corporatist* (Germany, Austria, Netherlands, Belgium, Norway, Sweden, Switzerland): highly developed news media systems, strong media professionalization and institutionalized self-regulation, and strong state intervention around support for PSBs and press subsidies;
3. *Liberal* (USA, Canada, Great Britain, Ireland): strong commercial media, strong professionalization, relatively weak media regulation, market-oriented system.

Hallin and Mancini identified the importance of comparative media systems analysis as lying in its ability to provide 'a clearer sense of the range of different kinds of institutional arrangements that have evolved to deal with the problems of communication in a democratic society' (2004, p. 14). The four key variables that informed their analysis were:

1. Development of a mass press, and whether newspapers were largely read by elites or had mass circulation;

2. Political parallelism, or the extent to which there was alignment – formal or informal – between media outlets and political parties;
3. Journalistic professionalism, and the extent to which media professionals enjoy autonomy, share professional norms and understand their primary vocation as being to the 'public interest';
4. The role of the state, as seen in the development of public service broadcasting and the extent to which commercial media are subject to strong external regulation.

Several critiques have been made of Hallin and Mancini's comparative framework. The conflation of the United States and Great Britain as exemplifying a liberal market model downplays the significance of the BBC to shaping not only the British media system but public service broadcasting on a global scale, which has no real parallel in the US case of the PBS. There is also the point, acknowledged by the authors in a later work (Hallin & Mancini, 2012), of how applicable these models are outside of a European context, or that of relatively stable liberal democracies (Voltmer, 2012). There are also changes over time, such as the growing commercialization of media and its relationship to the *mediatization of politics* (Mazzoleni & Schulz, 1999; Esser & Strömbäck, 2014), particularly as the influence of the media over politics increases and the relative strength of the traditional political parties is in decline.

A key question is the implications of globalization for comparative media systems. Is globalization, as Voltmer (2012, p. 231) suggests, a 'force for convergence [that] will eventually lead to the homogenization of media systems around the world'? Hallin and Mancini expressed the view that there was a tendency towards convergence in the direction of the Liberal model, and that globalization was a key aspect of this since 'in general the forces of the global market tend to displace the national political forces that once shaped the media' (Hallin & Mancini, 2004, p. 276). At the same time, they maintained that 'media system development is "path dependent", and that we cannot understand why media systems are the way they are without looking back at the historical roots of their development' (Hallin & Mancini, 2005, p. 218).

The importance of history and institutions

While the specifics of Hallin and Mancini's comparative media systems account can be contested, their work draws attention to the important point that institutions matter, and that the institutional framework of particular nations has its own history and forms of embeddedness in the socio-economic system. This insight has been most strongly developed in the institutionalist tradition of the social sciences, which has its roots in the work of scholars such as Émile Durkheim, Max Weber, Thorstein Veblen and Karl Polanyi, and which is 'concerned with studying the interactions between social values, technology, and economic institutions' (Stilwell, 2002, p. 2012). Karl Polanyi argued that economic relations are necessarily embedded in social institutions:

> The human economy ... is embedded and enmeshed in institutions, economic and non-economic. The inclusion of the non-economic is vital. For religion and government may be as important to the structure and functioning of the economy as monetary institutions or the availability of tools and machines themselves that lighten the toil of labor. (Polanyi, 1957, p. 34)

The most significant dissention from the proposition that institutions matter has traditionally come from economists, most notably those working within the dominant neoclassical tradition, for whom it has been argued 'all statements about "collectivities" – groups, institutions, societies – can be reduced to statements about the properties of individuals' (Ingham, 1996, pp. 245–246). But the new institutional economics of authors such as Douglass North, Oliver Williamson, Elinor Ostrom, Geoffrey Hodgson and others has been more attuned to the institutional and historical underpinnings of economic behaviour and market performance. Their understanding of institutions is necessarily a multi-layered one. It incorporated not only laws, policies and regulations that directly inform economic transactions, or what Williamson (2000) terms governance structures, but also the broader formal institutional environment that is underpinned by the political system, the legal system, bureaucratic norms, etc. Even more ambitiously, it refers to informal institutions, or what Thorstein Veblen described as 'the shared habits of thought' and the 'conventional standards, ideals, and canons of conduct that make up a community's system of life', and through which institutions act to shape the behaviours and practices of individuals (Veblen, 1961, p. 238).

Douglass North defined institutions as 'the humanly devised constraints that structure human interaction ... made up of formal constraints (rules, laws, conventions) and informal constraints (norms of behavior, conventions, and self imposed codes of conduct) and their enforcement characteristics' (North, 1994, p. 364). Geoffrey Hodgson has offered a comparable definition:

> Institutions are durable systems of established and embedded social rules and conventions that structure social interactions.... In part, the durability of institutions stems from the fact that they can usefully create stable

expectations of the behavior of others. Generally, institutions enable ordered thought, expectation and action, by imposing form and consistency on human activities. They depend on the thoughts and actions of individuals but are not reducible to them. (Hodgson, 2003, p. 163)

From the definitions of North and Hodgson, we can observe the following:

1. Institutions have a history that enables them to be durable over time;
2. Institutions include formal organizations, such as firms, trade unions, government agencies, universities etc., but also rules, habits, customs and conventions, of both a formal and an informal nature;
3. Institutions shape the behaviour of individuals and how they interact with one another;
4. Institutions do not necessarily exist 'outside' of individuals, as they shape the thoughts, expectations and actions of individuals;
5. At the same time, institutions have a concrete form that is over and above simply being the consequence of the rational decisions of individuals.

An understanding of the importance of both formal and informal institutions to the development of global media alerts us to the need to consider the significance of state forms themselves for the development of a nation's media and creative industries, and the risk that promises for reform are unlikely to be delivered upon due to the weakness of state capacities. This is partly captured in the notion of path dependency, which underpins the work of comparative media systems theorists such as Hallin and Mancini. *Path dependency* refers to the ways in which institutions conduct themselves in the present and future is shaped by their past, and the ways in which 'the range of possibilities for that development will have been constrained by the formative period of that institution' (Peters, 2012, p. 73). In considering why some PSBs have been seen to have autonomy from governments (such as the BBC or Japan's NHK), whereas others have been seen as de facto arms of the state (such as China's CCTV), the role of historical path dependency in shaping these contemporary institutions is vitally important to understand, as they initially appear as all being state-funded broadcasters.

An institutional perspective is also important to understand the motivations of state actors. Many policy theorists and political scientists approach state agencies as neutral arbiters between competing interests, or as a 'cipher' whose decisions simply reflect the outcomes of elite bargaining among powerful institutions that exist independently of them (Dunleavy & O'Leary, 1987, pp. 327–329). By contrast, institutionalists such as Skocpol (1985, p. 27) have argued that 'the formation ... [and] political capacities of interest groups and classes depend in significant measure on the structures and activities of the very states the social actors, in turn, seek to influence'. Such insights have also been applied to regulatory theory, around the issues of whether state agencies serve the 'public interest' or can be 'captured' by dominant interests among those regulated, and whether there are elements of self-interest in how regulators themselves promote their relationship to regulated industries (Christensen, 2011). The question of whether media regulators can retain a degree of autonomy and focus on the public interest, or are coerced or persuaded to support either state interests or powerful private interests, is a key factor in assessing media policy from a comparative perspective.

The developmental state, copyright and creative industries

The concept of the developmental state has been a significant application of institutional analysis to development thinking. It has often been observed that good intentions in the development field are thwarted in practice, either by problems within state institutions such as corruption, or by the more general issue of a lack of effective state capacity to implement policies on the ground. Hirschman (2013) told of how the aspirations of the first generation of modernization theorists in Latin America were thwarted as countries in the region turned from democracy to dictatorship, and how development advisors frequently found themselves working with military dictatorships against the will of the people. Critics argue that modernization theories continue to possess a technocratic dimension, often developing policies and programmes on behalf of elite state interests and 'neglecting to account for the influence on structural constraints on individual action and enterprise' (Melkote, 2010, p. 108).

Evans (1995) identified three archetypal state forms in developing nations. The first were *predatory states*, which were typically formed around an absolutist ruler and a small clique of supporters, possessed a weak and often corrupt bureaucracy, and largely used state power to appropriate resources and suppress civil opposition. An example of such a state would be the Democratic Republic of Congo, which has one of the lowest per capita incomes in the world and a history of poor and corrupt government, despite being rich in natural resources. The *fragmented intermediate state* has pockets of bureaucratic professionalism coexisting with other state agencies where personal ties and/or corruption predominate, where state authority is fragmented, and both intra-elite and elite-mass conflicts are common. India is sometimes cited as an example of such a state, where the gap between developmental aspirations and the on-the-ground experience speaks to weaknesses in state capacity to deliver on ambitious policy goals. It is notable that in such countries there are often successful regional governments, as with Kerala province in India (Issac, 2014), so a challenge can be how to implement best practices on a national scale.

Developmental states are the third state form on this continuum, and these are countries that have successfully organized resources and managed relations between international capital, local capital and the state in ways that have led to significant economic development. For Evans (1995, 1998), Weiss (2003), Kohli (2004) and others, East Asian states such as Taiwan, South Korea and Singapore have exemplified such a nation-building developmental agenda, with its historical roots being in Japanese industrial policy, and its keenest student generally being China.[2] Notably, they have done so by actively embracing the challenges presented by economic globalization rather than by denying them or trying to block them: a key component of their policies has been to harness public and private resources to build capacity in potential areas of international competitiveness (Evans, 1997; Weiss, 1997). Six elements of the developmental state have been identified as being critical (Williams, 2014, p. 7):

1. A comprehensive national plan that prioritizes development goals;
2. An elite state bureaucracy recruited through meritocratic processes;
3. A political system where the executive can provide effective leadership;
4. Pilot organizations within the bureaucracy that can pursue sector-specific and market-conforming interventions;
5. Linkages between state agencies, civil society organizations and private capital that can enable what Evans refers to as *embedded autonomy*, where bureaucratic independence can be reconciled with ready access to key information;
6. States with sufficient power, political will and capacity to direct capital towards national development goals.

The last of these has been particularly important in dealing with multinational corporations, where states seek to leverage technology transfer and knowledge transfer from foreign direct investment associated with the development of global production networks (Ernst & Kim, 2002). Michael Keane (2013, pp. 83–89) has described an analogous process of *cultural technology transfer*, where the interaction between international media companies and local capital, skills and talent enables the development of joint ventures which provide a springboard to local media industry development through technology transfer and the successful adaptation and 'modelling' of international formats and genres.

The developmental state concept was developed in the context of twentieth-century industrialization strategies, and at a time when countries such as South Korea and Taiwan were less democratic and open than is the case today. Williams (2014) has argued that the concept needs to be modified for the twenty-first century to deal with: the implications of the rise of a knowledge economy; recognition that development is a multifaceted concept, and cannot simply be equated with economic growth; the rapid movement of financial capital around the globe and the constraints this can place on nation-states; the global spread of democracy and the rise of non-governmental organizations (NGOs) and civil society movements; and acknowledgement of the ecological limitations of industrialization and economic growth. Evans (2014) has argued that the new challenges for developmental state strategies lie in: the implications of 'endogenous growth' economic models, which stress the importance of the application of new ideas to economic development; the focus on the quality of institutions, which include state bureaucracies but also areas such as education and health; and the challenge of how to enhance human well-being as well as incomes, and what Amartya Sen has termed 'expansion of the "capabilities" of people to lead the kind of lives they value – and have reason to value' (quoted in Evans, 2014, p. 224).

Two areas can be identified where developmental state concepts are of particular relevance to global media. The first is the uptake of *creative industries* policy discourses. While the creative industries idea was first developed in the United Kingdom, and has been elaborated upon in the academic sphere in Western Europe and places such as Australia (Flew, 2012b, pp. 34–37, 50–52), it has been in East Asia where there have been the strongest policy commitments made. Lee and Lim (2014) have argued that the 2000s saw a shift in cultural policy concerns in East Asian nations towards engagement with the knowledge economy and the creative industries, as growing competition in manufacturing-based developing economies – most notably from China – required a focus on knowledge, skills, innovation and creativity as a way of repositioning their increasingly post-industrial economies. At the same time, China has moved rapidly to identify the economic benefits of culture and to promote its arts, media, design and digital content industries, in what are variously termed 'cultural creative industries' and 'digital creative industries' strategies (Keane, 2013, pp. 36–43). Lee and Lim note that 'these countries are taking a top-down and hands-on approach to the development of their creative economy, regardless of how much bottom up entrepreneurialism is emphasized in the (Western) theory of creative industries' (2014, p. 10).

The second area where the question of state capacities is particularly relevant is that of copyright and intellectual property. The relationship of copyright to the media and creative industries has been the subject of recurring debates. On the one hand, creative industries are often defined as copyright industries, where the nexus between the capacity to generate creativity and new ideas and to be able to commercially exploit this intellectual property for financial gain is taken to be the distinctive difference between the creative industries and creative practice per se (e.g. Howkins, 2001). At the same time, the impact of the internet and digital media technologies has clearly been highly disruptive to traditional media and copyright-based industries, and many analysts and policy makers have concluded that overall economic well-being would be enhanced by extending 'fair use' provisions and developing alternative rights-handling arrangements as an alternative to the criminalization of copyright infringement (ALRC, 2013; Bakhshi *et al.*, 2013; Flew, 2015). These issues are of particular importance in the 'Global South', where the perception exists that copyright is a mechanism for transferring wealth from lower-income consumers in the developing world to Western copyright-based media conglomerates, enforced through treaties such as the Trade-Related Aspects of Intellectual Property Rights (TRIPS) agreement and international institutions dominated by the 'Global North', such as the World Trade Organization (WTO) and the World Intellectual Property Organization (WIPO) (Drahos & Braithwaite, 2002). In the context of such unequal power relations, illegal copying of media content using digital technologies may be seen less as piracy and more as a 'power of the weak' to resist economic domination through street-level entrepreneurship in the informal media economy (Lobato, 2012; Lobato & Thomas, 2014). Gray (2011) observed that Steven Seagal movies in Malawi could not be said to have been 'pirated' from Fox Studios as the distributor, as these and other Hollywood films found their way to Malawian video stores and local video houses by a highly circuitous and contingent route.

The problem is that rampant copyright piracy acts as a blockage to the development of media and creative industries in the developing world, by preventing the often fledgling new businesses from being able to generate a revenue stream for their content that is commensurate with the popularity of their work. In the case of the thriving Nigerian film industry ('Nollywood'), Lobato (2012, p. 60) has observed the need to go beyond 'informal globalization' of low-budget video-based content, towards being able to develop a sustainable local film industry that can 'shed its informal skin and become a mature business with global reach … the aim is to create bigger budget, conventionally funded movies, and to integrate the rough-and-ready video industries into the world of formal finance and banking'. Similar accounts have been given with the music industry in Africa (Pratt, 2008) and the Caribbean (James, 2008), where large-scale piracy subverts development of a sustainable and economically viable local music industry that can support local artists, denies local artists access to a revenue stream outside of the live performance circuit and discourages them from staying in their own country, leading to an exodus of creative talent and the loss of local capacity to further develop the sector. As international Agencies such as UNCTAD are identifying the opportunity to develop the creative economy in developing nations through 'industrial development strategies [that] can exploit the dynamism of the creative industries in generating growth in output, exports and employment' (UNCTAD, 2010, pp. 173–174), the legal, institutional and policy frameworks for media in these countries become an increasingly important developmental variable.

Globalization and the 'declining state' thesis

As we have noted throughout this book, a recurring feature of debates about globalization is that it has weakened the power of nation-states. It is generally observed that globalization is not the only factor behind the perceived crises of the contemporary nation-state – the influence of political ideologies such as neoliberalism is often also cited as an additional, and often complementary, factor – but a strong underlying premise of a significant part of the globalization literature is:

> A globalized world involves a dramatic power shift: one that restricts the scope for national institutions, actors, and policies while elevating the interests and preferences of non-national actors in a zero-sum logic … globalization has by and large become synonymous with state power erosion. (Weiss, 1999, p. 64)

Many examples can be cited of such arguments. We have considered the 'Golden Straitjacket' argument of Thomas Friedman (2001), where governments inevitably cede sovereignty in order to gain the benefits of prosperity, as well as the arguments of Marxists such as Hardt and Negri (2000) and world-systems theorists such as Leslie Sklair (2002) that real power in the world now resides with a small transnational elite. The political theorist Bob Jessop referred to a 'de-nationalization of the state', and a '"hollowing out" of the national state apparatus with old and new state capacities being reorganised territorially and functionally' (Jessop, 2000, p. 75). Influential theorists of globalization have argued that the power of nation-states is in decline. Anthony Giddens argued that 'nations lose some of the economic power they once had' in the wake of globalization, and become '"shell institutions" … that have become inadequate to the tasks they are called upon to perform' (Giddens, 2002, pp. 42, 44). Manuel Castells (2009, p. 19) proposed that 'under the conditions of multi-layered globalization, *the state becomes just a node (however important) of a particular network* … that overlaps with other significant networks in the construction of social practice' (emphasis added). Philip Howard has observed that Castells has consistently argued that 'a significant amount of economic, political, and cultural power has actually moved from the state to the media system', and that in the contemporary network society 'the power residing in media networks is stronger than that residing in states' (Howard, 2011, p. 20). Ulrich Beck argued that in an age of economic and cultural globalization, which governs the decline in nation-state power:

> Those who play only the national card in the global meta-game will lose. What is needed is a complete change in perspective ... the counter-power of states develops as they become transnationalized and cosmopolitanized. Only if states succeed in catching up with mobile capital and redefining and reorganizing their positions of power ... can the decline in state power and authority be halted internationally, indeed turned into its very opposite. (Beck, 2005, p. 9)

With regards to media globalization and its impact on national media policies, four propositions typically underpin the 'disappearing state' thesis.

1. *Economic globalization has seen an overall decline in the power and capacities of nation-states, as power has shifted to the global level and – to a lesser degree – the local level.*

The various authors cited above adhere to a version of this argument, which is a variant of the observation made by sociologist Daniel Bell in 1987 that 'the nation-state is becoming too small for the big problems of life, and too big for the small problems of life' (Bell, 1987, p. 14). To the extent that this is true, the question is: to what extent has the weakening of the power of nation-states been caused by economic globalization, i.e. is the relationship between the two a 'zero-sum' one? The data on foreign direct investment cited in Chapter 5 showed a continuous growth in foreign direct investment (FDI) from the early 1980s to 2007, and a dipping off thereafter. This would suggest that one long-term impact of the 2008 Global Financial Crisis may have been to slow FDI around the world. Insofar as developments such as the election of Donald Trump as US President in 2016 on a protectionist platform may herald a new era of trade wars and economic nationalism, then it could be that the period from the 1980s to 2008 can be understood as a particular historical interlude, rather than a decisive qualitative shift in global capitalism. This has been the argument of Hirst *et al.* (2009), who have proposed that economic globalization is more cyclical and wave-like in its nature, i.e. the 'first wave' of globalization, from 1870 to 1914, was followed by a period of retreat towards economic nationalism between 1914 and 1945.[3] More generally, the argument is that 'the level of integration, interdependence, openness ... of national economies in the present era is not unprecedented', and to 'register a certain skepticism over whether we have entered a radically new phase in the internationalization of economic activity' (Hirst *et al.*, 2009, p. 72).

The 'zero-sum' argument also typically posits the nation-state as powerless, or at least highly restricted, in its capacity to deal with transnational corporations and other globalizing forces. Even theorists of the 'developmental state', such as Evans, acknowledge that 'global capital has ... less reason to support devoting resources to building strong state apparatuses and pursuing national projects of capability expansion than national capital' (Evans, 2014, p. 236). But we do need to be careful not to overstate the novelty of such constraints. As early as 1976, the IMF intervened in the governing of the United Kingdom and Italy, as the pattern of deficit financing their governments were pursuing led to capital outflows and a crisis for their national currencies. IMF interventions in Latin American nations such as Mexico, Brazil and Argentina were also very much a feature of the 1980s and 1990s. Weiss (1997) notes that the international expansion of firms has in many instances been facilitated by national governments, in order to boost overall economic competitiveness and develop 'national champions' in global markets.

Another point is that, characteristically, the dominant form of expansion tends in the first instance to be regional: European companies expanding their operations in the European Union (EU) region, or companies in countries such as Japan, China, South Korea, Taiwan and Singapore expanding East Asian operations. To the extent that nation-states are disadvantaged or disempowered in the context of economic globalization, there is a need to look closely at questions of state capacity (size of national economy, nature of state bureaucracy, etc.) and dominant political ideologies (neoliberal, developmental, nationalist, populist, etc.) within those nations. Weiss has argued that:

> because domestic state capacities differ, so the ability to exploit the opportunities of international economic change – rather than simply succumb to its pressures – will be much more marked in some countries than in others ... the changes in process in different national systems are those of adaptation rather than of convergence on a single neoliberal model. (1997, p. 26)

2. *Global media corporations have promoted political ideologies of neoliberalism that have been deliberately used to weaken the powers of nation-states to regulate them.*

The argument that global media corporations have played a particularly important role in promoting neoliberal ideologies around the world, and hence weakening both the capacity and the likelihood of nation-states to regulate their activities, has been a staple of the critical political economy approach to global media. McChesney and Schiller argued that 'underlying the new communication technology has been a political force – the shift to neoliberal orthodoxy, which relaxed or eliminated barriers to commercial exploitation of media, foreign investment in communication systems, and concentrated media ownership' (2003, p. 6). In a similar vein, Miller *et al.* (2001, p. 4) argued that 'shifts towards a neo-liberal, multinational invest- ment climate ... have reinforced global Hollywood's strategic power over NICL [new international division of cultural labour]', while Sklair (2002) saw global media as being at the core of the cultural-ideology of global consumer- ism that reproduced the power of the transnational capitalist class.

More detailed consideration of such questions comes up against the big problem of identifying what exactly neoliberalism is. Is it primarily an analytical or a rhetorical concept? Is it essentially a synonym for capitalism and its dominant ideology, or does it refer to a distinctive mode of governing in the late twentieth/early twenty-first century? Is it essentially a pejorative term for things a particular author may disagree with, or does it refer to a coherent body of intellectual work? Springer *et al.* (2016) have proposed a minimal definition of neoliberalism as 'referring to the new political, economic, and social arrangements within society that emphasize market relations, re-tasking the role of the state, and individual responsibility ... neoliberalism is broadly defined as the extension of competitive markets into all areas of life' (p. 2). But even these authors, having produced a collec- tion of 53 essays on the subject, are forced to conclude that neoliberalism has become 'an adjective that can be added to almost anything', and 'risks ending up as some sort of totalizing rhetorical signifier or trope, rather than a concept we can use to reflect the specificity and particularity of human social life' (p. 11).

A bigger problem with neoliberalism is that, like globalization, it becomes a concept that assumes a much greater degree of institutional and policy homogeneity among nation-states than is in fact the case. There are some obvious exceptions to the claim that governments around the world have become increasingly neoliberal. China under the Communist Party led by Xi Jinping and Russia under Vladimir Putin's leadership would seem to be two obvious – and large – exceptions to the rule.[4] The developmental states of East Asia continue to provide an important point of contrast: even if they increasingly use market-conforming policy measures to promote interna- tional competitiveness, they still typically do so under a far greater degree of state direction than is found in the Anglo-American nations that are consid- ered to be the intellectual progenitors of neoliberal ideas (Weiss, 2003; Evans,

2014). Among the OECD (Organisation for Economic Co-operation and Development) nations, there has not been any notable tendency towards a reduced level of public expenditure as a percentage of GDP (Flew, 2014a), nor has there been a notable tendency towards policy convergence around identifiably 'neoliberal' ideas, or a 'race to the bottom' in abandoning either regulatory standards or levels of public welfare state provision (Drezner, 2001; Knill, 2005).

This is not to deny that a neoliberal policy regime can be adopted. It is rather to note, as Rodrik (2011, pp. 184–201) does, that when a strongly neoliberal or 'hyper-globalist' approach to policy has been adopted, as with Argentina and Russia in the first half of the 1990s, they have tended to come up very quickly against the limits of domestic politics to the imposition of a policy agenda seen to be significantly at odds with long-established formal and informal institutions and norms. Neoliberalism remains a largely ideational construct, not well grounded in policy or institutional norms, and resting upon what Barnett (2010, p. 275) describes as 'a pre-constructed normative framing of ... conceptual and moral binaries: market versus state; public versus private; consumer versus citizen ... self-interested egoism versus other-regarding altruism'. The possibility that policy makers typically engage across both sides of these divides, as they do in navigating the global and the local or national, is ruled out by virtue of the *a priori* ideological divides that have constructed the critical perspective on neoliberalism.

3. *The globally networked nature of the internet makes media regulation through national laws and policies less feasible, and the focus of governance needs to shift from national to supranational institutions.*

The rise of the global internet, and the convergence between internet-based digital networks and traditional media platforms, presents a raft of challenges for traditional forms of media policy (Flew, 2014a). The blurring of the relationship between media devices, platforms, services and content makes it increasingly difficult to retro-fit existing laws and regulations, developed for broadcasting, onto internet-based media. There is the vexing question of whether the major digital and social media platform providers are media companies, and hence subject to media-specific laws, as well as questions of parity between established and new media, and the differential treatment of similar media content across different platforms. Also, given that most of the content on Facebook, Twitter and other social media platforms has been generated by users themselves, to what extent is such content 'speech', and hence constitutionally protected in many parts of the world, as distinct from 'media content'?

At the same time, the internet is regulated, and is arguably becoming more regulated over time. Freedom House (2016) estimates that at least 64 per cent of the world's online user population are using the internet in countries where there is some form of content filtering or blocks placed on social media platforms by governments. At the same time, laws governing the internet are not purely negative in their impacts. The *Marco Civil da Internet*, passed by the Brazilian government in 2014, sought to safeguard net neutrality and provide privacy protections for Brazilian citizens using US-based social media platforms (Flew & Waisbord, 2015). Internet governance has evolved around a complex mix of international agreements and national regulations, and public regulation and industry self-regulation (DiNardis, 2013). But the applicability of international norms and agreements remains very much dependent upon local regulations and, as with other fields of law and regulation, there has not been a wholesale transfer of sovereign powers from nation-states to international institutions.

4. *Globally networked media have rendered media consumption patterns more global and cosmopolitan, rather than being tied to national media systems and nation-states.*

From a critical globalization perspective, Couldry and Hepp (2009) and Volkmer (2015) have questioned whether core concepts of media studies such as media cultures and the public sphere need to move outside of the 'container thinking' associated with a 'national-territorial frame' (Couldry & Hepp, 2009, pp. 33, 34), and register that media engagements in multicultural societies are increasingly transnational, transcultural, and not confined within the boundaries of nation-state-based media systems and logics. The growing porosity of nation-state boundaries, the globalization of communications flows, the significance of diasporic populations and the rise of non-state actors are all central features of contemporary global media. Certainly the rise of a parastatal entity such as ISIS would have been impossible without the global internet as a tool for recruitment of supporters. But the files leaked by Edward Snowden of the activities of the US National Security Agency (NSA) also remind us that while online content may flow internationally, the platforms on which it is hosted are territorially based, and are potentially subject to the intervention of nation-state agencies.

More generally, the literature on media consumption has consistently indicated that audience preferences have typically been strongly linked to locally produced material. This has been discussed with regards to broadcasting (Straubhaar, 2007; Xu *et al.*, 2013; Sparks, 2016), where preferences for local content or that from culturally proximate nations is an important counterpoint to claims about US-centric media and cultural imperialism. With regards to online content, more detailed studies await, but Taneja and Wu found that patterns of online content linking and Twitter links 'indicate Web users' tendency to show a predisposition toward local content' (2014, p. 299) as well as that from culturally proximate nations and regions.

Soft power and international broadcasting

One feature of global media in the 2000s and 2010s was a significant expansion in the operations of international broadcasting. Pioneers such as BBC World and America's CNN were joined by new satellite news services such as Al-Jazeera (based in Qatar), Arirang (South Korea), Australia Plus (Australia), Channel News Asia (Singapore), China Global Television Network (China), France24 (France), NDTV (India), Press TV (Iran), RT (Russia) and teleSUR (Venezuela). There was also significant expansion of the international operations of long-established public broadcasters such as Deutsche Welle (Germany) and NHK World (Japan). These global news channels frequently broadcast in multiple languages, with Arabic, English and Spanish being particularly common.

Most of these channels are state-funded, with the exceptions of CNN, NDTV and a few others, although many also carry commercials (in the case of BBC World, it carries commercials even though these are prohibited on the UK-based BBC channels). Sparks (2016, p. 63) makes the point that 'the explosion of international broadcast news in the last decade or so ... has been almost entirely the result of state action designed, directly or indirectly, to promote state objectives'. Of particular importance has been the idea that international broadcasters can be instruments of national *soft power* in the world. The Harvard University international relations theorist Joseph S. Nye defined soft power as 'the ability to get what you want through attraction rather than coercion or payments' (Nye, 2004, p. x), and the associated 'ability to shape the preferences of others' (p. 5).

Soft power initiatives are an important element of a nation's *public diplomacy*, or how a nation engages and communicates with foreign publics and promotes its national interests in international arenas by projecting a combination of its culture, political values and foreign policy objectives. Cultural diplomacy, as a subset of public diplomacy, involves 'a country's policy to facilitate the export of examples of its culture' in order to 'manage the international environment through making its cultural resources and achievements known overseas and/or facilitating cultural transmission abroad' (Cull, 2008, p. 33). Holden (2013) has argued that cultural diplomacy has a hierarchy of strategic goals, from increasing familiarity and awareness of a county to influencing behaviour and 'getting companies to invest, encouraging public support for your country's positions and convincing politicians to turn to it as an ally' (p. 22). Price (2003, p. 53) has described international broadcasting as an 'elegant term for ... the use of electronic media by one society to shape the opinion of the people and leaders of another'.

Among the most high-profile initiatives in international broadcasting have been the international expansion of China's CCTV (which became China Global Television Network in 2017) and the creation of RT (formerly Russia Today) by the Russian government in 2005. Chinese political leaders have enthusiastically engaged with soft power ideas since the 1990s (Flew, 2016c). Xi Jinping promised in a 2014 speech to 'strengthen our cultural soft power ... [and] disseminate the values of modern China ... so as to make our culture known through international communication and dissemination' (Xi, 2015, p. 179). Developing new foreign language services for China Central Television (CCTV), China Radio International (CRI) and the Xinhua News Agency, and investing heavily in the international expansion of these services have been an important part of China's 'soft power offensive', along with the hosting of major international events, development of film co-productions, and the international expansion of Confucius Institutes in universities around the world (Xin, 2012; Hartig, 2015). Rawnsley (2015) observed that while communication is at the heart of China's policy-making apparatus, and can thus respond quickly to new public diplomacy initiatives, this points to a recurring difficulty for Chinese international broadcasting, as it is seen to be embedded at the heart of the Chinese party-state and hence unable to gain the prestige that accrues to more established international broadcasters such as the BBC.[5]

Russia Today (now RT) was launched in 2005 to reach audiences outside of the Russian Federation. It has grown significantly since then, and has developed offshoots, such as the online Sputnik News. It was described at its launch by Russian President Vladimir Putin as an explicit alternative to CNN and the BBC, aiming to 'try to break the Anglo-Saxon monopoly on the global information streams' (Fisher, 2013). Its relationship to Russian soft power and foreign policy goals has often been quite explicit: Putin described it as an instrument of soft power in 2012, which he defined as being 'all about promoting one's interests and policies through persuasion and creating a positive perception of one's country, based not just on its material achievements but also its spiritual and intellectual heritage' (quoted in Rawnsley, 2015, p. 279). RT is distinctive in the international broadcasting space: whereas for most international broadcasters 'credibility (and therefore ... success) hinges on providing a professional and trustworthy news service' (Rawnsley, 2015, p. 274), RT has explicitly focused its global coverage on the gap between the rhetorical and political realities of major Western powers, most notably the US but also the European Union. It has been criticized as a propaganda tool of the Putin government and a major propagator of 'fake news' on the internet, and in 2017 was at the centre of a report prepared by the US Director of National Intelligence, Homeland Security and the CIA alleging Russian interference in the 2016 US Presidential election to assist Republican candidate Donald Trump.

The Russian and Chinese cases draw attention to some of the challenges presented with the use of international broadcasting services as instruments of cultural diplomacy and soft power. One is the question of credibility, and whether foreign audiences view such services as sufficiently distant from the governments that fund their operations. Joseph Nye has himself been highly critical of soft power strategies in countries such as Russia and China, arguing that they 'don't get' that soft power has its roots in a vibrant civil society and an attractive political culture, and is therefore incompatible with authoritarian regimes (Nye, 2013). Rawnsley (2015) has noted the considerable gap that exists between the potential audience size projected for such services and the actual audiences, which would be well below 1 per cent of the potential audience in nations to which they broadcast (cf. Sparks, 2016). At the same time, the fact that national governments are prepared to significantly invest in such international broadcasting services, and extend their operations into the online space, is a marker of their preparedness to engage actively with media globalization in order to enhance political, economic and cultural power in pursuit of strategic national objectives.

Cosmopolitanism, civil society and the internet

The rise of globalization theories in the 1990s and 2000s is related to the take-off and mass popularization of the internet over the same period. Giddens (2002, p. 37) argued that 'globalization is ... influenced above all by developments in systems of communication'. Castells proposed that the internet and digital networks were at the forefront of a new form of informational capitalism, where 'the core processes of knowledge generation, economic productivity, political/military power and media communication are already deeply transformed by the informational paradigm, and are connected to the global networks of wealth, power, and symbols working under such a logic' (1996, p. 21).

The relationship between the internet and digital media and new forms of politics and identity is, however, a complex one, and requires consideration of three other issues. The first is that of *cosmopolitanism* and the possibility of 'post-national' political identities. The proposition that one can, and should, be a 'citizen of the world' has a long history in modern philosophy, with Immanuel Kant's notion that all rational beings are members in a single moral community being one example, and the influence of discourses of inalienable human rights that informed the American and – particularly – the French Revolutions of the late eighteenth century being practical applications of cosmopolitan ideals (Kleingeld & Brown, 2013). Contemporary discourses around human rights, humanitarian disasters and environmental degradation have also acted as triggers to cosmopolitan identities, as they present ethical, moral and political challenges that clearly transcend national boundaries. Activist movements related to socialism, feminism, LGBT rights, religious freedoms and other issues have also been underpinned by 'partial cosmopolitanism' (Scholte, 2005, p. 220), insofar as the registering of a non-territorial identity as a political force requires a politics of recognition that by its nature must cross national boundaries (Fraser, 2007). The development of the internet also triggers its own cosmopolitan impulses as: it enables the formation of networks and shared identities across territorial boundaries; access to the internet can in itself be presented as a human rights issue; and it is a global public good, insofar as its effective operation requires the cooperation of national governments and a shared commitment to observe rules and norms and invest in relevant resources such as communications infrastructure (Seo, 2016).

The rise of *global civil society* has also been central to contemporary theories of globalization. Kaldor (2003) observes that the term 'civil society' has a number of possible definitions, ranging from a broad notion of those parts of society that were between the state and the family/household – which Jürgen Habermas (1974; cf. Thompson, 1990, pp. 110–114) broadly equates with the *public sphere* – to a more specific and activist-oriented definition, which refers to 'active citizenship, to growing self-organization outside formal political circles, and expanded space in which individual citizens can influence the conditions in which they live both directly through self-organization and through political pressure' (Kaldor, 2003, p. 8). In this latter definition, an expanded role for civil society is equated with a broadening of democracy. Two historical events, both of which preceded the internet, were particularly important in generating a renewed interest in the emancipatory possibilities of civil society. The first was the end of the Soviet Union and the fall of the communist one-party states of Eastern Europe: this was commonly equated with the self-organization of citizens prepared to challenge rule by authoritarian states, with innovative, bottom-up uses of communications media playing a critical role (Keane, 1988, 2005). Second, the formal establishment of the European Union in 1990 was seen as presenting the possibility of something more than a regional economic bloc, towards what Beck (2005, p. 96) termed a 'cosmopolitan union of states'. But it was argued that this could only occur if the governmental structures of both the EU and its member states were subject to ongoing scrutiny, challenge and contestation from the institutions of civil society. Global civil society was thus seen as offering 'possibilities for emancipation on a global scale', and of '"civilizing" or democratizing globalization [and] about the process through which groups, movements and individuals can demand a global rule of law, global justice and global empowerment' (Kaldor, 2003, p. 12).

The affordances of the internet and digital media have enabled new forms of social organization on the part of civil society and social movements. Lievrouw (2011) has observed the rise of new social movements with a preference for decentralized network organization over top-down collective action, combined with innovative uses of digital media and a distrust of mainstream communication channels. Bennett and Segerberg (2012) have referred to these global trends as the rise of a *logic of connective action*, which they contrast the long-established concept of a *logic of collective action*, which considers the ways in which political movements develop institutional forms to represent the interests of individuals and groups to achieve common goals. By way of contrast, connective action networks are 'typically far more individualized and technologically organized' (Bennett & Segerberg, 2012, p. 750), building upon a more 'affective politics' (Papacharissi, 2015) and drawing upon digital media to reduce the costs of enabling participating and collectively organizing. These 'action networks' can scale up rapidly 'through the combination of easily spreadable personal action frames and digital technology enabling such communication. This invites analytical attention to the network as an organizational structure in itself' (Bennett & Segerberg, 2012, pp. 752–753).

Mansell and Raboy (2011) observe that international communications policy coordination has a long history, going back as far as the International Telegraph Convention signed in Paris in 1865, and there has been inter-governmental coordination of radiofrequency spectrum going back to the 1920s. Article 19 of the United Nations (1948) Universal Declaration of Human Rights stated that:

Everyone has the right to freedom of opinion and expression; this right includes freedom to hold opinions without interference and to seek, receive and impart information and ideas through any media and regardless of frontiers.

In the 1970s, developing nations used UNESCO forums to critique international inequalities and power asymmetries in global information and communication, leading to demands for a New World Information and Communication Order (NWICO) (MacBride, 1980; Nordenstreng, 2012).

By contrast, the development of a Global Information Infrastructure (GII), driven by the Clinton administration in the 1990s to promote the global internet, was very much driven by the rich nations of the 'Global North', and sought to maximize market opportunities for the emerging global ICT giants (Schiller, 2000; Flew & McElhinney, 2006). Mansell and Raboy (2011, p. 7) described the GII and information society policies as:

> harbingers both of an emerging global regulatory system and of a future system of world governance ... characterized by the open leadership of a powerful group of countries, allied with the leading transnational companies ... and absent any participation, even nominal, of civil society nongovernmental actors.

In contrast to the largely state-led NWICO process and the corporate-driven GII, civil society organizations have played a key role in forums for global media and communications policy (GCMP) that have been developing over the 2000s. Padovani and Raboy (2010, p. 156; cf. Raboy, 2002) have identified the 'complex ecology of interdependent structures ... [and] vast array of formal and informal mechanisms working across a multiplicity of sites' as including the following:

1. *Global organizations*, such as those which have been traditionally a part of the United Nations structures, such as UNESCO and the International Telecommunications Union (ITU), as well as newer, more commercially focused entities such as the WTO and the WIPO;
2. *Multilateral exclusive 'clubs'*, such as the OECD and the Group of Eight (G8), which are collective groupings of the world's most powerful nations;
3. *Regional multistate groupings*, such as the EU and the Asia Pacific Economic Cooperation (APEC) group, as well as multilateral trade agreements such as the North American Free Trade Agreement (NAFTA) between the United States, Canada and Mexico;
4. *Transnational private sector organizations* which have gained recognition in official forums, including the Global Business Dialogue for e-commerce (GBDe) and the International Intellectual Property Alliance;
5. *Transnational civil society organizations*, or *INGOs*, such as the World Association of Community Radio Broadcasters (AMARC), Vidéazimut (film and video), the Association for Progressive Communication, the World Association for Christian Communication and Computer Professionals for Social Responsibility;
6. *'Transversal' regulatory sites* (Raboy, 2002, p. 8) which operate across institutional and categorical jurisdictions, such as the Internet Corporation

for Assigned Names and Numbers (ICANN), which is a loose federation of parties – principally business interests – that regulates online domain-name registration.

The resulting 'multistakeholderism' (Raboy, 2007, p. 345) was critical to the World Summit on the Information Society (WSIS) forums, held in Geneva in 2003 and Tunis in 2005. It was also important to the UNESCO Convention on the Protection and Promotion of the Diversity of Cultural Expressions, which came into effect in 2007, and the Internet Governance Forum (IGF), established in 2006. Padovani and Raboy (2010, p. 153). identify these new forms of civil society and INGO engagement as part of a 'shift from vertical, top-down and state-based modes of regulation to horizontal arrangements, while at the same time, governing processes have become more permeable to interventions from a plurality of players with stakes in media and communication'. For civil society organizations more generally, they have 'identified the media as essential to the development of a democratic public sphere ... as progressive politics come to be redefined in keeping with the new political challenges of globalization' (Raboy, 2007, p. 344).

The limits of cosmopolitanism and civil society

Noting the achievements of multilateral forums related to media and communications policy, and to internet governance, also draws attention to their limitations. While the WSIS can be interpreted as 'a laboratory experimenting with a new distribution of power involving emerging as well as established social forces' (Raboy, 2004, p. 355), it was also the case that many of the civil society organizations that participated in WSIS were deeply dissatisfied with its outcomes. The Civil Society Declaration to the WSIS (Civil Society WSIS, 2003) argued that communication rights could only be made meaningful if they were connected to questions of social justice on both a local and a global scale, and that this required the transfer of resources to the least developed nations, and broadening access to ICTs among the most marginalized people (e.g. people such as refugees, those displaced by wars and asylum seekers).

In a manner similar to the NWICO debates and the critiques of modernization theories, they were critical of what they saw as undue faith in technological solutions to social, cultural and political problems, such as the ICTs for Development agenda. Pickard (2007) critiqued the multi-stakeholder framework as allowing corporate interests to co-opt civil society organizations into deregulatory agendas. Proposals to link communication rights to human rights have also come up against the opposition of particular member states, such as China, Saudi Arabia, Iran and Russia, to proposals to guarantee freedoms of expression, association and information, as well as the right to privacy. At the same time, proposals by nations such as Brazil, India and South Africa for greater United Nations oversight of ICANN, to make it less of a US-based technologists' club, have been successfully blocked by the United States and its allies, with the strong lobbying of leading technology companies such as Google, despite recommendations to this effect coming out of the WSIS (Take, 2012).

Examples of the limits of multilateral forums such as WSIS and the IGF could be multiplied, but they point to a similar issue, which is that the power of such forums arises from the preparedness of powerful national governments to cede decision-making responsibilities to them, and that there is always the scope to revoke such power. Raboy (2007, p. 346) acknowledges that there is a 'blindspot regarding how "international" or "global" these debates really are, given the weak and often heavily skewed participation of both government and non-governmental actors from the South'. But the problems run deeper, in that the legitimacy of such multilateral forums is intimately tied to the preparedness of nation-state governments to acknowledge their right to make binding decisions, and to be prepared to implement policies that arise from such decision-making processes.

It is therefore surely premature to argue, as Mansell and Raboy (2011, p. 4) do, that 'the arena [of media and communications policy] has shifted from the nation-state to the global'. Moreover, the likelihood of such a shift may have been diminishing over time, rather than increasing. Implicit in the assumptions around GCMP, whether supportive or critical, is the likelihood of a degree of policy convergence among nation-states around certain norms associated with global media platforms and networks such as the internet. But the two major nations in terms of the number of internet users – China and the United States – have fundamentally different norms and expectations around matters such as the role of the state vis-à-vis private companies, the right to privacy and freedom of information, the extent to which communications infrastructure should be driven by the market and private investors, and much more. Just as there is strong evidence that national broadcast media systems continue to be primarily shaped by national cultures and nation-state policies and regulations (Pertierra & Turner, 2013; Turner, 2015), it would also appear to be premature to associate the development of the internet with the decline of nation-state regulation and national identities, and the rise of cosmopolitan identities and global civil society to fill the political vacuum.

Notes

1   The Peace of Westphalia was enacted in Europe in 1648, and marked the end of 80 years of religiously inspired wars. It required governments to cease supporting co-religionists abroad in conflicts with their own states, thereby

placing matters such as religious freedom within the sovereign domain of individual states. It established the principles that the sovereignty of states could be guaranteed through diplomatic agreements, meaning that norms were established against interference in another state's domestic political affairs.

2   This has also been referred to as the 'flying geese' model of regional development (Ozawa, 2009). Where one nation in the East Asian region takes a lead in its development strategy, this has positive developments for other nations in expanding markets, but also provides lessons about institutional frameworks that best facilitate economic growth and transformation. This means that a premium is placed upon policy makers in East Asia learning from the successful strategies of other nations. The metaphor refers to how geese fly in formation, with each goose taking turns in leading the flock in flight.

3   There are also issues with the use of aggregate FDI data as a proxy for economic globalization. A very large proportion of FDI occurs in the extractive industries such as mining, agriculture and energy, and these companies are typically also the most transnational in terms of the percentage of assets held outside of their national base. But such corporations have always been transnational by the nature of their business operations, which require them to identify and extract resources from around the globe. The claim that the corporations have become more transnational in their operations rests upon developments in manufacturing and services, and here the evidence of global expansion exists, but is less rapid than is sometimes assumed, particularly in services. See Glyn & Sutcliffe, 1999; Dicken, 2003 for an elaboration of these arguments.

4   Indeed, in a 'Communiqué on the Current State of the Ideological Sphere' circulated by the Communist Party of China (CCP) in late 2013 (known in the West as Document 9), neoliberalism was identified as a 'false ideological tendency' against which CCP members were required to struggle, alongside Western constitutional democracy, promotion of civil society, universal values, Western styles of journalism, and 'historical nihilism', or a disregard for China's history and the central role of the CCP in it (ChinaFile, 2015).

5   In 2017 CCTV International became the China Global Television Network (CGTN). This rebranding gave a strong focus to multi-platform delivery, and drew upon a network of journalists from over 70 countries. It described its mission as being to 'cover the whole globe, reporting news from a Chinese perspective. Our mission is to create a better understanding of international events across the world, bridging continents and bringing a more balanced view to global news reporting'. Notably, it has its headquarters in the CCTV building in Chaoyang, Beijing, so it remains strongly connected to the CCTV network.

CHAPTER 8

Conclusion

A new nationalism?

There is a pervasive sense that accounts of globalization, and with them global media, may be at a crossroads. It has been argued in this book that the impact of changes associated with global media, from access to a greater diversity of viewpoints to online activism to the emergence of global production networks for media content, have been profound, and that the global media environment of the twenty-first century differs in major ways from that of twentieth century mass media. At the same time, there is an awareness that the globality of media, and the universalism of some of the trends identified, is frequently overstated. Just as national audiences tended to prefer their own broadcast content on television, so too does it appear that online communities prefer to go to nation-specific information content in key areas such as news. While global production networks are increasingly pervasive in the production of digital media content, local and national governments nonetheless seek to develop media capitals that offer location-based advantages to media companies, while promoting their 'national champions' in global media markets where necessary. The rise of 'soft power' discourses has seen nation-states increasingly investing in the international distribution of media content, so as to help frame global interpretations of their own nations and to shape their national 'brand' identity in global media culture. While the internet and the dominant digital and social media platforms are considerably more deterritorialized than traditional national broadcasters, they can be and are subject to nation-state regulations, as well as forms of supranational governance through institutions whose ultimate legitimacy rests upon maintaining the support and confidence of key national governments.

But 2016 was a year that presented its own challenges to the dominant narratives around media globalization, and globalization more generally. On 23 June 2016, voters in the United Kingdom narrowly elected to leave the European Union in the so-called 'Brexit' referendum, thus overturning over 40 years of consensus among the major political parties, as well as among employer organizations and trade unions, about British membership of the European Union being in its own national interest. Even more dramatically, on 8 November 2016 Donald Trump was elected the 45th President of the United States, on a populist and explicitly nationalist platform to 'Make America Great Again'. One of Trump's first acts as president was to withdraw from the Trans-Pacific Partnership that had been led by the Obama Administration and involved 12 Pacific Rim nations. Trump also promised to make migration to the United States more difficult for people of selected – predominantly Muslim – nations, and to build a wall to prevent people entering the US illegally from Mexico. In a speech to the Conservative Political Action Committee on 25 February 2017, Trump highlighted the extent to which he saw his presidency as being about serving national interests, rather than advancing global priorities:

> Global cooperation, dealing with other countries, getting along with other countries is good, it's very important. But there is no such thing as a global anthem, a global currency or a global flag. This is the United States of America that I'm representing. I'm not representing the globe, I'm representing your country. (Trump, 2017)

The return to a populist nationalism was by no means a phenomenon peculiar to the English-speaking world. In France, Marine Le Pen's *Front National* regularly attracts at least 20 per cent of the national vote on a platform that is both anti-globalist and anti-Muslim, with Geert Wilders' Party for Freedom in the Netherlands, the Freedom Party in Austria, the *Alternative für Deutschland* in Germany and other parties in Europe have had electoral success with comparable nationalist and 'Eurosceptic' political positions. Leaders such as Viktor Orbán in Hungary, Radosław Kaczyński in Poland and Vladimir Putin in Russia have also been associated with a strong anti-globalist nationalism. This may yet be a fringe phenomenon of the so-called 'alt-right', whose historical moment may pass with a few adverse electoral results or changes in international affairs. But populist nationalism became more politically mainstream in the 2010s. To take one example, the UK Prime Minister Theresa May said in her October 2016 address to the Conservative Party conference that 'if you believe you're a citizen of the world, you're a citizen of nowhere. You don't understand what the very word "citizenship" means' (May, 2016).

Such developments mean that the backdrop for considering approaches to global media has shifted sharply in recent years. One could contrast Trump's 'America First' rhetoric, for instance, with statements made by US Vice-President Al Gore in launching the Global Information Infrastructure initiative at the ITU in Buenos Aires in 1994, where he proposed that the global internet 'can at last create a planetary information network that transmits messages and images with the speed of light from the largest city to the smallest village on every continent', and that 'from these connections we will derive robust and sustainable economic progress, strong democracies, better solutions to global and local environmental challenges, improved health care, and – ultimately – a greater sense of shared stewardship of our small planet' (Gore, 1994). It also differs from the assumptions that underpinned supranational institutions such as the World Trade Organization, whose first President, Renato Ruggiero, was confident that 'globalization, by which I mean a multiplicity of interlocking economic relationships among national economies, is a natural outgrowth of technological advances in communications and transport' (Ruggiero, 1998).

It is too early to say that globalization is in retreat. It is very clear that the Trump administration remains as committed as its predecessors to the projection of US military force globally, so it is not a turn to isolationism. It is also now apparent that China is positioning itself to be a leading advocate of globalization and free trade. Chinese President Xi Jinping took the opportunity provided by the World Economic Forum in Davos in January 2017 to reinforce China's endorsement of economic globalization and international institutions that support free trade, arguing that:

> Whether you like it or not, the global economy is the big ocean that you cannot escape from. Any attempt to cut off the flow of capital, technologies, products, industries and people between economies, and channel the waters in the ocean back into isolated lakes and creeks is simply not possible. Indeed, it runs counter to the historical trend. (Xi, 2017)

We do need to be aware, nonetheless, that the period since 2016 may have marked a sea-change in political perspectives on globalization, which will in turn impact upon the development of global media, and needs to inform the judgements we make of competing analytical frameworks for understanding global media.

Assessing the competing frameworks

Modernization theories have been subject to so many permutations, and so many critiques since they first emerged as the sociological underpinning of development communication, that it can be difficult to know if an assessment is worthwhile. But the question of how communications technologies can be utilized to improve the lives of people, and particularly the poorest and most disadvantaged people in the world, remains vitally important. Enghel (2015, p. 11) has described this as the proposition that:

> Strategic communication interventions can and must play a positive role in the production of social change is the central tenet of development communication, understood here as a subset of both communication and media studies and international development studies, as well as a practical and institutional component of international development cooperation.

Enghel's revised definition of strategic communication is important, since it establishes that evaluation of strategic communication initiatives informed by modernization approaches are never simply an academic exercise. Development communication 'is not only a field of study. It is also a (more or less) professional practice, and an institutional project with a geopolitical underpinning and a specific governance structure' (Enghel, 2015, p. 12).

The top-down approaches to development communication that informed the first modernization-based projects were strongly critiqued by those arguing the need for more bottom-up, participatory approaches to communication and social change. While the sociology of Max Weber guided the first generation of modernization theorists, with its question of how to cultivate 'modern minds' through communication technologies, the participatory paradigm was influenced by social change theorists such as Paulo Friere, who understood communication in terms of dialogue and participation, and prioritized the role of existing cultural resources in communities for enabling change and adaptation, rather than viewing 'traditional culture' as an obstacle to change. Methodologies such as participatory action research became increasingly important in development communication, as did theories associated with feminism, postcolonialism and post-structuralism, as the view was taken that there is no universal model of or single pathway to development.

But the 2000s saw reconciliation of the traditional diffusionist paradigm of development communication with the more participatory and social change-oriented approaches. Huesca (2003) observed that the methodological pluralism of participatory communication had, ironically, come to redeem the dominant paradigm, as the combination of top-down and bottom-up approaches suited development agencies who wanted to increase both NGO and business involvement in development projects. Morris (2003, p. 227) argued that while the participatory approach often defined itself in opposition to the more traditional models, the diffusionist and participatory approaches were not polar opposites since 'the diffusion model has evolved in a participatory direction since its initial formulation, and participatory projects necessarily involve some element of information transfer'. Mefalopulos (2008) made the point that participatory communications approaches had increasingly been adopted by the United Nations, the World Bank and others precisely because they promised more cost-effective service delivery by requiring local stakeholders to take ownership of project design and implementation. Models of multi-stakeholder engagement were also critical to programmes such as ICT for Development (ICT4D) and global symposia such as the World Summit on the Information Society (WSIS).

Contemporary modernization approaches to development communication can thus be reconciled with globalization theories, since both stress the role played by NGOs and civil society organizations, the need for values plurality in a post-Cold War, multi-polar world and the scope for diffuse forms of local adaptation in the take-up and use of ostensibly 'Western' digital ICTs. At the same time, the absence of overt theorizing about the political-economic context of media and communication in developing nations, combined with an implicit media-centrism arising from the need to prove that programmes centred on the use of ICTs for development communication 'made a difference', continues to leave a vacuum where the critical analysis of media and power should sit.

Critical political economy approaches to global media have been the most influential approaches intellectually in the field, and have had political influence as providing the foundations for critique of the dominant policy paradigms, particularly in the developing world. The framework combines media economics with neo-Marxist critical theory, aligning insights about the tendency towards concentration of ownership and control over the means of communication and the contradictory position of media professionals under capitalism with theories of ideological domination and class hegemony. In the global media field, it has historically been associated with dependency theories, world-systems theories and critiques of Western cultural imperialism. More recent accounts of political economy approaches to global media identify its priorities in these terms:

Political economy mixes social struggle and social science, with an abiding concern for class interests and other forms of inequality. It focuses on material power, the capacity to mobilize resources, the warp and woof of history, and the correlation of meanings with economic and political interests. It sees culture as created through struggle, with an emphasis on social power as a determinant, examining the relationships between political consciousness and industrial organization, state and citizen, and government, labor, and capital. (Miller & Kraidy, 2016, p. 37)

Understood as an economic approach to media, critical political economy has been at the forefront of critiques of *digital capitalism*. Critical political economists have drawn attention to the complex interplay between the powerful emergent economic interests of the ICT industries and the capacity of dominant Western governments, most notably that of the United States, to reshape national and supranational policy and regulatory regimes to enable these powerful corporate players to expand their operations globally, and to forestall more critical voices from the 'Global South'. This focus on situating media in the context of political-economic relations is in contrast to more technocratic approaches that understand the internet in media-centric terms, as a form of communications technology whose properties and affordances are inherently democratic and liberating.

At the same time, critical political economy needs to be attuned to structural shifts taking place within global capitalism, which may see the rise of some corporate interests and the relative decline of others. While tendencies towards media concentration remain a feature of most parts of the world (Noam, 2016), the rise of the ICT-based giants (Google, Apple, Microsoft, Facebook, etc.) has challenged traditional conceptions of what constitutes a media business and a media industry. The rise of these companies as controllers of platforms and integrators of content, rather than its direct producers, has challenged the traditional media conglomerates, who have traditionally been content producers and distributors and strongly reliant on copyright as a basis for profitability. Critical political economy needs to avoid simply focusing upon bigness *per se* as a measure of economic power, as the market dynamics of global capitalism remain fluid and waves of 'creative destruction' coexist with the tendencies of monopoly capitalism towards ownership concentration and the exercise of market power. The ability to absorb such changes requires political economists to be open to a range of perspectives in heterodox economics, including institutional and evolutionary perspectives, alongside the dominant neo-Marxist paradigm (Winseck, 2011; Cunningham *et al.*, 2015).

It is in relation to claims that global media promote a dominant ideology of global capitalism, variously termed neoliberalism, globalism and consumerism, that the strongest concerns exist around the critical political economy approach. The main lines of critique around 'first generation' political economists related to the difficulties involved in substantiating the claim that exposure to Western film and television content led to people in developing nations aligning their worldviews to dominant Western values, as well as the relative neglect of the dynamism of media systems outside of the dominant US and Western European models. Similar issues can be raised with assumptions that access to the global internet and mobile phones has a similar incorporating effect upon the fast-growing digital populations of the Global South. The relatively limited range of studies undertaken thus far on local preference for nationally based internet content (Taneja & Wu, 2014) indicate patterns similar to those for broadcast media that are not simply explained by language or by the blocking of 'outside' sites (e.g. the 'Great Firewall of China'). The example of *shanzhai* culture and its proliferation in China through cultural products such as mobile phones that closely resemble those of the dominant Western brands indicates that hybridity and local adaptation continue to be vital elements of how global culture is re-appropriated in local contexts, as critics of the cultural imperialism thesis have long argued.

There has also been the question of what an anti-globalist or anti-neoliberal ideology may look like. Carroll and Sapinski (2016) argue that one of the characteristics of the rise of what – following Sklair (1997, 2002) – they term a transnational capitalist class (TCC) has been a turn away from identification with nation-states and national populations. Associated with the rise of the TCC has been a shift in the role of the state from being one of 'promoting "its" capitalists as leading agents of a national economy' towards a global 'supra-class identity', represented by transnational entities such as the World Economic Forum (WEF) which meets annually at Davos, Switzerland. Perhaps not surprisingly, then, opposition to such a transnational elite – what Samuel Huntington termed 'Davos Man' (Tett, 2017) – has taken the form of nationalism as much as it has anti-capitalism. While it has long been acknowledged that anti-globalization movements could take the form of nationalism and right-wing populism, there has been a strong underlying assumption that anti-globalist movements would predominantly evolve in the direction of global anti-capitalism, through the connective logics of political organization through digital technologies and counter-hegemonic organizational forms such as the World Social Forum (Hardt & Negri, 2004; Kahn & Kellner, 2007).

The idea that opposition to globalization and transnational elites may be led by people who would themselves appear to be a part of such elites, such as Donald Trump in the US, Nigel Farage in the UK and Marine Le Pen in France, has thrown into question that the dominant social divide in contemporary global capitalism would be between a transnational capitalist class and its governing allies on the one hand, and a globally networked anti-capitalism movement on the other. The political left – with which critical political economists typically align themselves – has rejected the nativist nationalism of such movements and has strongly supported the rights of refugees and the value of multicultural societies. At the same time, this has had a paradoxical dimension, as many on the left have also had concerns with economic globalization, such as the movement of production offshore, the ability to lower wages and conditions through global competition and the undemocratic nature of multilateral trade agreements and supranational forms of governance.[1] There have thus been shared concerns from figures on the left such as US presidential candidate Bernie Sanders and the more populist movements of the nationalist right.

Globalization theories constitute a diverse range of works whose general features are to see global media and communication as being central to a fundamental transformation of systems of production and consumption, forms of culture and identity, and practices of power and governance. Authors such as Giddens, Castells, Appadurai, Beck, Tomlinson, Pieterse and others have identified cultural hybridization rather than cultural domination as the core consequence of global media and culture, seeing relationships between culture and identity on the one hand, and nation states and national media systems on the other, as becoming increasingly deterritorialized, leading to a proliferation of identities that are less and less connected to nation-states. Associated with the proposition that the power of nation-states is in decline, these authors draw links between the rise of cosmopolitan, 'post-national' identities and the growing role played by non-governmental organizations and civil society in using power and shaping governance, arguing that, as Ulrich Beck put it, 'those who play only the national card in the global meta-game will lose ... [and] the counter-power of states develops as they become transnationalized and cosmopolitanized' (Beck, 2005, p. 9).

Several important contributions of globalization theorists have been identified in this book. The significance of the concept of *glocalization* was noted, where global cultural forms are repurposed for different local contexts, with the *shanzhai* culture in China being perhaps the latest manifestation of such phenomena (Chubb, 2014). The complexities of defining a national cultural identity in multicultural societies have drawn attention to the significance of *cultural hybridity*, where more and more people are 'in between' cultures, and diasporic media become a key resource for forging new forms of identity in such fluid circumstances. The need for forms of media policy and regulation has also been noted, with complex forms of co-regulation, self-regulation and multi-stakeholder governance arising as alternative forms of 'nodal governance' (Burris *et al.*, 2015) to traditional forms of state regulation of the media.

At the same time, a number of weaknesses in the account of globalization theorists have been noted. The most significant is the underestimation of the continuing significance of nation-states. The assumption that global media flows are no longer able to be regulated by nation-states has not been borne out in practice. At the same time, attempts to develop supranational forms of media governance have struggled in the face of relative indifference from key national governments. One consequence of media globalization has also been a push for nation-states to invest – selectively – in their own systems of media production and distribution, through mechanisms as diverse as developing media capitals and creative clusters to promoting cultural diplomacy and 'soft power' objectives through international broadcasting.

Such empirical difficulties are emblematic of a recurring tendency to overstate the degree to which transnational corporations have been able to disconnect their operations from national governments. The corollary has been a tendency to understate the continuing pull of national identity and the symbols of national cultures, in the face of the 'global supermarket' of identities offered by capitalist globalization. Television studies theorists have long picked up the tendency for media consumers to prefer the content that is most local and familiar to them when presented with choices between local and imported content, and this continues to be central to the dynamics of global internet culture. It is only in a relatively small number of nations where levels of migration have been such as to promote a genuine multiculturalism: in most of the largest nations in the world, cultural diversity is a feature of their national populations but is not something driven by large-scale migration from other parts of the world, or involving people with major cultural differences to the host population.[2]

Post-globalization

The international political economist Robert Gilpin, in *Global Political Economy: Understanding the International Economic Order* (Gilpin, 2001), considers two alternative modes of global governance to a framework based primarily around the interaction between national systems and nation-states. The first is that of *neoliberal institutionalism*, which is broadly the system to manage and promote globalization that concentrates the minds of both its advocates and its critics. Building upon the liberal institutional order established in the wake of World War II (often referred to as the Bretton Woods system), new agreements such as the General Agreement on Trade in Services (GATS, signed in 1994), and new institutions such as the World Trade Organization (WTO, established in 1995), were developed with the explicit aim of consolidating a system of international governance that would ensure the hegemony of market-conforming institutions to manage the global economic system. In the wake of the collapse of the Soviet Union in 1991, and the seeming historical triumph of liberal democracy and market capitalism over communism and planned economies, such an institutional regime seemed to be a basis for the twenty-first century, particularly when China acceded to the WTO in 2001.

A variety of issues confront such attempts at a global institutional order. The divergence between national systems is a recurring issue, and the assumption that 'the process of convergence will eventually lead to worldwide acceptance of the policy prescriptions of neoclassical economics and a free market following the American model' (Gilpin, 2001, p. 381) have not come to pass. Indeed, as Jeremy Tunstall (2008) has famously argued, American dominance of global media has been declining since the 1990s. For Tunstall, this decline in US leadership particularly occurred in the wake of the Iraq War, which both exposed gaps in the credibility of US news media sources when reporting on their own government and encouraged nations as diverse as Russia, Qatar, China and Venezuela to invest heavily in the international broadcasting of their own news media to provide alternative perspectives on global affairs. The sense of a 'democratic deficit' surrounding multilateral institutions was strongly voiced in 1999 by protestors against the inaugural meeting of the WTO in Seattle, and has if anything intensified since then. Finally, the need for shared agreement on liberal norms and values has been sorely tested by the rise of Al-Qaeda and ISIS, the 'War on Terror' and associated abuses of human rights, and terrorist and state terror actions around the globe. All of these developments, and the underlying anxieties that they trigger, undermine the sense of security and confidence around relations between states that must underwrite a preparedness to cede power to multilateral institutions.

The second possibility that Gilpin discussed is what he termed the *new medievalism*, premised on the notion that:

> The concept of national sovereignty ... is breaking down because of both internal and external developments; states are fragmenting into sub-states as a result of ethnic and regional conflicts and, at the same time, are being eclipsed by rising non-state and super-state actors such as multinational firms, international organizations, and especially, nongovernmental organizations. (2001, pp. 390–391)

Both globalization theorists and some digital media theorists have seen the current period as a historical watershed where:

> The once dominant hierarchic order of nation-states [is] being supplanted by horizontal networks of states, voluntary organizations, and international institutions. This development in turn leads to cooperative problem solving by concerned individuals and groups from around the world, in place of the undisputed loyalty formerly owed by the citizen to the sovereign. A world of multiple allegiances and responsibilities is envisioned ... in which subnational, national, and supranational institutions will share authority over individuals. (Gilpin, 2001, p. 391)

While Gilpin's concern is with global governance, the framework outlined here shaped more critical discourses around alternatives to capitalist globalization. Hardt and Negri's (2004) conception of the *multitude* envisaged a digitally networked 'cognitariat' (Berardi, 2005), engaging collectively beyond borders to produce new forms of common struggle and a new global polity. In the more reformist vein, the cosmopolitan social democracy proposed by globalization theorists such as Held (2004) identified NGOs as central players in new forms of global assembly that could work collaboratively with nation-states to generate new forms of global governance. At different points in the 2000s, possibilities along these lines periodically appeared – the WSIS providing one example in the communication sphere – and there was considerable growth in intergovernmental forums where NGOs had a role and international civil society forums that critiqued neoliberal globalization, as well as the protest movements associated with Occupy, the *Indignados* and the Arab Spring (Castells, 2012). All of these movements and forums were strongly powered by digital technology and the possibility of collective political action, or what Bennett and Segerberg (2012) termed *connective* action, beyond the nation-state.

The possibilities of such a cosmopolitan globalization were always overstated, just as the coherence of the neoliberal institutional order was overestimated. The case of China post-WTO accession was perhaps emblematic: it could become an increasingly important part of the global economic order without in any way ceding its territorial sovereignty or opening up its system of governance to international civil society or the global media on terms other than its own. While critical Western scholars spoke of a neoliberal 'Washington Consensus', the growing economic significance of China led to some referring to a 'Beijing consensus', where globalization and national sovereignty are seen as soulmates rather than as antinomies (Cho & Jeong, 2008). The consolidation of Vladimir Putin's power in Russia was accompanied by a crackdown on Western NGOs operating in the country, as well as the proclamation of new doctrines of Russian exceptionalism such as 'sovereign democracy'. While the political pendulum may yet swing back towards cosmopolitan globalism, and away from a resurgent nationalism, the signs are very mixed, particularly since the election of Donald Trump as US President in 2016. In contrast to the orthodoxy of critical political economists that international free trade agreements largely served US interests, Trump tapped into a rich vein of domestic protectionism, to argue that trade agreements and global corporations had operated against the interests of American workers. Trump's threats to leave institutions such as the World Trade Organization contrast to the work of his predecessors – both Republican and Democrat – who were at the forefront of promoting such global institutions. At the same time, Trump's scepticism about free trade clearly has echoes among Democrats, notably supporters of the unsuccessful Democratic Party candidate Bernie Sanders.

We have seen the media as being at the forefront of globalization, and the trajectory of media as being an increasingly global one. With regards to broadcasting, satellite and cable delivery were seen as challengers to nationally based terrestrial systems. The internet was global from its inception, largely developing 'behind the backs' of national governments, until the 1990s and subsequent decades saw its global expansion increasingly driven by corporate interests. But it is apparent that national governments never really left the stage, and that the openness of global media could be managed at a national level by those states that had both the resources and the political will to do so. Seemingly global ICT corporations remain highly reliant upon national governments for their operations, and governments increasingly look to these corporations to assist them in their own tasks, from counter-terrorism and surveillance to monitoring copyright infringements. But the media can only ultimately be as global as those who consume its content wish it to be, and in thinking about how we conceive of culture and identity in an age of global media, we can see that national and territorial identities continue to coexist with more deterritorialized and cosmopolitan forms of subjectivity.

Notes

1   These debates have played themselves out most sharply in the nations of the European Union. While most of the left and centre-left in Europe are broadly pro-EU, responses to the Greek financial crisis and the unwillingness to countenance debt relief to the left-wing SYRIZA-led government threw into sharp relief political questions of 'whose Europe' was being represented by the EU and its institutions. Movements such as Another Europe is Possible and Democracy in Europe 2025 (DiEM25), launched by former SYRIZA Finance Minister Yanis Varoufakis, have sought to democratize the EU, and many Members of the European Parliament (MEPs) are concerned about its image as a technocratic super-state remote from ordinary citizens. But in Britain the 2016 EU Referendum and its aftermath revealed deep divisions on this issue within the UK Labour Party. In a position at odds with the majority of his pro-EU MPs, its leader, Jeremy Corbyn, and Shadow Chancellor, John McDonnell, championed a 'People's Brexit' (Sabin, 2017), echoing the earlier left position of figures such as Tony Benn, who saw the EU as essentially undemocratic and saw socialism as only achievable within nation-states.

2   Of the world's 50 most populous nations, only 11 had net migration rates of greater than 500,000 over the period from 1965 to 2015: United States, Russia, Germany, United Kingdom, France, South Africa, Spain, Saudi Arabia, Turkey, Canada and Australia. Not surprisingly, the highest rates of net migration are to the high income countries on this list, notably the US, the UK, Germany, France and Canada (World Bank, 2016).

Bibliography

Adam, G. (1975) 'Multinational Corporations and Worldwide Sourcing', in Radice, H. (ed.) *International Firms and Modern Imperialism*. Harmondsworth: Penguin, pp. 89–103.

Aglietta, M. (1987) *A Theory of Capitalist Regulation*. Translated by David Fernbach (2nd ed.). London: Verso.

Albarran, A. (2010) *The Media Economy*. New York: Routledge.

Allen, J. (2002) 'Symbolic Economies: The "Culturalization" of Economic Knowledge', in du Gay, P. & Pryke, M. (eds) *Cultural Economy*. London: SAGE, pp. 39–58.

Allor, M. (1995) 'Relocating the Site of the Audience', in Boyd-Barrett, O. & Newbold, C. (eds) *Approaches to Media: A Reader*. London: Arnold, pp. 543–553.

Amin, A. (2000) 'The Economic Base of Contemporary Cities', in Bridge, G. & Watson, S. (eds) *A Companion to the City*. Oxford: Blackwell, pp. 115–129.

Amin, A. (2001) 'Globalization: Geographical Aspects', in Smelser, N.J. & Baltes, P.B. (eds) *International Encyclopedia of the Social and Behavioral Sciences*. Amsterdam: Elsevier, pp. 6271–6277.

Amin, A. (2002) 'Spatialities of Globalisation', *Environment and Planning A*, 34(3), 385–399.

Amin, A. (2003) 'Industrial Districts', in Sheppard, E. & Barnes, T.J. (eds) *A Companion to Economic Geography*. Oxford: Blackwell, pp. 149–168.

Amin, S. (1980) *Accumulation on a World Scale*. New York: Monthly Review Press.

Amsden, A. (1989) *Asia's Next Giant: South Korea and Late Industrialization*. Oxford: Oxford University Press.

Anderson, B. (1991) *Imagined Communities: Reflections on the Origins and Spread of Nationalism* (2nd ed.). London: Verso.

Ang, I. (1991) *Desperately Seeking the Audience*. London: Routledge.

Ang, I. (1996) *Living Room Wars: Rethinking Media Audiences for a Postmodern World*. New York: Routledge.

Ang, I., Hawkins, G. & Dabboussy, L. (2008) *The SBS Story*. Sydney: UNSW Press.

Appadurai, A. (1990) 'Disjuncture and Difference in the Global Cultural Economy', in Featherstone, M. (ed.) *Global Culture: Nationalism, Globalization and Modernity*. London: SAGE, pp. 295–310.

Appadurai, A. (1996) *Modernity at Large: Cultural Dimensions of Globalization*. Minneapolis, MI: University of Minnesota Press.

Ausfilm (2000) *A Bigger Slice of the Pie: Policy Options for a More Competitive International Film and Television Production Industry in Australia*. Report prepared by Malcolm Long Associates, November.

Australian Law Reform Commission [ALRC] (2013) *Copyright and the Digital Economy: Final Report 122*. Sydney: ALRC. Retrieved from www.alrc.gov.au/publications/copyright-report-122 (Accessed 13 December 2017).

Bagdikian, B. (2000) *The Media Monopoly* (6th ed.). Boston, MA: Beacon.

Baker, E. (2007) *Media Concentration and Democracy: Why Ownership Matters*. Cambridge: Cambridge University Press.

Bakhshi, H., Hargreaves, I. & Mateos-Garcia, J. (2013) *A Manifesto for the Creative Economy*. Retrieved from www.nesta.org.uk/sites/default/files/a-manifesto-for-the-creative-economy-april13.pdf (Accessed 25 January 2017).

Ballon, P. (2014) 'Old and New Issues in Media Economics', in Donders, K., Pauwels, C. & Loisen, J. (eds) *The Palgrave Handbook of European Media Policy*. Basingstoke: Palgrave, pp. 70–95.

Baran, P. (1973) *The Political Economy of Growth* (2nd ed.). Harmondsworth: Penguin.

Baran, P. & Sweezy, P.M. (1968) *Monopoly Capital*. Harmondsworth: Penguin.

Barber, B.J. (2000) 'Jihad vs. McWorld', in Lechner, F. & Boli, J. (eds) *The Globalization Reader*. Malden, MA: Blackwell, pp. 21–26.

Barnett, C. (2010) 'Publics and Markets: What's Wrong with Neoliberalism?' in Smith, S.J., Pain, R., Marston, S.A. & Jones III, J.P. (eds) *The SAGE Handbook of Social Geographies*. London: SAGE, pp. 269–297.

Barney, D. (2004) *The Network Society*. Cambridge: Polity Press.

Barrett, M. (1991) *The Politics of Truth: From Marx to Foucault*. Cambridge: Polity Press.

Bauer, J. (2014) 'Platforms, Systems Competition, and Innovation: Reassessing the Foundations of Communications Policy', *Telecommunications Policy*, *38*(8–9), 662–673.

Bauman, Z. (1996) 'From Pilgrim to Tourist – or a Short History of Identity', in Hall, S. & du Gay, P. (eds) *Questions of Cultural Identity*. London: SAGE, pp. 18–36.

Beck, U. (2000) *What is Globalization?* Cambridge: Polity.

Beck, U. (2005) *Power in the Global Age: A New Global Political Economy*. Malden, MA: Polity.

Beck, U. (2006) *The Cosmopolitan Vision*. Translated by Ciaran Cronin. Cambridge: Polity.

Bell, D. (1980) 'The Social Framework of the Information Society', in Forester, T. (ed.) *Microelectronics Revolution*. Cambridge, MA: MIT Press, pp. 500–549.

Bell, D. (1987) 'The World and the United States in 2013', *Daedalus*, *116*(3), 1–31.

Bell, D. & Oakley, K. (2015) *Cultural Policy*. London: Routledge.

Beltrán, L.R. (1976) 'Alien Premises, Objects, and Methods in Latin American Communication Research', *Communication Research*, *3*(2), 107–134.

Bennett, T. (1998) *Culture: A Reformer's Science*. Allen & Unwin: Sydney.

Bennett, W.L. & Segerberg, A. (2012) 'The Logic of Connective Action: Digital Media and the Personalization of Contentious Politics', *Information, Communication & Society*, *15*(5), 739–768.

Benyon, J. & Dunkerley, D. (2002) *The Globalization Reader: An Introduction to Global Studies*. New York: Routledge.

Berardi, F. (2005) 'What does Cognitariat Mean? Work, Desire and Depression', *Cultural Studies Review*, 11(2), 57–63.

Berg, E. & Besharov, D. (2016) 'Patterns of Global Migration', in Besharov, D. & Lopez, M. (eds) *Adjusting to a World in Motion: Trends in Global Migration and Migration Policy*. Oxford: Oxford University Press, pp. 57–76.

Best, J. & Paterson, M. (2010) *Cultural Political Economy*. London: Routledge.

Bhabha, H. (1994) *The Location of Culture*. London: Routledge.

Billig, M. (1995) *Banal Nationalism*. London: SAGE.

Boas T. & Gans-Morse J. (2009) 'Neo-Liberalism: From New Liberal Philosophy to Anti-Liberal Slogan', *Studies in Comparative International Development*, 44(1), 137–161.

Bocock, R. (1992) 'The Cultural Formations of Modern Society', in Hall, S. & Gieben, B. (eds) *Formations of Modernity*. Cambridge: Polity with the Open University, pp. 229–274.

Boyd-Barrett, O. (1977) 'Media Imperialism: Towards an International Framework for the Analysis of Media Systems', in Curran, J., Gurevitch, M. & Woolacott, J. (eds) *Mass Communication and Society*. London: Edward Arnold, pp. 116–135.

Boyd-Barrett, O. (1995) 'Political Economy', in Boyd-Barrett, O. & Newbold, C. (eds) *Approaches to Media: A Reader*. London: Arnold, pp. 185–194.

Boyd-Barrett, O. (1998) 'Media Imperialism Reformulated', in Thussu, D.K. (ed.) *Electronic Empires: Global Media and Local Resistance*. London: Edward Arnold, pp. 157–176.

Boyd-Barrett, O. (2015) *Media Imperialism*. London: SAGE.

Boyne, R. (1990) 'Culture and the World-System', in Featherstone, M. (ed.) *Global Culture: Nationalism, Globalization and Modernity*. London: SAGE, pp. 57–62.

Braithwaite, J. (2006) 'The Regulatory State?', in Rhodes, R.A.W., Binder, S. & Rockman, B. (eds) *The Oxford Handbook of Political Institutions*. Oxford: Oxford University Press, pp. 407–430.

Brewer, A. (1980) *Marxist Theories of Imperialism*. London: Routledge & Kegan Paul.

Brzeski, P. (2015) *China Box Office Grows Astonishing 48.7 Percent in 2015, Hits $6.78 Billion*. Retrieved 1 November 2016. Retrieved from www.hollywoodreporter.com/news/china-box-office-grows-astonishing-851629 (Accessed 12 June 2017).

Burris, S., Drahos, P. & Shearing, C. (2015) 'Nodal Governance', *Australian Journal of Legal Philosophy*, 30(1), 30–58.

Cable, V. (1995) 'The Diminished Nation-State: A Study in the Loss of Economic Power', *Daedalus*, 124, 23–53.

Calhoun, C. (1997) *Nationalism*. Milton Keynes: Open University Press.

Callon, M., Meadel, C. & Rabeharisoa, V. (2004) 'The Economy of Qualities', in Amin, A. & Thrift, N. (eds) *The Cultural Economy Reader*. Malden, MA: Blackwell, pp. 58–79.

Carroll, W.K. & Sapinski, J.P. (2016) 'Neoliberalism and the Transnational Capitalist Class', in Springer, S., Birch, K. & MacLeavy, J. (eds) *The Handbook of Neoliberalism*. London: Routledge, pp. 39–49.

Castells, M. (1996) *The Rise of the Network Society: The Information Age: Economy, Society and Culture*. Malden, MA: Blackwell.

Castells, M. (2000) 'Materials for an Exploratory Theory of the Network Society', *British Journal of Sociology*, 51(1), 5–24.

Castells, M. (2001) *The Internet Galaxy: Reflections on the Internet, Business, and Society.* New York: Oxford University Press.

Castells, M. (2009) *Communication Power.* New York: Oxford University Press.

Castells, M. (2012) *Networks of Outrage and Hope: Social Movements in the Internet Age.* Cambridge: Polity.

Castles, S. (1997) 'Multicultural Citizenship: A Response to the Dilemma of Globalization and National Identity?', *Journal of Intercultural Studies*, *18*(1), 5–22.

Castles, S. & Davidson, A. (2000) *Citizenship and Migration: Globalization and the New Politics of Belonging.* Basingstoke: Macmillan.

Castles, S. & Miller, M.J. (2003) *The Age of Migration* (3rd ed.). London: Macmillan.

Chevalier, J. & Buckles, D. (2012) *Participatory Action Research: Theory and Methods for Engaged Inquiry.* London: Routledge.

China Hollywood Society (2014) *About Co-Productions.* Retrieved from www.chinahollywood.org/about-co-productions (Accessed 7 November 2016).

ChinaFile. (2015) *Document 9: A ChinaFile Translation.* Retrieved from www.chinafile.com/document-9-chinafile-translation (Accessed 26 January 2017).

Cho, Y. & Jeong, J. (2008) 'China's Soft Power: Discussions, Resources, and Prospects', *Asian Survey*, *48*(3), 453–472.

Christensen, J.G. (2011) 'Competing Theories of Regulatory Governance: Reconsidering Public Interest Theories of Regulation', in Levi-Faur, D. (ed.) *Handbook of the Politics of Regulation.* Cheltenham: Edward Elgar, pp. 96–110.

Christopherson, S. (2011) 'Hard Jobs in Hollywood: How Concentration in Distribution Affects the Production Side of the Media Entertainment Industry', in Winseck, D. & Jin, D.Y. (eds) *The Political Economies of Media: The Transformation of the Global Media Industries.* London: Bloomsbury, pp. 179–190.

Chu, Y. (2002) 'The Consumption of Cinema in Contemporary China', in Donald, S., Keane, M., and Hong, Y. (eds) *Media in China: Consumption, Content and Crisis.* London: Routledge Curzon, pp. 43–54.

Chubb, A. (2014) 'China's *Shanzhai* Culture: "Grabism" and the Politics of Hybridity', *Journal of Contemporary China*, *24*(2), 260–279.

Civil Society WSIS. (2003) *Shaping Information Societies for Human Needs: Civil Society Declaration to the World Summit on the Information Society.* Geneva: WSIS Civil Society Plenary. Retrieved from www.itu.int/net/wsis/docs/geneva/civil-society-declaration.pdf. (Accessed 13 December 2017).

Clift, B. (2014) *Comparative Political Economy: States, Markets and Global Capitalism.* New York: Palgrave Macmillan.

Coe, N., Kelly, P. & Yeung, H.W.C. (2007) *Economic Geography: A Contempporary Introduction.* Malden, MA: Blackwell.

Coleman, J. & Almond, G. (1960) *The Politics of the Developing Areas.* Princeton, NJ: Princeton University Press.

Coleman, W.D. & Sajed, A. (2012) *Fifty Key Thinkers on Globalization.* London: Routledge.

Collins, R., Garnham, N. & Locksley, G. (1988) *The Economics of Television.* London: SAGE.

Compaine, B. & Gomery, D. (2001) *Who Owns the Media? Competition and Concentration in the Mass Media Industry* (3rd ed.). Mahwah, NJ: Lawrence Erlbaum Associates.

Compaine, B. (2001) 'The Myths of Encroaching Global Media Ownership', *Open Democracy*. Retrieved from www.opendemocracy.net/debates/debate-8-24.jsp. Posted 8 November (Accessed 14 November 2004).

Cooke, P. (2002) *Knowledge Economies: Clusters, Learning and Cooperative Advantage*. London: Routledge.

Couldry, N. & Hepp, A. (2009) 'What Should Comparative Media Research be Comparing? Towards a Transcultural Approach to "Media Cultures"', in Thussu, D.K. (ed.) *Internationalizing Media Studies*. London: Routledge, pp. 32–47.

Crawford, K. & Lumby, C. (2013) 'Networks of Governance: Users, Platforms, and the Challenges of Networked Media Regulation', *International Journal of Technology Policy and Law*, 1(3), pp. 270–282.

Crotty, J., Epstein, G. & Kelly, P. (1998) 'Multinational Corporations in the Neo-Liberal Regime', in Baker, D., Epstein, G., and Pollin, R. (eds) *Globalization and Progressive Economic Policy*. Cambridge: Cambridge University Press, pp. 117–143.

Cubitt, S. (2012) 'Avatar and Utopia', *Animation: An Interdisciplinary Journal*, 7(3), 227–237.

Cull, N. (2008) 'Public Diplomacy: Taxonomies and Histories', *The Annals of the American Academy of Political and Social Science*, 616(1), 31–54.

Cunningham, S. (2013) *Hidden Innovation: Policy, Industry and the Creative Sector*. Brisbane: University of Queensland Press.

Cunningham, S., Flew, T. & Swift, A. (2015) *Media Economics*. Basingstoke: Palgrave.

Curran, J. (1990) 'The New Revisionism in Mass Communication Research: A Reappraisal', *European Journal of Communication*, 5(2), 135–164.

Curran, J. (2005) 'Mediations of Democracy', in Curran, J. & Gurevitch, M. (eds) *Mass Media and Society*. London: Arnold, pp. 122–149.

Curran, J., Fenton, N. & Freedman, D. (2012) *Misunderstanding the Internet*. London: Routledge.

Curran, J. & Park, M.-J. (2000) 'Beyond Globalization Theory', in Curran, J. & Park, M.-J. (eds) *Dewesternizing Media Studies*. London: Routledge, pp. 3–18.

Currid, E. (2007) *The Warhol Economy: How Fashion, Art and Music Drive New York City*. Princeton, NJ: Princeton University Press.

Currie, D.H. & Thobani, S. (2003) 'From Modernization to Globalization: Challenges and Opportunities', *Gender, Technology and Development*, 7(2), pp. 149–170.

Curtin, M. (2007) *Playing to the World's Biggest Audience: The Globalization of Chinese Film and TV*. Berkeley, CA: University of California Press.

Curtin, M. (2009) 'Thinking Globally: From Media Imperialism to Media Capital', in Holt, J. & Perren, A. (eds) *Media Industries: History, Theory, Method*. Malden, MA: Wiley-Blackwell, pp. 108–119.

Curtin, M. (2010) 'Comparing Media Capitals: Hong Kong and Mumbai', *Global Media and Communication*, 6(3), 263–270.

Darling-Wolf, F. (2009) 'Hybridity', in Foss, K.A. & Littlejohn, S.W. (eds) *Encyclopedia of Communication Theory*. London: SAGE, pp. 483–485.

Davies, G. (2014) *The BBC and Public Value*. London: Social Market Foundation.

Dayan, D. & Katz, E. (1994) *Media Events: The Live Broadcasting of History*. Cambridge, MA: Harvard University Press.

Dean, M. (2014) *Governmentality: Power and Rule in Modern Societies* (2nd ed.). London: SAGE.

Dequech, D. (2003) 'Cognitive and Cultural Embeddedness: Combining Institutional Economics and Economic Sociology', *Journal of Economic Issues*, *37*(2), 461–470.

Deutsch, K.W. (1994) 'Nationalism and Social Communication', in Hutchinson, J. & Smith, A.D. (eds) *Nationalism*. Oxford: Oxford University Press, pp. 24–31.

Deuze, M. (2007) *Media Work*. Malden, MA: Polity Press.

Dicken, P. (2003) '"Placing" Firms: Grounding the Debate on the "Global"', in Peck, J. & Yeung, H.W. (eds) *Remaking the Global Economy*. London: SAGE, pp. 27–44.

Dicken, P. (2007) *Global Shift: Mapping the Changing Contours of the World Economy* (5th ed.). London: SAGE.

DiNardis, L. (2013) 'The Emerging Field of Internet Governance', in Dutton, W.H. (ed.), *The Oxford Handbook of Internet Studies*. Oxford: Oxford University Press, pp. 555–575.

Dirlik, A. (2003) 'Global Modernity? Modernity in an Age of Global Capitalism', *European Journal of Social Theory*, *6*(3), 275–292.

Doremus, P., Keller, W., Pauly, L. & Reich, S. (1998) *The Myth of the Global Corporation*. Princeton, NJ: Princeton University Press.

Douglas, M. (1987) *How Institutions Think*. London: Routledge.

Doyle, G. (2013) *Understanding Media Economics* (2nd ed.). London: SAGE.

Drahos, P. & Braithwaite, J. (2002) *Information Feudalism*. London: Earthscan.

Drezner, D. (2001) 'Globalization and Policy Convergence', *International Studies Review*, *3*(1), 53–78.

Du Gay, P. & Pryke, M. (2002) 'Cultural Economy: An Introduction', in du Gay, P. & Pryke, M. (eds) *Cultural Economy*. London: SAGE, pp. 1–19.

Dunleavy, P. & O'Leary, B. (1987) *Theories of the State: The Politics of Liberal Democracy*. Chicago, IL: New Amsterdam Books.

Dunning, J. (2015) *The Globalization of Business:* (3rd ed.). New York: Routledge.

During, S. (1993) 'Introduction', in During, S. (ed.) *The Cultural Studies Reader*. London: Routledge, pp. 1–25.

Earl, P.E. & Peng, T-C. (2012) 'Brands of Economics and the Trojan Horse of Pluralism', *Review of Political Economy*, *24*(3), 451–467.

Eco, U. (1976) *A Theory of Semiotics*. Bloomington, IN: Indiana University Press.

Eisenstadt, S. (1966) *Modernization, Protest and Change*. Englewood Cliffs, NJ: Prentice-Hall.

Eisenstein, E. (1993) *The Printing Revolution in Early Modern Europe*. Cambridge: Cambridge University Press.

Enghel, F. (2015) 'Towards a Political Economy of Communication in Development?' *Nordicom Review*, *36*, 11–24.

Ernst, D. & Kim, L. (2002) 'Global Production Networks, Knowledge Diffusion, and Local Capacity Formation', *Research Policy*, *31*(10), 1417–1429.

Esping-Anderson, G. (1990) *The Three Worlds of Welfare Capitalism*. Princeton, NJ: Princeton University Press.

Esser, F. & Strömbäck, J. (2014) 'Mediatization of Politics: Towards a Theoretical Framework', in Esser, F. & Strömbäck, J. (eds) *Mediatization of Politics: Understanding the Transformation of Western Democracies*. Basingstoke: Palgrave Macmillan, pp. 3–28.

Evans, G. (2009) 'Creative Cities, Creative Spaces and Urban Policy', *Urban Studies*, 46(5/6), 1003–1040.

Evans, P. (1995) *Embedded Autonomy: States and Industrial Transformation*. Princeton, NJ: Princeton University Press.

Evans, P. (1997) 'The Eclipse of the State? Reflections on Stateness in an Era of Globalization', *World Politics*, 50(1), 62–87.

Evans, P. (1998) 'Transferable Lessons? Re-examining the Institutional Prerequisites of East Asian Economic Policies', *Journal of Development Studies*, 34(6), 66–86.

Evans, P. (2014) 'The Developmental State: Divergent Responses to Modern Economic Theory and the Twenty-First Century Economy', in Williams, M. (ed.) *The End of the Developmental State?* London: Routledge, pp. 220–239.

Fair, J. (1989) '29 Years of Theory and Research on Media and Development: The Dominant Paradigm Impact', *International Communication Gazette*, 44(2), 129–150.

Finckenstein, K. von (2011) *Speech to the Banff World Media Festival*. Retrieved from www.crtc.gc.ca/eng/com200/2011/s110613.htm (Accessed 25 February 2017).

Finn, A., McFayden, S. & Finn, C. (2004) *Media Economics: Applying Economics to New and Traditional Media*. Thousand Oaks, CA: SAGE.

Fisher, M. (2013) 'In case you weren't clear on Russia Today's relationship to Moscow, Putin clears it up', *Washington Post*. Retrieved from www.washingtonpost.com/news/worldviews/wp/2013/06/13/in-case-you-werent-clear-on-russia-todays-relationship-to-moscow-putin-clears-it-up/ (Accessed 13 December 2017).

Fiske, J. (1998) 'Television: Popularity and Polysemy', in Dickinson, R., Harindranath, R. & Linne, O. (eds) *Approaches to Audiences: A Reader*. London: Arnold, pp. 194–204.

Flew, T. (2005) 'Creative Economy', in Hartley, J. (ed.) *Creative Industries*. Oxford: Blackwell, pp. 344–360.

Flew, T. (2006) 'The Social Contract and Beyond in Broadcast Media Policy', *Television and New Media*, 7(3), 282–305.

Flew, T. (2007) *Understanding Global Media* (1st ed.). Basingstoke: Palgrave.

Flew, T. (2011) 'Media as Creative Industries: Conglomeration and Globalization as Accumulation Strategies in an Age of Digital Media', in Winseck, D. & Jin, D.Y. (eds) *The Political Economies of Media: The Transformation of the Global Media Industries*. London: Bloomsbury, pp. 84–100.

Flew, T. (2012a) 'Michel Foucault's The Birth of Biopolitics and Contemporary Neo-Liberalism Debates', *Thesis Eleven: Critical Theory and Historical Sociology*, 108(1), 42–63.

Flew, T. (2012b) *The Creative Industries: Culture and Policy*. London: SAGE.

Flew, T. (2014a) 'Convergent Media Policy', in Dearman, P. & Greenfield, C. (eds) *How We Are Governed: Investigations of Communication, Media and Democracy*. Newcastle, UK: Cambridge Scholars Publishing, pp. 10–30.

Flew, T. (2014b) 'Six Theories of Neoliberalism', *Thesis Eleven*, 124(1), 49–71.

Flew, T. (2015) 'Copyright and Creativity: An Ongoing Debate in the Creative Industries', *International Journal of Cultural and Creative Industries*, 2(3), 4–17.

Flew, T. (2016a) 'Convergent Media Policy: Reflections Based Upon the Australian Case', in Simpson, S., Puppis, M. & Van den Bulck, H. (eds) *European Media Policy for the Twenty-First Century*. London: Routledge, pp. 219–237.

Flew, T. (2016b) 'National Media Regulations in an Age of Convergent Media: Beyond Globalization, Neoliberalism and Internet Freedom Theories', in Flew, T., Iosifidis, P. & Steemers, J. (eds) *Global Media and National Policies: The Return of the State*. Basingstoke: Palgrave Macmillan, pp. 75–91.

Flew, T. (2016c) 'Evaluating China's Aspirations for Cultural Soft Power in a Post-Globalization Era', *Media International Australia*, *159*(1), 32–42.

Flew, T. & McElhinney, S. (2006) 'Globalization and the Dynamics of New Media Industries', in Lievrouw, L. & Livingstone, S. (eds) *The Handbook of New Media: Student Edition*. Los Angeles, CA: SAGE, pp. 287–306.

Flew, T. & Waisbord, S. (2015) 'The Ongoing Significance of National Media Systems in the Context of Media Globalization', *Media, Culture & Society*, *37*(4), 620–636.

Florida, R. (2002) *The Rise of the Creative Class*. New York: Basic Books.

Florida, R. (2008) *Who's Your City? How the Creative Economy is Making Where You Live the Most Important Decision of Your Life*. New York: Basic Books.

Forde, S. (2011) *Challenging the News: The Journalism of Alternative and Community Media*. Basingstoke: Palgrave Macmillan.

Fortune. (2016) *Global 500*. Retrieved from http://beta.fortune.com/global500 (Accessed 13 December 2017).

Foster, J.B. (2000) Monopoly Capital at the Turn of the Millennium. *Monthly Review*, *51*(11), 1–17.

Foster, J.B. & McChesney, R.W. (2003) 'The Commercial Tidal Wave', *Monthly Review*, *54*(10), 1–16.

Foucault, M. (1982) 'The Subject and Power', in Dreyfus, H.L. & Rabinow, P. (eds) *Michel Foucault: Beyond Structuralism and Hermeneutics*. Chicago, IL: University of Chicago Press, pp. 208–226.

Foucault, M. (1988) 'On Power', in Kritzman, L. (ed.) *Michel Foucault: Politics, Philosophy, Culture: Interviews and Other Writing 1977–1984*. New York: Routledge, pp. 96–109.

Foucault, M. (2008) *The Birth of Biopolitics: Lectures at the College de France 1978–79*. Edited by M. Senellart. Translated by G. Burchell. Basingstoke: Palgrave Macmillan.

Frank, A. (1973) *The Development of Underdevelopment* (2nd ed.). New York: Monthly Review Press.

Fraser, N. (2007) 'Transnationalizing the Public Sphere: On the Legitimacy and Efficacy of Public Opinion in a Post-Westphalian World', *Theory, Culture & Society*, *24*(4), 7–30.

Freedman, D. (2008) *The Politics of Media Policy*. Cambridge, UK: Polity Press.

Freedman, D. (2014) 'Metrics, Models and the Meaning of Media Ownership', *International Journal of Cultural Policy*, *20*(2), 170–185.

Freedman, D. (2015) 'Paradigms of Media Power', *Communication, Culture & Critique*, *8*(2), 273–289.

Freedom House. (2016) *Freedom on the Net 2016*. Retrieved from http://freedomhouse.org/report/freedom-net/freedom-net-2016 (Accessed 26 January 2017).

Friedman, T. (2001) *The Lexus and the Olive Tree: Understanding Globalization*. New York: St Martin's Press.

Friedman, T. (2005) *The World is Flat: A Brief History of the Globalized World in the Twenty-First Century*. London: Allen Lane.

Freidrichs, J. (2001) 'The Meaning of New Medievalism', *European Journal of International Relations*, 7(4), 475–501.

Frobel, F., Heinrichs, J. & Kreye, O. (1980) *The New International Division of Labor: Structural Unemployment in Industrialised Countries and Industrialisation in Developing Countries*. Translated by P. Burgess. Cambridge: Cambridge University Press.

Frow, J. & Morris, M. (1996) 'Australian Cultural Studies', in Storey, J. (ed.) *What is Cultural Studies? A Reader*. London: Edward Arnold, pp. 344–367.

Fuchs, C. (2015) *Culture and Economy in the Age of Social Media*. London: Routledge.

García Canclini, N. (1995) *Hybrid Cultures: Strategies for Entering and Leaving Modernity*. Translated by S. Lopez and E. Schiappari. Minneapolis, MI: Minnesota University Press.

Garnham, N. (1990) *Capitalism and Communication*. London: SAGE.

Garnham, N. (1995) 'Political Economy and Cultural Studies: Reconciliation or Divorce?', *Critical Studies in Mass Communication*, 12(1), 62–71.

Gellner, E. (1983) *Nations and Nationalism*. Oxford: Basil Blackwell.

Gibson, M. (2007) *Culture and Power: A History of Cultural Studies*. Sydney: UNSW Press.

Giddens, A. (1990) *The Consequences of Modernity*. Stanford, CA: Stanford University Press.

Giddens, A. (1997) 'The Globalizing of Modernity', in Sreberny-Mohammadi, A., Winseck, D., McKenna, J. & Boyd-Barrett, O. (eds) *Media in Global Context: A Reader*. London: Edward Arnold, pp. 19–26.

Giddens, A. (2001) *The Global Third Way Debate*. Cambridge: Polity.

Giddens, A. (2002) *Runaway World: How Globalization is Reshaping Our Lives*. London: Profile.

Gilmore, J. & Pine, J. (2011) *The Experience Economy*. Boston, MA: Harvard Business Review Press.

Gilpin, R. (1987) *The Political Economy of International Relations*. Princeton, NJ: Princeton University Press.

Gilpin, R. (2001) *Global Political Economy: Understanding the International Economic Order*. Princeton, NJ: Princeton University Press.

Gilpin, R. (2002) 'A Realist Perspective on International Governance', in Held, D. & McGrew, A. (eds) *Governing Globalization: Power, Authority and Global Governance*. Cambridge: Polity, pp. 237–248.

Gitlin, T. (1995) 'Media Sociology: The Dominant Paradigm', in Boyd-Barrett, O. & Newbold, C. (eds) *Approaches to Media: A Reader*. London: Arnold, pp. 21–32.

Glyn, A. & Sutcliffe, B. (1999) 'Still Underwhelmed: Indicators of Globalization and their Misrepresentation', *Review of International Political Economy*, 31(1), 111–131.

Goldsmith, B., Ward, S. & O'Regan, T. (2010) *Local Hollywood: Global Film Production and the Gold Coast*. Brisbane: University of Queensland Press.

Gomery, D. (1989) 'Media Economics: Terms of Analysis', *Critical Studies in Mass Communication*, 6(1), 43–60.

Gorman, L. & McLean, D. (2009) *Media and Society into the 21st Century: A Historical Introduction* (2nd ed.). Malden, MA: Wiley-Blackwell.

Gore, A. (1994) 'Remarks Prepared for Delivery by Vice-President Al Gore to the International Telecommunications Union', 21 March. Retrieved from www.itu.int/itudoc/itu-d/wtdc/wtdc1994/speech/gore.html (Accessed 19 July 2013).

Govil, N. (2009) 'Thinking Nationally: Domicile, Distinction, and Dysfunction in Global Media Exchange', in Holt, J. & Perren, A. (eds) *Media Industries: History, Theory, Method*. Malden, MA: Wiley-Blackwell, pp. 132–143.

Grabe, M. & Myrick, J. (2016) 'Informed Citizenship in a Media-centric Way of Life', *Journal of Communication*, 66(2), 215–235.

Grainge, P. (2008) *Brand Hollywood: Selling Entertainment in a Global Media Age*. London: Routledge.

Grant, P. & Wood, C. (2004) *Blockbusters and Trade Wars: Popular Culture in a Globalized World*. Vancouver: Douglas & McIntyre.

Gray, J. (2011) 'Mobility Through Piracy, or How Steven Seagal Got to Malawi', *Popular Communication*, 9(2), pp. 99–113.

Grossberg, L. (2010) *Cultural Studies in the Future Tense*. Durham, NC: Duke University Press.

Grossberg, L., Nelson, C. & Treischler, P. (1992) 'Cultural Studies: An Introduction', in Grossberg, L., Nelson, C. & Treischler, P. (eds) *Cultural Studies*. New York: Routledge, pp. 1–22.

Habermas, J. (1974) 'The Public Sphere', *New German Critique*, 3, 49–55.

Hall, P. (2000) 'Creative Cities and Urban Development', *Urban Studies*, 37(4), 637–649.

Hall, P.A. & Soskice, D. (2001) 'An Introduction to Varieties of Capitalism', in Hall, P.A. & Soskice, D. (eds) *Varieties of Capitalism: The Institutional Foundations of Comparative Advantage*. Oxford: Oxford University Press, pp. 1–86.

Hall, P. & Taylor, R. (1996) 'Political Science and the Three New Institutionalisms', *Political Science*, 44(6), 936–957.

Hall, S. (1977) 'Culture, the Media, and the "Ideological Effect"', in Curran, J., Gurevitch, M. & Woollacott, J. (eds) *Mass Communication and Society*. London: Edward Arnold, pp. 315–348.

Hall, S. (1982) 'The Rediscovery of "Ideology": Return of the Repressed in Media Studies', in Gurevitch, M., Bennett, T., Curran, J. & Woollacott, J. (eds) *Culture, Society and the Media*. London: Methuen, pp. 56–90.

Hall, S. (1986) 'Cultural Studies; Two Paradigms', in Collins, R., Curran, J., Garnham, N., Scannell, P., Schlesinger, P. & Sparks, C. (eds) *Media, Culture and Society: A Critical Reader*. London: SAGE, pp. 33–48.

Hall, S. (1993a) 'Culture, Community, Nation', *Cultural Studies*, 7(3), 349–363.

Hall, S. (1993b) 'Encoding/Decoding', in During, S. (ed.) *The Cultural Studies Reader*. London: Routledge, pp. 90–103.

Hall, S. (1996a) 'The Problem of Ideology: Marxism without Guarantees', in Morley, D. & Chen, K.-H. (eds) *Stuart Hall: Critical Dialogues in Cultural Studies*. London: Routledge, pp. 25–46.

Hall, S. (1996b) 'Who Needs "Identity"?', in Hall, S. & du Gay, P. (eds) *Questions of Cultural Identity*. London: SAGE, pp. 1–17.

Hall, S. & Jefferson, T. (1976) *Resistance Through Rituals: Youth Sub-cultures in Post-War Britain*. London: Hutchinson.

Hallin, D. & Mancini, P. (2004) *Comparing Media Systems: Three Models of Media and Politics*. Cambridge: Cambridge University Press.

Hallin, D. & Mancini, P. (2005) 'Comparing Media Systems', in Curran, J. & Gurevitch, M. (eds) *Mass Media and Society*. London: Arnold, pp. 215–235.

Hallin, D. & Mancini, P. (2012) 'Conclusion', in Hallin, D. & Mancini, P. (eds) *Comparing Media Systems Beyond the Western World*. Cambridge: Cambridge University Press, pp. 278–304.

Halloran, J. (1995) 'The Context of Mass Communication Research', in Boyd-Barrett, O. & Newbold, C. (eds) *Approaches to Media: A Reader*. London: Arnold, pp. 33–42.

Hamelink, C. (2015) *Global Communication*. London: SAGE.

Hannerz, U. (1990) 'Cosmopolitans and Locals in World Culture', in Featherstone, M. (ed.) *Global Culture: Nationalism, Globalization and Modernity*. London: SAGE, pp. 237–252.

Hardt, M. & Negri, A. (2000) *Empire*. Cambridge, MA: Harvard University Press.

Hardt, M. & Negri, A. (2004) *Multitude*. London: Penguin.

Hardy, J. (2014) *Critical Political Economy of the Media: An Introduction*. London: Routledge.

Hartig, F. (2015) *Chinese Public Diplomacy: The Rise of the Confucius Institute*. London: Routledge.

Harvey, D. (1989) *The Condition of Postmodernity: An Enquiry into the Origins of Cultural Change*. Cambridge, MA: Blackwell.

Harvey, D. (2005) *A Brief History of Neoliberalism*. Oxford: Oxford University Press.

Held, D. (1983) 'Frankfurt School', in Bottomore, T., Harris, L., Kiernan, V.G. & Miliband, R. (eds) *A Dictionary of Marxist Thought*. Oxford: Blackwell, pp. 183–188.

Held, D. (1989) 'The Decline of the Nation State', in Hall, S. & Jacques, M. (eds) *New Times: The Changing Face of Politics in the 1990s*. London: Lawrence & Wishart, pp. 191–204.

Held, D. (2004) *Global Covenant: The Social Democratic Alternative to the Washington Consensus*. Cambridge: Polity.

Held, D. (2006) *Models of Democracy* (3rd ed.). Cambridge: Polity.

Held, D. & McGrew, A. (eds) (2002) *Governing Globalization: Power, Authority and Global Governance*. Cambridge: Polity.

Held, D., McGrew, A., Goldblatt, D. & Perraton, J. (1999) *Global Transformations: Politics, Economics and Culture*. Cambridge: Polity Press.

Hendy, D. (2013) *Public Service Broadcasting*. Basingstoke: Palgrave Macmillan.

Herman, E. & Chomsky, N. (1988) *Manufacturing Consent: The Political Economy of the Mass Media*. New York: Pantheon Books.

Hernandez-Ramos, P. & Schramm, W. (1989) 'Development Communication: History and Theories', in Barnouw, E. (ed.) *International Encyclopedia of Communication*, pp. 9–12.

Hesmondhalgh, D. (2013) *The Cultural Industries* (3rd ed.). London: SAGE.

Hirst, P., Thompson, G. & Bromley, S. (2009) *Globalization in Question* (3rd ed.). Cambridge: Polity.

Hirschmann, A.O. (2013) 'The Rise and Decline of Development Economics', in Hirschmann, A.O. & Adelman, J. (eds) *The Essential Hirschmann*. Princeton, NJ: Princeton University Press, pp. 49–73.

Ho, V. & Fung, A. (2016) 'Cultural Policy, Chinese National Identity and Globalization', in Flew, T., Iosifidis, P. & Steemers, J. (eds) *Global Media and National Policies: The Return of the State*. Basingstoke: Palgrave Macmillan, pp. 122–138.

Hobsbawm, E. (1990) *Nations and Nationalism since 1780: Programme, Myth, Reality*. Cambridge: Cambridge University Press.

Hodgson, G. (2003) 'The Hidden Persuaders: Institutions and Individuals in Economic Theory', *Cambridge Journal of Economics*, *27*(2), 157–175.

Holden, J. (2013) *Influence and Attraction: Culture and the Race for Soft Power in the 21st Century*. London: British Council. Retrieved from www.britishcouncil.org/sites/default/files/influence-and-attraction-report.pdf (Accessed 13 December 2017).

Holt, J. & Malčić, S. (2015) 'The Privacy Ecosystem: Regulating Digital Identity in the United States and European Union', *Journal of Information Policy*, *5*(2), 155–178.

Holton, R. (1998) *Globalization and the Nation-State*. Basingstoke: Macmillan.

Horwitz, R. (1989) *The Irony of Regulatory Reform: The Deregulation of American Telecommunications*. New York: Oxford University Press.

Hout, W. (1993) *Capitalism and the Third World: Development, Dependence and the World System*. Aldershot: Edward Elgar.

Howard, P. (2011) *Castells and the Media*. Cambridge: Polity.

Howkins, J. (2001) *The Creative Economy: How People Make Money from Ideas*. London: Allen Lane.

Huesca, R. (2003) 'Participatory Approaches to Communication for Development', in Mody, B. (ed.) *International and Development Communication: A 21st-Century Perspective*. Thousand Oaks, CA: SAGE, pp. 209–226.

Huntington, S. (1993) 'The Clash of Civilizations?', *Foreign Affairs*, *72*(3), 22–49.

Hutchison, D. (2004) 'Protecting the Citizen, Protecting Society', in Allen, R.C. & Hill, A. (eds) *The Television Studies Reader*. London: Routledge, pp. 64–78.

Ingham, G. (1996) 'Some Recent Changes in the Relationship between Economics and Sociology', *Cambridge Journal of Economics*, *20*(2), 243–275.

Inglis, F. (2004) *Culture*. Cambridge: Polity.

Innis, H.A. (1991) *The Bias of Communication*. Edited by P. Heyer and D. Crowley. Toronto: University of Toronto Press.

Interbrand. (2016) *Rankings – 2015 – best global brands – best brands*. Retrieved 25 September 2016. Retrieved from http://interbrand.com/best-brands/best-global-brands/2015/ranking/ (Accessed 13 December 2017).

International Telecommunications Union. (2016) *ICT Facts and Figures 2016*. Geneva: ITU. Retrieved from www.itu.int/en/ITU-D/Statistics/Documents/facts/ICTFacts Figures2016.pdf (Accessed 13 December 2017).

Iosifidis, P. (2016) 'Globalisation and the Re-emergence of the Regulatory State', in Flew, T., Iosifidis, P. & Steemers, J. (eds) *Global Media and National Policies: The Return of the State*. Basingstoke: Palgrave Macmillan, pp. 16–31.

Isar, Y.R., Hoelscher, M. & Anheier, H.K. (2012) 'Cities as Policy Actors', in Anheier, H.K. & Isar, Y.R. (eds) *Cities, Cultural Policy and Governance*. Los Angeles, CA: SAGE, pp. 1–12.

Issac, T. (2014) 'Politics of Democratic Decentralization and the Developmental State: A Study of the Kerala Experience', in Williams, M. (ed.) *The End of the Developmental State*. London: Routledge, pp. 197–219.

Iwabuchi, K. (2002) *Recentering Globalization: Popular Culture and Japanese Transnationalism*. Durham, NC: Duke University Press.

Jackson, W. (2009) *Economics, Culture and Social Theory*. Cheltenham, UK: Edward Elgar.

James, V. (2008) 'The IPRs and the Music Industries in the Caribbean', in Barrowclough, D. & Kozul-Wright, Z. (eds) *Creative Industries and Developing Countries: Voice, Choice and Economic Growth*. London: Routledge, pp. 213–247.

Jenks, C. (1993) *Culture*. London: Routledge.

Jensen, K.B. & Rosengren, E. (1990) 'Five Traditions in Search of the Audience', *European Journal of Communication*, 5(2), 207–238.

Jessop, B. (2000) 'The State and the Contradictions of the Knowledge-Driven Economy', in Bryson, J.R., Daniels, P.W., Henry, N.D. & Pollard, J. (eds) *Knowledge, Space, Economy*. London: Routledge, pp. 63–78.

Jessop, B. (2002) *The Future of the Capitalist State*. Cambridge: Polity.

Jiafeng, W. (2009) 'Some Reflections on Modernization Theory and Globalization Theory', *Chinese Studies in History*, 43(1), 72–98.

Jordan, T. (1999) *Cyberpower: The Culture and Politics of Cyberspace and the Internet*. London: Routledge.

Kahn, R. & Kellner, D. (2007) 'Resisting Globalization', in Ritzer, G. (ed.) *The Blackwell Companion to Globalization*. Malden, MA: Blackwell, pp. 662–674.

Kaldor, M. (2003) *Global Civil Society: An Answer to War*. Cambridge: Polity.

Karim, K. (2003) *The Media of Diaspora: Mapping the Globe*. London: Routledge.

Karlsson, C. & Picard, R. (2011) *Media Clusters and Media Cluster Policies*. Stockholm: Centre of Excellence for Science and Innovation Studies. Retrieved from https://ideas.repec.org/p/hhs/cesisp/0246.html (Accessed 13 December 2017).

Karppinen, K. (2012) *Rethinking Media Pluralism*. New York: Fordham University Press.

Katz, E. & Lazarsfeld, P. (1995) 'The Two-Step Flow of Mass Communication', in Boyd-Barrett, O. & Newbold, C. (eds) *Approaches to Media: A Reader*. London: Hodder Arnold, pp. 124–134.

Katz, E. & Liebes, T. (1990) The Export of Meaning: Cross-Cultural Readings of Dallas. Oxford: Oxford University Press.

Keane, J. (1988) *Democracy and Civil Society*. London: Verso.

Keane, J. (2005) 'Eleven Theses on Markets and Civil Society', *Journal of Civil Society*, 1(1), 25–34.

Keane, M. (2013) *Creative Industries in China*. Cambridge: Polity.

Keane, M. (2015) *The Chinese Television Industry*. London: BFI Publishing.

Keane, M. (2016) 'Going Global or Going Nowhere? Chinese Media in a Time of Flux', *Media International Australia*, 159(1), 13–21.

Kellner, D. (1995) 'Cultural Studies, Multiculturalism and Media Culture', in Dines, G. & Humez, J.M. (eds) *Gender, Race and Class in Media: A Text-Reader*. Thousand Oaks, CA: SAGE, pp. 5–17.

Kellner, D. & Pierce, C. (2007) 'Media and Globalization', in Ritzer, G. (ed.) *The Black-well Companion to Globalization*. Malden, MA: Blackwell, pp. 383–395.

Klein, N. (2000) *No Logo: Taking Aim at the Brand Bullies*. New York: Saint Martin's Press.

Knill, C. (2005) 'Introduction: Cross-National Policy Convergence: Concepts, Approaches and Explanatory Factors', *Journal of European Public Policy*, *12*(5), 764–774.

Kohli, A. (2004) *State-Directed Development*. Cambridge: Cambridge University Press.

Kokas, A. (2016) *Hollywood: Made in China – Understanding the Relationship Between Two Global Production Brands*. Berkeley, CA: University of California Press.

Koshy, V., Waterman, H. & Koshy, E. (2011) *Action Research in Healthcare*. London: SAGE.

Kraidy, M. (2005) *Hybridity, or the Cultural Logic of Globalization*. Philadelphia, PA: Temple University Press.

Kleingeld, P. & Brown, E. (2013) 'Cosmopolitanism', *Stanford Encyclopedia of Philosophy*. Retrieved from https://plato.stanford.edu/entries/cosmopolitanism/ (Accessed 27 January 2017).

Kurlantzick, J. (2012) *The global human rights regime*. Retrieved from www.cfr.org/human-rights/global-human-rights-regime/p27450 (Accessed 5 December 2016).

Kuwahara, Y. (2014) *The Korean Wave: Korean Popular Culture in Global Context*. Basingstoke: Palgrave Macmillan.

Landry, C. (2000) *The Creative City: A Toolkit for Urban Innovators*. London: Earthscan.

Larkin, B. (2008) *Signal and Noise: Media, Infrastructure, and Urban Culture in Nigeria*. Durham, NC: Duke University Press.

Larrain, J. (1983) *Marxism and Ideology*. London: Macmillan.

Lash, S. & Urry, J. (1994) *Economies of Signs and Space*. Thousand Oaks, CA: SAGE.

Lash, S. & Urry, J. (1987) *The End of Organised Capitalism*. Cambridge: Polity.

Lee, H.-K. & Lim, L. (2014) 'Cultural Policies in East Asia: An Introduction', in Lee, H.-K. & Lim, L. (eds) *Cultural Policies in East Asia: Dynamics between the State, Arts and Creative Industries*. Basingstoke: Palgrave Macmillan, pp. 1–14.

Lee, T. (2016) 'Forging an "Asian" Media Fusion: Singapore as a 21st Century Media Hub' *Media International Australia*, *158*(1), 80–89.

Lenin, V. (1965) *Imperialism: The Highest Stage of Capitalism*. Moscow: Progress Press.

Lerner, D. (1958) *The Passing of Traditional Society*. Glencoe, IL: Free Press.

Lerner, D. (1963) 'Towards a Communication Theory of Modernization', in Pye, L. (ed.) *Communications and Political Development*. Princeton, NJ: Princeton University Press, pp. 327–350.

Lerner, D. (1968) 'Modernization', in Sills, D. (ed.) *International Encyclopedia of the Social Sciences*. New York: Macmillan, pp. 386–395.

Leye, V. (2007) 'UNESCO, ICT Corporations and the Passion of ICT for Development: Modernization Resurrected', *Media, Culture & Society*, *29*(6), 972–993.

Lievrouw, L.A. (2011) *Alternative and Activist New Media*. Cambridge: Polity.

Lievrouw, L.A. & Livingstone, S. (eds) (2006) *The Handbook of New Media: Student Edition*. Thousand Oaks, CA: SAGE.

Lobato, R. (2012) *Shadow Economies of Cinema*. London: BFI.

Lobato, R. & Thomas, J. (2014) *The Informal Media Economy*. Cambridge: Polity Press.

Locker, M. (2014) 'Did North Korea Hack Sony Pictures Over The Interview?' *Vanity Fair*. Retrieved from www.vanityfair.com/hollywood/2014/11/north-korea-james-franco-seth-rogen (Accessed 13 December 2017).

Looseley, D. (1995) *The Politics of Fun: Cultural Policy and Debate in Contemporary France*. Oxford: Berg.

Lukes, S. (2005) *Power: A Radical View* (2nd ed.). Basingstoke: Palgrave.

Lyotard, J.-F. (1984) *The Postmodern Condition: A Report on Knowledge*. Translated by G. Bennington and B. Massumi. Minneapolis, MI: University of Minnesota Press.

MacBride, S. (1980) *Many Voices, One World: Communications and Society Today and Tomorrow*. Paris: UNESCO.

Mansell, R. (2004) 'Political Economy, Power and New Media', *New Media & Society*, 6(1), 96–105.

Mansell, R. & Raboy, M. (2011) 'Foundations of the Theory and Practice of Global Media and Communication Policy', in Mansell, R. & Raboy, M. (eds) *Handbook of Global Media and Communication Policy*. Malden, MA: Wiley-Blackwell, pp. 1–20.

Manyozo, L. (2012) *Media, Communication and Development: Three Approaches*. Thousand Oaks, CA: SAGE.

Markusen, A. (1996) 'Sticky Places in Slippery Space: A Typology of Industrial Districts', *Economic Geography*, 72, 293–313.

Marshall, A. (1980) *Principles of Economics* (8th ed.). London: Macmillan.

Marx, K. & Engels, F. (1983) 'Manifesto of the Communist Party', in Giddens, A. & Held, D. (eds) *Classes, Power and Conflict: Classical and Contemporary Debates*. London: Macmillan, pp. 19–24.

Massey, D. (1985) 'New Directions in Space', in Gregory, D. & Urry, J. (eds) *Social Relations and Spatial Structures*. London: Macmillan, pp. 9–19.

Mathews, G. (2000) *Global Culture/Individual Identity: Searching for Home in the Cultural Supermarket*. London: Routledge.

Mattelart, A. (1994) *Mapping World Communication: War, Progress, Culture*. Translated by S. Emanuel & J.A. Cohen. Minneapolis, MI: University of Minnesota Press.

Mattelart, A. (2003) *The Information Society: An Introduction*. Thousand Oaks, CA: SAGE.

Matthews, J. & Maguire, J.S. (2014) 'Thinking with Cultural Intermediaries', in Maguire, J.S. & Matthews, J. (eds) *The Cultural Intermediaries Reader*. London: SAGE, pp. 1–12.

May, T. (2016) 'Speech to the Conservative Party conference', 5 October. Retrieved from www.telegraph.co.uk/news/2016/10/05/theresa-mays-conference-speech-in-full/ (Accessed 13 December 2017).

Mazzoleni, G. & Schulz, W. (1999) '"Mediatization" of Politics: A Challenge for Democracy?', *Political Communication*, 16(3), 247–261.

McChesney, R. (1999) *Rich Media, Poor Democracy: Communication Politics in Dubious Times*. Urbana-Champaign, IL: University of Illinois Press.

McChesney, R. (2001a) 'Global Media, Neoliberalism, and Imperialism', *Monthly Review* 52 (10), 1–19.

McChesney, R. (2001b) 'Policing the Thinkable', *Open Democracy*. Retrieved from www.opendemocracy.net/media-globalmediaownership/article_56.jsp (Accessed 13 December 2017).

McChesney, R. (2008) *The Political Economy of Media: Enduring Issues, Emerging Dilemmas*. New York: Monthly Review Press.

McChesney, R. (2013) *Digital Disconnect: How Capitalism is Turning the Internet Against Democracy*. New York: New Press, The.

McChesney, R. & Herman, E. (1997) *The Global Media: The New Missionaries of Global Capitalism*. London: Cassell.

McChesney, R. & Schiller, D. (2003) *The Political Economy of International Communication: Foundations for the Emerging Global Debate about Media Ownership and Regulation*. Geneva: United Nations Research Institute for Social Development. Retrieved from www.unrisd.org/80256B3C005BCCF9/search/C9DCBA6C7DB78C2AC1256B DF0049A774?OpenDocument. (Accessed 13 December 2017).

McClelland, D. (1961) *The Achieving Society*. Princeton, NJ: Princeton University Press.

McGuigan, J. (2004) *Rethinking Cultural Policy*. Buckingham: Open University Press.

McLuhan, M. & Fiore, Q. (1967) *The Medium is the Massage*. New York: Bantam.

McMillin, D. (2007) *International Media Studies*. Malden, MA: Blackwell.

McNair, B., Flew, T., Harrington, S. & Swift, A. (2017) *Politics, Media and Democracy in Australia*. London: Routledge.

McPhail, T. (2009) *Global Communication: Theories, Stakeholders, and Trends* (3rd ed.). Malden, MA: Wiley-Blackwell.

McQuail, D. (2005) *Mass Communication Theory* (5th ed.). London: SAGE.

McRobbie, A. (2016) *Be Creative: Making a Living in the New Culture Industries*. Cambridge: Polity.

Mefalopulos, P. (2008) *Development Communication Sourcebook: Broadening the Boundaries of Communication*. Washington, DC: World Bank Publications.

Meikle, G. (2016) *Social Media: Communication, Sharing and Visibility*. London: Routledge.

Melkote, S.R. (2010) 'Theories of Development Communication', in Thussu, D.K. (ed.) *International Communication: A Reader*. London: Routledge, pp. 105–121.

Meyrowitz, J. (1985) *No Sense of Place: The Impact of Electronic Media on Social Behavior*. New York: Oxford University Press.

Michael, J. (1990) 'Regulating Communications Media: From the Discretion of Sound Chaps to the Arguments of Lawyers', in Ferguson, M. (ed.) *Public Communications: The New Imperatives*. London: SAGE, pp. 40–60.

Mihelj, S. (2011) *Media Nations*. Basingstoke: Palgrave.

Miller, D. & Slater, D. (2000) *The Internet: An Ethnographic Approach*. Oxford: Berg.

Miller, T. & Kraidy, M. (2016) *Global Media Studies*. Cambridge: Polity.

Miller, T., Govil, N., McMurria, J. & Maxwell, R. (2001) *Global Hollywood*. London: British Film Institute.

Miller, T., Govil, N., McMurria, J., Maxwell, R. & Wang, T. (2005) *Global Hollywood 2* (2nd ed.). London: British Film Institute.

Mirrlees, T. (2013) *Global Entertainment Media: Between Cultural Imperialism and Cultural Globalization*. New York: Routledge.

Moran, A. (2004) 'Television Formats in the World/The World of Television Formats', in Moran, A. & Keane, M. (eds) *Television Across Asia: Television Industries, Programme Formats and Globalization*. London: Routledge, pp. 1–8.

Morley, D. (1989) 'Changing Paradigms in Audience Studies', in Seiter, E., Borchers, H., Kreutzner, G. & Warth, E.-M. (eds) *Remote Control: Television, Audiences and Cultural Power*. London: Routledge, pp. 16–43.

Morley, D. (2009) 'For a Materialist, Non-media-centric Media Studies', *Television & New Media*, *10*(1), 114–116.

Morley, D., Moores, S. & Krajina, Z. (2014) 'Non-media-centric Media Studies: A Cross-Generational Conversation', *European Journal of Cultural Studies*, *17*(6), 682–700.

Moore, B. (1967) *Social Origins of Dictatorship and Democracy: Lord and Peasant in the Making of the Modern World*. London: Allen Lane.

Morris, N. (2003) 'A Comparative Analysis of the Diffusion and Participatory Models in Development Communication', *Communication Theory*, *13*(2), 225–248.

Mosco, V. (2009) *The Political Economy of Communication* (2nd ed.). Los Angeles, CA: SAGE.

Mowlana, H. (2012) 'International Communication: The Journey of a Caravan', *Journal of International Communication*, *18*(2), 267–290.

Murdock, G. & Golding, P. (1973) 'For a Political Economy of Mass Communication', in Miliband, R. & Saville, J. (eds) *The Socialist Register 1973*. London: Merlin Press, pp. 203–234.

Murdock, G. & Golding, P. (2005) 'Culture, Communications and Political Economy', in Curran, J. & Gurevitch, M. (eds) *Mass Media and Society* (4th ed.). London: Arnold, pp. 60–83.

Murphy, E., Fox-Rogers, L. & Redmond, D. (2014) 'Location Decision Making of "Creative" Industries: The Media and Computer Game Sectors in Dublin, Ireland', *Growth and Change*, *46*(1), 97–113.

Murray, R. (1971) 'The Internationalization of Capital and the Nation-State', *New Left Review*, (67), 84–109.

Murray, R. (1989) 'Fordism and Post-Fordism', in Hall, S. & Jacques, M. (eds) *New Times: The Changing Face of Politics in the 1990s*. London: Lawrence & Wishart, pp. 38–53.

Nafziger, W. (2006) *Economic Development* (4th ed.). Cambridge: Cambridge University Press.

Napoli, P. (2009) 'Media Economics and the Study of Media Industries', in Perren, A. & Holt, J. (eds) *Media Industries: History, Theory, and Method*. Malden, MA: Wiley-Blackwell, pp. 161–170.

Newbold, C. (1995) 'The Media Effects Tradition', in Boyd-Barrett, O. & Newbold, C. (eds) *Approaches to Media: A Reader*. London: Arnold, pp. 118–123.

Noam, E. (2009) *Media Ownership and Concentration in America*. New York: Oxford University Press.

Noam, E. (2016) *Who Owns the World's Media?: Media Concentration and Ownership around the World*. Oxford: Oxford University Press.

Nordenstreng, K. (2012) 'The New World Information and Communication Order: An Idea that Refuses to Die', in Valdivia, A.N. (ed.) *International Encyclopedia of Media Studies*. Chichester: Wiley-Blackwell, pp. 477–499.

Nordenstreng, K. & Varis, T. (1974) *Television Traffic – A One-Way Street? A Survey and Analysis of the International Flow of Television Programme Material*. Paris: UNESCO.

North, D. (1990) *Institutions, Institutional Change and Economic Performance*. Cambridge: Cambridge University Press.

North, D. (1994) 'Economic Performance Through Time', *American Economic Review*, 84(3), 359–368.

Nye, J. (2004) *Soft Power: The Means to Success in World Politics*. New York: Public Affairs.

Nye, J. (2013) 'What China and Russia Don't Get About Soft Power', *Foreign Policy*. Retrieved from http://foreignpolicy.com/2013/04/29/what-china-and-russia-dont-get-about-soft-power/ (Accessed 13 December 2017).

Ogan, C., Bashir, M., Camaj, L., Luo, Y., Gaddie, B., Pennington, R., Rana, S. & Salih, M. (2009) 'Development Communication: The State of Research in an Era of ICTs and Globalization', *International Communication Gazette*, 71(8), 655–670.

Ozawa, T. (2009) *The Rise of Asia: The 'Flying-Geese' Theory of Tandem Growth and Regional Agglomeration*. Cheltenham: Edward Elgar.

Padovani, C. & Raboy, M. (2010) 'Mapping Global Media Policy: Concepts, Frameworks, Methods', *Communication, Culture & Critique*, 3(2), 150–169.

Papacharissi, Z. (2015) *Affective Publics: Sentiment, Technology, and Politics*. New York: Oxford University Press.

Parsons, T. (1951) *The Social System*. London: Routledge & Kegan Paul.

Pertierra, A. & Turner, G. (2013) *Locating Television: Zones of Consumption*. London: Routledge.

Peters, B. (2012) *Institutional Theory in Political Science: The New Institutionalism* (3rd ed.). London: Continuum.

Picard, R. (1989) *Media Economics: Concepts and Issues*. London: SAGE.

Picard, R. (2011a) 'Economic Approaches to Media Policy', in Mansell, R. & Raboy, M. (eds) *The Handbook of Global Media and Communications Policy*. Malden, MA: Wiley-Blackwell, pp. 355–365.

Picard, R. (2011b) *The Economics and Financing of Media Companies*. New York: Fordham University Press.

Pickard, V. (2007) 'Neoliberal Visions and Revisions in Global Communications Policy from NWICO to WSIS', *Journal of Communication Inquiry*, 31(2), 118–139.

Pierskala, J. & Hollenbach, F. (2013) 'Technology and Collective Action: The Effect of Cell Phone Coverage on Political Violence in Africa', *American Political Science Review*, 107(2), 207–223.

Pieterse, J. (2015) *Globalization and Culture: Cultural Mélange* (3rd ed.). Lanham, MD: Rowman & Littlefield.

Poggi, G. (1990) *The State: Its Nature, Development, and Prospects*. Cambridge: Polity.

Polanyi, K. (1957) 'The Economy as an Instituted Process', in Polanyi, K., Arensberg, C.M. & Pearson, H.W. (eds) *Trade and Markets in the Early Empires: Economies in History and Theory*. New York: Free Press, pp. 29–52.

Porter, M. (1998) 'Clusters and the New Economics of Competition', *Harvard Business Review*, 76(6), 77–91.

Porter, M. (2000) 'Locations, Clusters, and Company Strategy', in Clark, G., Feldman, M. & Gertler, M. (eds) *The Oxford Handbook of Economic Geography*. Oxford: Oxford University Press, pp. 253–274.

Prahalad, C. (2005) *The Fortune at the Bottom of the Pyramid*. Philadelphia, PA: Wharton School Publishing.

Pratt, A.C. (2008) 'The Music Industry and its Potential Role in Local Economic Development: The Case of Senegal', in Barrowclough, D. & Kozul-Wright, Z. (eds) *Creative Industries in Developing Countries: Voice, Choice and Economic Growth*. London: Routledge, pp. 130–145.

Price, M. (2003) 'Public Diplomacy and the Transformation of International Broadcasting', *Cardoza Arts and Entertainment Law Journal*, 21(1), 51–85.

de Propris, L. & Hypponen, L. (2008) 'Creative Clusters and Governance: The Dominance of the Hollywood Film Cluster', in Cooke, P. & Lazzeretti, L. (eds) *Creative Cities, Creative Clusters and Local Economic Development*. Cheltenham: Edward Elgar, pp. 258–286.

Pye, L. (1963) *Communication and Political Development*. Princeton, NJ: Princeton University Press.

Raboy, M. (2002) 'Media Policy in the New Communications Environment', in Raboy, M. (ed.) *Global Media Policy in the New Millennium*. Luton: University of Luton Press, pp. 3–16.

Raboy, M. (2004) 'The WSIS as a Political Space in Global Media Governance', *Continuum: Journal of Media and Cultural Studies*, 18(3), 345–359.

Raboy, M. (2007) 'Broadening Media Discourses: Global Media Policy Defining the Field', *Global Media and Communication*, 3(3), 343–347.

Rawnsley, G. (2015) 'To Know Us is to Love Us: Public Diplomacy and International Broadcasting in Contemporary Russia and China', *Politics*, 35(3–4), 273–286.

Rennie, E. (2006) *Community Media: A Global Introduction*. Lanham, MD: Rowman & Littlefield.

Rice, R.E. & Haythornthwaite, C. (2006) 'Perspectives on Internet Use: Access, Involvement and Interaction', in Lievrouw, L.A. & Livingstone, S. (eds) *Handbook of New Media*. Los Angeles, CA: SAGE, pp. 92–113.

Ritzer, G. (2004) *The McDonaldization of Society* (3rd ed.). Pine Forge Press: Thousand Oaks, CA.

Ritzer, G. (2007) 'Introduction', in Ritzer, G. (ed.) *The Blackwell Companion to Globalization*. Malden, MA: Blackwell, pp. 1–12.

Roach, C. (1990) 'The Movement for a New World Information and Communication Order: A Second Wave?', *Media, Culture & Society*, 12(3), 283–307.

Roach, C. (1997) 'The Western World and the NWICO? United They Stand?', in Golding, P. & Harris, P. (eds) *Beyond Cultural Imperialism: Globalization, Communication and the New International Order*. London: SAGE, pp. 94–116.

Robbins, B. (1998) 'Actualy Existing Cosmopolitanism', in Cheah, P. & Robbins, B. (eds), *Cosmopolitics: Thinking and Feeling Beyond the Nation*. Minneapolis, MI: University of Minnesota Press, pp. 1–19.

Robertson, R. (1992) *Globalization: Social Theory and Global Culture*. London: SAGE.

Robertson, R. & Lechner, F. (1985) 'Modernization, Globalization and the Problem of Culture in World-Systems Theory', *Theory, Culture and Society*, 2(3), 103–117.

Robertson, R. & White, K.E. (2007) 'What is Globalization?', in Ritzer, G. (ed.) *The Blackwell Companion to Globalization*. Malden, MA: Blackwell, pp. 54–66.

Robins, K. & Morley, D. (1995) *Spaces of Identity: Global Media, Electronic Landscapes and Cultural Boundaries*. New York: Routledge.

Rodrik, D. (2011) *The Globalization Paradox: Democracy and the Future of the World Economy*. New York: W. W. Norton & Co.

Rogers, E. (1969) *Modernization among Peasants: The Impact of Communication*. New York: Holt, Rinehart & Winston.

Rogers, E. (1974) 'Communication in Development', *Annals of The American Academy of Political and Social Science, 412*(1), 44–54.

Rogers, E. (1976) 'Communication and Development: The Passing of the Dominant Paradigm', *Communications Research, 3*(2), 213–240.

Rogers, E. & Antola, L. (1985) 'Telenovelas: A Latin American Success Story', *Journal of Communication, 35*(4), 24–35.

Ruccio, D. (2008) 'Economic Representations', *Cultural Studies, 22*(6), 892–912.

Ruggiero, R., 1998, 'A Borderless World', Address to the OECD Ministerial Conference, Ottawa, 7 October, www.wto.org/english/news_e/sprr_e/ott_e.htm (Accessed 13 December 2017).

Rugman, A. (2000) *The End of Globalization*. London: Random House.

Rustad, M. & Kulevska, S. (2015) 'Reconceptualizing the Right to be Forgotten to Enable Transatlantic Data Flows', *Harvard Journal of Law and Technology, 28*(2), 349–418.

Sabin, L. (2017) 'Labor "Will Fight for a People's Brexit"', *Morning Star*. Retrieved from http://morningstaronline.co.uk/a-6728-Labour-Will-Fight-for-a-Peoples-Brexit#. WjCwMVT1VYg (Accessed 13 December 2017).

Sachs, J. (2005) *The End of Poverty: Economic Possibilities for Our Time*. New York: Allen Lane.

dos Santos, T. (1973) 'The Structure of Dependence', in Wilber, C.K. (ed.) *The Political Economy of Development and Underdevelopment* (1st ed.). New York: Random House, pp. 99–107.

Sarakakis, K. (2012) 'Cities as Geopolitical Spaces for the Global Governance of Culture', in Anheier, H. & Isar, Y.R. (eds) *Cities, Cultural Policy and Governance*. Los Angeles, CA: SAGE, pp. 17–31.

Sassen, S. (2006) *Territory, Authority, Rights: From Medieval to Global Assemblages*. Princeton, NJ: Princeton University Press.

Schiller, D. (2000) *Digital Capitalism: Networking the Global Market System*. Cambridge, MA: MIT Press.

Schiller, H.I. (1969) *Mass Communications and American Empire*. Boston, MA: Beacon Press.

Schiller, H. I. (1976) Communication and Cultural Domination. New York: International Arts and Sciences Press.

Schiller, H.I. (1991) 'Not Yet the Post-Imperialist Era', *Critical Studies in Mass Communication, 8*(1), pp. 13–28.

Schiller, H.I. (1996) *Information Inequality: The Deepening Social Crisis in America*. London: Routledge.

Schlesinger, P. (1991a) *Media, State, and Nation: Political Violence and Collective Identities*. London: SAGE.

Schlesinger, P. (1991b) 'Media, the Political Order and National Identity', *Media, Culture and Society, 13*(3), 297–308.

Schlesinger, P. (1997) 'From Cultural Defence to Political Culture: Media, Politics and Collective Identity in the European Union', *Media, Culture and Society, 19*(3), 369–391.

Scholte, J. (2005) *Globalization: A Critical Introduction* (2nd ed.). Basingstoke: Palgrave Macmillan.

Schramm, W. (1964) *Mass Media and National Development: The Role of Information in Developing Societies.* Stanford, CA: Stanford University Press.

Schudson, M. (1994) 'Culture and the Integration of Modern Societies', *International Social Science Journal, 46*(1), 63–80.

Schwab, K. (2017) *The Fourth Industrial Revolution.* London: Penguin.

Scott, A.J. (2004) 'Cultural-Products Industries and Urban Economic Development: Prospects for Growth and Market Contestation in Global Context', *Urban Affairs Review, 39*(4), 461–490.

Scott, A.J. (2005) *On Hollywood: The Place, the Industry.* Oxford: Oxford University Press.

Scott, A.J. (2008) *Social Economy of the Metropolis.* Oxford: Oxford University Press.

Scott, A.J., Agnew, J., Soja, E.W. & Storper, M. (2008) 'Global City-Regions', in Scott, A.J. (ed.) *Global City-Regions: Trends, Theory, Policy.* Oxford: Oxford University Press, pp. 11–30.

Sen, A. (2003) 'Development as Capability Expansion', in Fukuda-Parr, S. & Shiva Kumar, A.K. (eds), *Readings in Human Development: Concepts, Measures and Priorities for a Development Paradigm.* New York: Oxford University Press, pp. 26–45.

Seo, S. (2016) 'A Theory of Global Public Goods and their Provisions', *Journal of Public Affairs, 16*(4), 394–405.

Servaes, J. (1989) *One World, Many Cultures: Towards Another Paradigm on Communication for Development.* Leuwen: ACCO.

Servaes, J. (1999) *Communication for Development: One World, Multiple Cultures.* New York: Hampton Press.

Shade, L. (2003) 'Here comes the DOT Force!: The New Cavalry for Equity?', *Gazette: The International Journal for Communication Studies, 65*(2), 107–120.

Shaw, M. (1997) 'The Theoretical Challenge of Global Society', in Sreberny-Mohammadi, A., Winseck, D., McKenna, J. & Boyd-Barrett, O. (eds) *Media in Global Context: A Reader.* London: Edward Arnold, pp. 27–36.

Siapera, E. (2010) *Cultural Diversity and Global Media: The Mediation of Difference.* Malden, MA: Wiley-Blackwell.

Siapera, E. (2012) *Understanding New Media.* London: SAGE.

Siebert, F.S., Peterson, T. & Schramm, W. (1956) *Four Theories of the Press.* Urbana, IL: University of Illinois Press.

Sinclair, J., Jacka, E. & Cunningham, S. (1996) *New Patterns in Global Television: Peripheral Vision.* Oxford: Oxford University Press.

Sinclair, J. (1999) *Latin American Television: A Global View.* New York: Oxford University Press.

Sinclair, J. (2003) '"The Hollywood of Latin America": Miami as Regional Center in Television Trade', *Television and New Media, 4*(3), 211–229.

Sinclair, J. (2012) *Advertising, the Media and Globalization: A World in Motion.* London: Routledge.

Sinclair, J. & Straubhaar, J. (2013) *Latin American Television Industries.* London: BFI.

Sinclair, J., Cunningham, S. & Jacka, E. (1998) 'Global and Regional Dynamics of International Television Flows', in Thussu, D.K. (ed.) *Electronic Empires: Global Media and Local Resistance.* London: Arnold, pp. 177–192.

Skidelsky, R. (2003) *John Maynard Keynes, 1883–1946: Economist, Philosopher, Statesman*. London: Penguin.

Sklair, L. (1997) 'Classifying the Global System', in Sreberny-Mohamadi, A., Winseck, D., McKenna, J. & Boyd-Barrett, O. (eds) *Media in Global Context: A Reader*. London: Arnold, pp. 37–47.

Sklair, L. (1998) 'Social Movements and Global Capitalism', in Jameson, F. & Miyoshi, M. (eds) *The Cultures of Globalization*. Durham, NC: Duke University Press, pp. 291–311.

Sklair, L. (2002) *Globalization: Capitalism and its Alternatives* (3rd ed.). New York: Oxford University Press.

Skocpol, T. (1985) 'Bringing the State Back In: Current Research', in Evans, P., Rueschmeyer, D. & Skocpol, T. (eds) *Bringing the State Back in*. Cambridge: Cambridge University Press, pp. 3–37.

Smith, A. (1991) 'Towards a Global Culture?', in Featherstone, M. (ed.) *Global Culture: Nationalism, Globalization and Modernity*. London: SAGE, pp. 171–192.

Smythe, D. (1977) 'Communication: Blindspot of Western Marxism', *Canadian Journal of Social and Political Theory*, 1(3), 1–27.

de Sola Pool, I. (1963) 'The Mass Media and Politics in the Modernization Process', in Pye, L. (ed.) *Communications and Political Development*. Princeton, NJ: Princeton University Press, pp. 234–253.

Sparks, C. (2007) *Globalization, Development, and the Mass Media*. London: SAGE.

Sparks, C. (2012) 'Media and Cultural Imperialism Reconsidered', *Chinese Journal of Communication*, 5(3), 281–299.

Sparks, C. (2016) 'Global Integration, State Policy and the Media', in Flew, T., Iosifidis, P. & Steemers, J. (eds) *Global Media and National Policies: The Return of the State*. Basingstoke: Palgrave Macmillan, pp. 49–73.

Spencer, P. & Wollman, H. (2002) *Nationalism: A Critical Introduction*. Edited by H. Wollman. Los Angeles, CA: SAGE.

Spivak, G.C. (1990) *The Post-Colonial Critic: Interviews, Strategies, Dialogues*. Edited by S. Harasym. New York: Routledge.

Springer, S., Birch, K. & MacLeavy, J. (2016) 'An Introduction to Neoliberalism', in Springer, S., Birch, K. & MacLeavy, J. (eds) *The Handbook of Neoliberalism*. London: Routledge, pp. 1–14.

Star, S.L. & Bowker, G.C. (2006) 'How to Infrastructure', in Lievrouw, L. & Livingstone, S. (eds) *The Handbook of New Media: Student Edition*. Los Angeles, CA: SAGE, pp. 230–245.

Steger, M. (2005) *Globalism* (2nd ed.). Lanham, MD: Rowman & Littlefield.

Steger, M. (2009) *Globalization: A Very Short Introduction* (2nd ed.). New York: Oxford University Press.

Steinert, H. (2003) *The Culture Industry*. Cambridge: Polity Press.

Stilwell, F. (2002) *Political Economy: The Contest of Economic Ideas*. Oxford: Oxford University Press.

Storey, J. (1996) *What is Cultural Studies? A Reader*. London: Edward Arnold.

Storper, M. (1997) *The Regional World*. New York: Guildford Press.

Storper, M. & Venables, A. (2004) Buzz: Face-to-Face Contact and the Urban Economy. *Journal of Economic Geography*, 4(2), 351–370.

Storper, M. & Scott, A.J. (2009) 'Rethinking Human Capital, Creativity and Urban Growth', *Journal of Economic Geography*, *9*(1), 147–167.

Strange, S. (1995) 'The Defective State', *Daedalus*, *124*, 55–74.

Straubhaar, J. (1991) 'Beyond Media Imperialism: Assymetrical Interdependence and Cultural Proximity', *Critical Studies in Mass Communication*, *8*(1), 39–59.

Straubhaar, J. (1997) 'Distinguishing the Global, Regional and National Levels of World Television', in Sreberny-Mohammadi, A., Winseck, D., McKenna, J. & Boyd-Barrett, O. (eds) *Media in Global Context: A Reader*. London: Edward Arnold, pp. 284–298.

Straubhaar, J. (2007) *World Television: From Global to Local*. Los Angeles, CA: SAGE.

Streeter, T. (1996) *Selling the Air: A Critique of the Policy of Commercial Broadcasting in the United States*. Chicago, IL: University of Chicago Press.

Sum, N.L. & Jessop, B. (2015) *Towards a Cultural Political Economy*. Cheltenham: Edward Elgar.

Sundaram, R. (2005) 'Developmentalism Redux?', in Lovink, G. & Zehle, S. (eds) *Incommunicado Reader: Information Technology for Everyone Else*. Amsterdam: Institute of Network Cultures, pp. 115–121.

Syvertsen, T., Enli, G., Mjos, O.J. & Moe, H. (2014) *The Media Welfare State: Nordic Media in the Digital Era*. Ann Arbor, MI: The University of Michigan Press.

Take, I. (2012) Regulating the Internet Infrastructure: A comparative appraisal of the legitimacy of ICANN, ITU, and the WSIS. *Regulation & Governance*, *6*(4), 499–523.

Taneja, H. & Wu, A.X. (2014) 'Does the Great Firewall Really Isolate the Chinese? Integrating Access Blockage with Cultural Factors to Explain Web User Behavior', *The Information Society*, *30*(5), pp. 297–309.

Tett, G. (2017) 'Davos Man has No Clothes', *Foreign Policy*. Retrieved from http://foreignpolicy.com/2017/01/16/davos-man-has-no-clothes-globalization/ (Accessed 13 December 2017).

Thomas, P. (2010) 'Digital Divide', in Littlejohn, S.W. & Foss, K.A. (eds) *Encyclopedia of Communication Theory*. Los Angeles, CA: SAGE, pp. 310–312.

Thompson, J.B. (1990) *Ideology and Modern Culture*. Cambridge: Polity Press.

Thompson, J.B. (1995) *The Media and Modernity*. Stanford, CA: Stanford University Press.

Thompson, J.E. & Krasner, S. (1989) 'Global Transactions and the Consolidation of Sovereignty', in Czempiel, E.O. & Rosenau, J.N. (eds) *Global Changes and Theoretical Challenges*. Lexington, MA: Lexington Books, pp. 195–219.

Throsby, D. (2010) *The Economics of Cultural Policy*. Cambridge: Cambridge University Press.

Thussu, D.K. (2006) *International Communication: Continuity and Change* (2nd ed.). London: Arnold.

Thussu, D.K. (2010) *International Communication: A Reader*. London: Routledge.

Tinic, S. (2005) *On Location: Canada's Television Industry in a Global Market*. Toronto: University of Toronto Press.

Todaro, M.D. & Smith, S. (2015) *Economic Development* (12th ed.). New York: Pearson.

Tomlinson, J. (1991) *Cultural Imperialism*. London: Pinter.

Tomlinson, J. (1999) *Globalization and Culture*. Cambridge: Polity Press.

Tomlinson, J. (2003) 'Globalization and Cultural Identity', in Held, D. & McGrew, A. (eds) *The Global Transformations Reader*. Cambridge: Polity, pp. 269–277.

Tomlinson, J. (2007) 'Cultural Globalization', in Ritzer, G. (ed.) *The Blackwell Companion to Globalization*. Malden, MA: Blackwell, pp. 352–366.

Towse, R. (2010) *A Handbook of Cultural Economics*. Cheltenham: Edward Elgar.

Tracey, M. (1988) Popular Culture and the Economics of Global Television. *Intermedia*, *16*(3), 53–69.

Trump, D. (2017) 'Speech to the Conservative Political Action Conference', 25 February. Retrieved from http://time.com/4682023/cpac-donald-trump-speech-transcript/. (Accessed 13 December 2017).

Tunstall, J. (1978) *The Media Are American*. New York: Columbia University Press.

Tunstall, J. (2008) *The Media Were American: U.S. Mass Media in Decline*. Oxford: Oxford University Press.

Turner, G. (2015) *Re-inventing the Media*. London: Routledge.

UNCTAD (2003) *World Investment Report*. Geneva: United Nations.

UNCTAD (2006) *World Investment Report*. Geneva: United Nations.

UNCTAD (2007) *World Investment Report*. Geneva: United Nations.

UNCTAD (2010) *The Creative Economy Report 2010*. Geneva: United Nations.

UNCTAD (2016) *World Investment Report 2016*. Geneva: UNCTAD. Retrieved from http://unctad.org/en/PublicationsLibrary/wir2016_en.pdf (Accessed 13 December 2017).

UNESCO (2004) *UNESCO and the Issue of Cultural Diversity: Review and Strategy, 1946–2004*. Paris: UNESCO.

Union of International Associations (UIA) (2015) *The Yearbook of International Organizations*. Retrieved from www.uia.org/yearbook (Accessed 13 December 2017).

United Nations (1948) *Universal Declaration of Human Rights*. Retrieved from www.un.org/en/universal-declaration-human-rights/ (Accessed 13 December 2017).

United Nations (2003) *We Can End Poverty: Millennium Development Goals and Beyond 2015*. New York: United Nations. Retrieved from http://un.org/millenniumgoals/2015_MDG_Report/pdf (Accessed 13 December 2017).

United Nations Development Program. (2001) *Human Development Report 2001: Making New Technologies Work for Human Development*. New York: Oxford University Press.

Unwin, T. (2009) 'ICT4D Implementation: Policies and Partnerships', in Unwin, T. (ed.) *ICT4D: Information and Communication Technology for Development*. Cambridge: Cambridge University Press, pp. 125–175.

Van Cuilenburg, J. and McQuail, D. (2003) 'Media Policy Paradigm Shifts: Towards a New Communications Policy Paradigm', *European Journal of Communication*, *18*(2), 181–207.

Varis, T. (1974) 'Global Traffic in Television', *Journal of Communication*, *24*(1), 102–109.

Varis, T. (1984) 'The International Flow of Television Programs', *Journal of Communication*, *34*(1), 143–152.

Veblen, T. (1961) 'The Limitations of Marginal Utility', in Veblen, T. (ed.) *The Place of Science in Modern Civilization*. New York: Russell & Russell, pp. 231–251.

Volkmer, I. (2015) 'Globalization Research in New Dimensions of Public Interdependence', *Communication Research and Practice*, *1*(3), 258–266.

Voltmer, K. (2012) 'How Far Can Media Systems Travel? Applying Hallin and Mancini's Comparative Framework outside the Western World', in Hallin, D. & Mancini, P. (eds)

Comparing Media Systems Beyond the Western World. Cambridge: Cambridge University Press, pp. 224–245.

Wade, R. (1990) *Governing the Market: Economic Theory and the Role of Government in East Asian Industrialization*. Princeton, NJ: Princeton University Press.

Wade, R. (2002) 'Bridging the Digital Divide: New Route to Development or New Form of Dependency?', *Global Governance: A Review of Multilateralism And International Organizations*, 8(4), 443–466.

Waisbord, S. (2000) 'Media in South America: Between the Rock of the State and the Hard Place of the Market', in Curran, J. & Park, M.-J. (eds) *Dewesternizing Media Studies*. London: Routledge, pp. 50–62.

Waisbord, S. (2001) *Family Tree of Theories, Methodologies and Strategies in Development Communication*. Washington, DC: Rockefeller Foundation. Retrieved from http://m.communicationforsocialchange.org/pdf/familytree.pdf (Accessed 13 December 2017).

Waisbord, S. (2004) 'McTV: Understanding the Global Popularity of Television Formats', *Television & New Media*, 5(4), 359–383.

Waisbord, S. (2016) 'The "Post-State" Argument and its Problems: Lessons from Media Policy Reforms in Latin America', in Flew, T., Iosifidis, P. & Steemers, J. (eds) *Global Media and National Policies: The Return of the State*. Basingstoke: Palgrave Macmillan, pp. 32–48.

Wallerstein, I. (1974) 'The Rise and Future Demise of the World Capitalist System: Concepts for Comparative Analysis', *Comparative Studies in Society And History*, 16(4), 387–415.

Wallerstein, I. (1990) 'Culture as the Ideological Battleground of the Modern World-System', in Featherstone, M. (ed.) *Global Culture: Nationalism, Globalization and Modernity*. London: SAGE, pp. 31–57.

Wallerstein, I. (1997) 'The National and the Universal: Can there be such a thing as World Culture?', in King, A.D. (ed.) *Culture, Globalization and the World-System*. Minneapolis, MI: University of Minnesota Press, pp. 91–106.

Wallerstein, I. (2000) 'A Left Politics for the 21st Century? Or, Theory and Praxis once again', *New Political Science*, 22(2), 143–159.

Walmart. (2016) *Walmart Annual Report 2016*. Retrieved from www.annualreports.com/Company/wal-mart-stores-inc. (Accessed 13 December 2017).

Warren, B. (1980) *Imperialism: Pioneer of Capitalism*. London: Verso.

Wasko, J. (2003) *How Hollywood Works*. Thousand Oaks, CA: SAGE.

Wasko, J. (2004) 'The Political Economy of Communications', in Downing, J., McQuail, D., Schlesinger, P. & Wartella, E. (eds) *SAGE Handbook of Media Studies*. Thousand Oaks, CA: SAGE, pp. 309–330.

Waters, M. (2000) *Globalization* (2nd ed.). New York: Routledge.

Weber, M. (1946) *From Max Weber: Essays in Sociology*. Edited by H.H. Gerth & C.W. Mills. New York: Oxford University Press.

Weber, M. (1978) *Economy and Society (2 vols.)*. Edited by G. Roth & C. Wittich. Berkeley, CA: University of California Press.

Weiss, L. (1997) 'Globalization and the Myth of the Powerless State', *New Left Review*, 225, 3–27.

Weiss, L. (1999) 'Globalization and National Governance: Antinomies or Inter-dependence?', in Cox, M., Booth, K. & Dunne, T. (eds) *The Interregnum: Controversies in World Politics 1989–1999*. Cambridge: Cambridge University Press, pp. 59–88.

Weiss, L. (2003) 'Introduction: Bringing Domestic Institutions Back In', in Weiss, L. (ed.) *States in the Global Economy: Bringing Domestic Institutions Back In*. Cambridge: Cambridge University Press, pp. 1–33.

Wikipedia (2017) 'List of Sovereign States', Retrieved from http://en.wikipedia.org/wiki/List_of_sovereign_states (Accessed 13 December 2017).

Wilber, C.K. & Jameson, K.P. (1988) 'Paradigms of Economic Development and Beyond', in Wilber, C.K. & Jameson, K.P. (eds) *The Political Economy of Development and Underdevelopment*. New York: Random House, pp. 3–27.

Wilkins, K.G. (2008) 'Development Communication', in Donsbach, W. (ed.) *International Encyclopedia of Communication*. Malden, MA: Blackwell, pp. 1229–1238.

Williams, M. (2014) 'The Developmental State in the 21st Century', in Williams, M. (ed.) *The End of the Developmental State*. London: Routledge, pp. 1–29.

Williams, R. (1965) *The Long Revolution*. Harmondsworth: Penguin.

Williams, R. (1973) 'Base and Superstructure in Marxist Cultural Theory', *New Left Review*, (82), 3–16.

Williams, R. (1976) *Keywords: a Vocabulary of Culture and Society*. London: Fontana.

Williams, R. (1977) *Marxism and Literature*. Oxford: Oxford University Press.

Williamson, O.E. (2000) 'The New Institutional Economics: Taking Stock, Looking Forward', *Journal of Economic Literature*, 38(3), 595–613.

Winseck, D. (2011) 'The Political Economies of Media and the Transformation of the Global Media Industries', in Winseck, D. & Jin, D.Y. (eds) *The Political Economies of Media: The Transformation of the Global Media Industries*. London: Bloomsbury, pp. 3–47.

World Bank. (2016) *Net Migration*. Retrieved from http://data.worldbank.org/indicator/SM.POP.NETM (Accessed 5 March 2017).

Xi, J. (2015) *The Governance of China*. Beijing: Foreign Languages Press.

Xi, J. (2017) *Opening Plenary Address to the World Economic Forum 2017*.

Xin, X. (2012) *How the Market Is Changing China's News: The Case of Xinhua News Agency*. Lanham, MD: Lexington Books.

Xu, X., Fu, W. & Straubhaar, J. (2013) 'National Self-sufficiency in Broadcast Television Programming: Examining the Airtime Shares of Homemade versus U.S.-made Programs', *Journal of Broadcasting & Electronic Media*, 57(4), 543–561.

Yeh, E.Y. (2010) 'The Deferral of Pan-Asian: A Critical Appraisal of Film Marketization in China', in Curtin, M. & Shah, H. (eds) *Reorienting Global Communication – Indian and Chinese Media beyond Borders*. Urbana, IL: University of Illinois Press, pp. 183–200.

Zhao, Y. (2008) *Communication in China: Political Economy, Power, and Conflict*. Lanham, MD: Rowman & Littlefield Publishers.

Zhao, Y. (2010) 'Whose Hero? The "Spirit" and "Structure" of a Made-in-China Global Blockbuster', in Curtin, M. & Shah, H. (eds) *Reorienting Global Communication – Indian and Chinese Media beyond Borders*. Urbana, IL: University of Illinois Press, pp. 161–182.

Index